T0155825

Enterprise Architecture Patterns

Thierry Perroud · Reto Inversini

Enterprise Architecture Patterns

Practical Solutions for Recurring IT-Architecture Problems

 Springer

Thierry Perroud
Büren an der Aare
Switzerland

Reto Inversini
Schalunen
Switzerland

ISBN 978-3-642-42894-4   ISBN 978-3-642-37561-3 (eBook)
DOI 10.1007/978-3-642-37561-3
Springer Heidelberg New York Dordrecht London

ACM Computing Classification (1998): J.1, D.2, K.6

Printed on acid-free paper

Springer is part of Springer Science+Business Media (www.springer.com)

Acknowledgments

We would like to thank the following persons for their support, advice, and generously given time to review the manuscript of this book: First and foremost Ralf Gerstner our editor at Springer – we stretched his patience many times and always received kind advice and professional support. Our thanks go to all our reviewers who pointed out our mistakes in clear light: Emanuel Haldi and Martin Mannarella. We would also like to thank Patric Geissbühler and Rahel Gaukel for their input and encouragement. For all the discussions and input we would like to thank our teams, the Enterprise Architects and the Security Architects of FOITT. As many sushis, zukedons, and miso soups have been eaten during the writing of this book, we would like to thank Mr. Tanaka's Kabuki restaurant in Berne, Switzerland for his outstanding cuisine.

This book would not have been possible without the encouragements and indulgence of our beloved – we know that we have been sitting behind our computers way too long! We therefore dedicate this book to Monika and Martina.

Reto would like to thank his parents for having bought him a computer when he was 12 and thus enabling him to make his first steps in programming.

Contents

Part II Pattern Catalog

Part I
Fundamentals

Chapter 1
Introduction

«We cannot escape history.»
Abraham Lincoln in Annual Message to Congress, Dec. 1,
1862.

Abstract This chapter introduces the idea of patterns, describes the motivation and intent of the book, and explains the audience being addressed by this book.

1.1 A Brief History of Patterns

Looking back in history is always a good way to understand the present. So is it when trying to judge the suitability of the concept of patterns in the domain of Enterprise Architecture. Understanding that the concept of patterns is far older than the best known use in the software engineering business gives way to new applications of this approach.

It is deeply human to think in patterns and it has been done for eons, beginning with hunting and collecting for food. Indeed, patterns can be observed in nature. The fact that chances are high to have meat for dinner when hunting at dawn near a waterhole, might be considered as a simple pattern.

We are used to think in patterns and to apply patterns – even when we are not aware of it. In our daily life we are surrounded by visual, aural, behavioral, and other kinds of patterns. We are in a certain way conditioned to recognize and apply patterns, which help us to survive. Patterns help us to navigate through the jungle of information and to extract only the relevant information without drowning in the flood. It is certainly an extremely effective mechanism to protect ourselves and to help us to take decisions. Sometimes it is better to not know every detail to take the adequate measures (Doerner 2003). Even while you are reading this book, you do not read every letter – perhaps not even every chapter (which is a pity, as we put a lot of time into writing this book) as you are trained from your experience in recognizing certain reoccurring sentence patterns. On a more semantic level you certainly make analogy while reading the text – you recall perhaps other books in which things are said differently but similarly?

The use of patterns gives us a certain confidence that a situation that has been mastered using a specific pattern may be mastered again using the same pattern again

T. Perroud and R. Inversini, *Enterprise Architecture Patterns*,
DOI: 10.1007/978-3-642-37561-3_1, © Springer-Verlag Berlin Heidelberg 2013

in a similar situation. Many heuristic methods, which are used to come to an optimal solution as rapidly as possible, rely in fact on our explicit or implicit knowledge of patterns. Many of the patterns have been « coded » into our way of thinking by evolution, our history, our cultural and social background, and more. Even history itself follows patterns (we all know the expression «history repeats itself»).

Patterns may also be used to learn something. For example, jazz musicians practice their musical and rhythmical patterns to copy a certain style or to improve their faculty to improvise by recalling these patterns on stage.

Imagine building a new city without ever having built something bigger than isolated farmhouses. Following the path of an imaginary architect, he certainly would travel to a big city, gazing at all the streets and buildings, at the market place, the churches, and the town hall. By looking, walking around, and visiting other cities he would slowly begin to see a pattern how cities are built. When he starts planning his own city, he would certainly reuse some of these patterns. It is no surprise that the description of patterns is the topic of a well-known book in the «real» architect's community: Christopher Alexander wrote «A Pattern Language» (Alexander et al. 1977), a book that reflects also the mindset of the 1960s: Everybody should be able to build a town or a house using the patterns in the book. The patterns are available for everyone – without distinction of social classes.

In the Information and Communication Technology (ICT) literature the term pattern has been used for

- Software development: Best known are the «Design Patterns» by «The Gang of Four» (Gamma et al. 1995). All the patterns are describing ways to create (software) objects, to control the access to objects, or to define the behavior of an object. The patterns are described using interaction and object diagrams as well as C-code. The authors refer to Alexander in the following way (Chap. 6, page 356): «Alexander claims his patterns will generate complete buildings. We do not claim that our patterns will generate complete programs.»
- A way to structure the layering of enterprise applications, the business logic to be programmed, and handle session states (Fowler 2002). Fowler uses the term pattern in a way similar to the aforementioned book. The difference lies in the classification of the patterns in terms of layers (presentation, domain, data source). The patterns are described for application developers. The notations used are class and interaction diagrams, database tables, C#, JAVA, and (X)HTML code. Interesting to mention is the defined scope of the book, as described on page 97: «Digging into patterns for message-based work is a sizeable topic on its own, and that is why I ducked out of it for this book.»
- Or describing interfaces between applications and intermediary systems [communication patterns, integration patterns, messaging (Fowler 2002)]. Hohpe and Woolf (2004) and Chappell (2004) are closely related to each other, as the second book uses the same pictograms for the notation of the patterns. Both books deal heavily with integration issues of applications and services (message routing, service calls, loose coupling, standard-based protocols, etc.) and are intended for application developers as well as for ICT architects (software, solution, or enterprise).

- Recently, the concept of pattern has reached the Enterprise Architecture community: An initiative led by the TU Munich (Ernst 2008), supported by different enterprises has published a catalog of different kinds of Enterprise Architecture-related patterns. These patterns are classified into three types: I-pattern (Implementation), V-pattern (Views), and M-pattern (Methodology).
- It is interesting to mention that all the books follow the same formal «pattern»: The first part is an introduction to the topic (narrative or introductive), followed generally by a case study using some of the depicted patterns and then, as a third part, a catalog of those patterns is presented to the reader. You will recognize this pattern by looking at our table of contents.

Nowadays, displaying a solution schema in the shape of a reusable pattern is a procedure that is well established in Information Technology since several years. ICT professionals tend more and more to think in patterns, thus reducing the complexity of modern infrastructure and preventing from reinventing the wheel with every new project.

It is interesting to observe how the degree of abstraction of the pattern in Information Technology rose from year to year. This evolution can even be observed in the development of Enterprise Architecture frameworks. The Open Group Architecture Framework (TOGAF) for example, states:

> «Patterns for system architecting are very much in their infancy. They have been introduced into TOGAF essentially to draw them to the attention of the systems architecture community as an emerging important resource, and as a placeholder for hopefully more rigorous descriptions and references to more plentiful resources in future versions of TOGAF.» (TOGAF 2009, page 293)

It may well be said that using patterns in their various shapes is commonly considered a good or even best practice approach.

We would take any bet that the use of patterns in Information Technology is going to increase over the years and to conquer new areas. In a more and more complex environment (virtualization, cloud computing, model-driven development, interacting web services, etc.) the idea of solution schemes for reoccurring problems is a most helpful approach avoiding to get lost in the jungle of ideas, concepts, and technologies.

Patterns may be used not only in the description of rather technical environments but for information as well. With the ever-increasing amount of data, the retrieval of information is getting more and more important. The organization of information often takes reoccurring shapes, such as many enterprises storing redundant information and a clever combination of different information sources would not only reduce the amount of storage needed but would also render information more accessible. Looking at social networks where incredible amounts of personal data are stored and combining this fact with the tendency of humans to stick to habits, the potential of a pattern-based analysis of this data is huge. But leaving the field of a rather technical analysis of environments also increases the need for ethical behavior while analyzing information and trying to extract certain patterns.

1.2 Audience

The book has been written in a form that every ICT professional should be able to read and draw conclusions from. The main audience, however, are persons responsible for planning, designing, and implementing the ICT of an enterprise, mainly Enterprise Architects, Solution Architects, Project Managers, Business Analysts, and to some degree, Software Architects and Security Architects. As one can see a lot of people are involved in Enterprise Architecture discussions and therefore, instead of listing all the possible stakeholders it should be noted that everyone affected directly or indirectly by architectural decisions could take advantage by reading this book.

1.3 Motivation

Enterprise Architecture is influencing many areas of ICT, be it directly or by slowly changing the environment where ICT projects happen. As ICT is pervading everyday life, the same may be said for the ICT in an enterprise. As the density of various ICT applications and domains is ever-increasing the need for an organizing and regulating concept is getting more and more important. Enterprise Architecture is trying to answer the question of «how our ICT environment should be built in a way that it supports our business goals in the most efficient way.» Working for several years on organizing and streamlining the architecture of a governmental organization, we began to recognize reoccurring problems that also seemed to exist in other organizations, not only governmental but also in privately held enterprises. This led to the thought that maybe the same concept could be adapted to the domain of Enterprise Architecture that has been successfully used in Software Architecture/ Software Engineering – the concept of Design Patterns. As TOGAF mentions the possibility of EA patterns it does not formulate them in detail. After having adapted the idea during a diploma thesis (Inversini 2009), we concluded that this concept is suited also to the domain of Enterprise Architecture as reoccurring problems and solution schemas can be observed regularly. Such patterns are motivated by ever returning needs originating from the business architecture of an enterprise: Nearly every enterprise faces the challenge to establish an identity and access management or has the need to share data securely with partners. In addition, every enterprise has office automation, web presence, and many business applications.

An Enterprise Architecture Pattern thus describes a solution for fulfilling requirements emanating from the business architecture of any company using ICT means. The solution is described by introducing a solution scheme that contains a name, the problem, the context, the forces governing the pattern, the solution, the consequences arising when using this pattern, and the resulting context. Actually, every pattern in the catalog is worth a book of itself – we tried to convey the most important facts in the proposed concise form of an Enterprise Architecture Pattern.

The goal of the book is not only to prove that the concept of patterns is well suited for the domain of Enterprise Architecture but also to provide a means for simplifying the life of the Enterprise Architects. We hope that the patterns will help as a guide for the development of your Enterprise Architecture – as a source for inspiration or as a reference book.

1.4 Organization of the Book

The first part of the book introduces you to the fascinating domain of Enterprise Architecture in a general form: What is Enterprise Architecture? Why do we need it? What are patterns? Why are these helpful to an architect? After having answered these questions, the concept of an Enterprise Architecture Pattern (EAP) is discussed in-depth, thus concluding Chap. 2 of the book. In Chap. 3 we will give an overview of all the patterns arranged in a catalog and show their relationship in a pattern map. Chapter 4 gives further reasons to use EAPs. In Chap. 5 the idea of describing the ICT Architecture using patterns is put to test in a case study. The case study is based on a (fictional) company. Starting by describing the business architecture and identifying the relevant patterns from the catalog, we show how this concept can be applied to a real-world scenario. Although introducing and building up the pattern world are not the only important parts, yet one can say that indeed, they are the easiest. The hard work is followed by governing the use of patterns and learning to live with their impact, such as having to judge new projects not only for their short-term benefits but also for their long-term implications for the enterprise. To better understand the symbols we use in this book, we have put them together in Chap. 6. Chapters 7, 8, and 9 contain the detailed catalog of EAP provided for everyday use as well as an inspirational treasure chest for developing and deriving new patterns. The catalog is built-up in categories and for each pattern the business drivers, the invariance (the degree of confidence with which we believe a certain pattern may be used without further modifications), the affecting forces, the standardized notation, the interdependences on other patterns, and the benefits of using the pattern are shown.

References

Alexander C, Ishikawa S, Silverstein M (1977) Pattern language: towns, buildings constructions. Oxford University Press, New York

Ernst A (2008) Enterprise architecture management patterns. http://www.hillside.net/plop/2008/papers/ACMVersions/ernst.pdf. Accessed 21 June 2013

Chappell D (2004) Enterprise service bus. O'Reilly, USA

Doerner D (2003) Die Logik des Misslingens. Rowohlt Taschenbuch Verlag, Berlin

Fowler M (2002) Patterns of enterprise application architecture. Addison-Wesley, USA

Gamma E, Helm R, Johnson R, Vlissides J (1995) Design patterns. Elements of reusable object-oriented software. Addison-Wesley, USA

Hohpe G, Woolf B (2004) Enterprise integrations patterns. Addison-Wesley, USA

Inversini R (2009) Entwurfsmuster für IKT Architekturen. http://static.sws.bfh.ch/download/MAS-06-01-13-doc.pdf. Accessed 28 July 2011

TOGAF (2009) The Open Group architecture framework. http://pubs.opengroup.org/architecture/togaf9-doc/arch/. Accessed 28 July 2011

Chapter 2
Theory

«My theory is to enjoy life, but the practice is against it.»
Charles Lamb

Abstract An enterprise architecture pattern (EAP) is based on the concepts and ideas of Architecture Enterprise frameworks such as TOGAF, NAF, or Zachman. We first give a short description of Enterprise Architecture, followed by the main concepts conveyed by the frameworks, such as views and viewpoints, architectural domains, architecture bricks, etc. This is followed by a list of stakeholders who might use the patterns in this book. We then explain in detail what an EAP is, define the graphical notations of the different views, and describe the structure of an EAP.

2.1 Enterprise Architecture: Explain It to Your Girlfriend

A number of books and articles have been written on Enterprise Architecture. We do not try to write a new one, or present a revolutionary way of defining it. Yet, we do need to write a few words on Enterprise Architecture, as it is the vessel on which we transport our concept of patterns. In the following sections we give a brief overview of the concepts behind Enterprise Architecture. You may find more in-depth information in the reference list at the end of this chapter.

If you had to explain the rather abstract discipline of «Enterprise Architecture» to a friend or relative, who is not in the Information Technology business, you certainly would try to make an analogy with something that the person could know from his or her own experience: «Planning and overview the building of a house», «Urban planning and sustainability» or «Draw plans for different craftsmen» would be common approaches to try to explain this topic. After your expert talk, your discussion partner will certainly have one understanding: Architecture, be it in the house construction business or in information technology, is a planning discipline, involving many different people with different skills. The architect is expected to overview, coordinate the different craftsmanship, and address the requirements of all the people involved through adequate views of the building (or information system) to be built or renovated. He will have to translate the

T. Perroud and R. Inversini, *Enterprise Architecture Patterns*,
DOI: 10.1007/978-3-642-37561-3_2, © Springer-Verlag Berlin Heidelberg 2013

requirements of the sponsor into a feasible architecture, present options depending on costs and budget, and measure the progress of the as-is architecture in relation to the to-be architecture. As in real architecture, the Enterprise Architecture is not «l'art pour l'art» – you do not do it just because of the beauty of it, but to align your Information Technology investments with the business needs and strategies. This is the main goal. In addition to this, one of the agreeable by-products of an Enterprise Architecture initiative is to order things, make classification, to clarify terms, and to introduce a sustainable way to document your business processes, the application landscape, and the underlying infrastructure. Every architect adheres to a more or less rigorous methodology to document his doing. This ensures transparency, traceability, and minimizes the risks of wrong decisions by using well-proven techniques and documentation standards.

There is no scientific definition of Enterprise Architecture, but a lot of smart people have thought about it and have formulated their understanding in books, articles, forums, blogs, and conferences in the last few years (Perks and Beveridge 2003; Wikipedia EA 2011; NIH 2008; Lankhorst 2005). In the context of this book we use the definitions related to the vast field of Enterprise Architecture as given by TOGAF (2009). In order to facilitate the understanding of the EAP in this book, the following definitions will be of help to the reader:

Enterprise: The highest level (typically) of description of an organization that typically covers all missions and functions. An enterprise will often span multiple organizations.

Architecture: 1. A formal description of a system, or a detailed plan of the system at component level, to guide its implementation (ISO/IEC 42010 2007).
2. The structure of components, their interrelationships, and the principles and guidelines governing their design and evolution over time.

Architecture Framework: A conceptual structure used to develop, implement, and sustain an architecture.

Architecture Domain: The architectural area being considered. There are four architecture domains within TOGAF: business, data, application, and technology.

Patterns: A technique for putting building blocks into context; for example, to describe a reusable solution to a problem. Building blocks are what you use: patterns can tell you how you use them, when, why, and what tradeoffs you have to make in doing so.

In this book, we deal with a simplification of the real world to address the concerns of different stakeholders. We therefore use the following definitions as well:

Model: A representation of a subject of interest. A model provides a smaller scale, simplified, and/or abstract representation of the subject matter. A model is constructed as a «means to an end». In the context of Enterprise Architecture, the subject matter is the entire enterprise or a part of it and the end is the ability to construct «views» that address the concerns of particular stakeholders; i.e., their «viewpoints» in relation to the subject matter.

View: The representation of a related set of concerns. A view is what is seen from a viewpoint. An architecture view may be represented by a model to demonstrate to stakeholders their areas of interest in the architecture. A view does not have to be visual or graphical in nature.

Viewpoint: A definition of the perspective from which a view is taken. It is a specification of the conventions for constructing and using a view (often by means of an appropriate schema or template). A view is what you see; a viewpoint is where you are looking from – the vantage point or perspective that determines what you see.

As most of these kinds of disciplines have roots in a very technological environment (e.g., information technology), the Enterprise Architecture has gained maturity by taking more and more the views and viewpoints of the business and its strategies.[1] Nowadays, every definition of Enterprise Architecture encompasses all the levels, beginning at the business architecture down to the technology. This understanding of Enterprise Architecture can also be observed in how the role of the «Enterprise Architecture» identified by the Gartner Group (Pettey and Stevens 2009), the 4th states:

> «Doing Only Technical Domain-Level Architecture: This dated EA approach is still in use in some organizations and is even narrower in scope than technical architecture. Holistic EA best practice is much broader as it includes business, information, and solutions architecture.»

Enterprise Architecture acts like a master plan for the whole enterprise; it takes into account the business strategy, goals, vision and principles, aspects of business operations, automation of processes, data processing, and the necessary technological infrastructure. Moreover, the Enterprise Architecture enables the communication among the different stakeholders and promotes a common glossary.

Why Do We Need an Enterprise Architecture?
An Enterprise Architecture fulfills primarily one goal: Aligning the IT-related activities with the goals of the enterprise. This encompasses all investments, the management of the resources (hardware, software, facilities, people) in the different architecture layers, the strategic planning of the evolution of the overall Enterprise Architecture, and of course an up-to-date of the actual situation. With a consistent and well-managed EA the enterprise will be able to minimize the risks of wrong investments, to contribute to the value delivery according to business goals, and to react more flexibly to changes in the business environment and derived requirements.

---

[1] The same can be said, for example, of the IT infrastructure library (ITIL): Versions 1 and 2 were more oriented toward technology, whereas version 3 now encompasses strategies and business viewpoints.

To achieve this, the Enterprise Architecture delivers artifacts that help to manage the complexity of all architecture layers in the form of models, blueprints, policies, a glossary, and principles to adhere to. The principles are the cornerstone of every Enterprise Architecture: They are high-level statements with a direct link to an IT strategy and business goals, and are motivated by a rationale and the implications that ensue when applying. Last but not least an EA principle enables the enterprise to measure how well the goals of the IT strategy are being reached and thus contribute to the overall performance management.

Layers of an Enterprise Architecture
To cope with the complexity of the relations between all the elements of an Enterprise Architecture and the different views and viewpoints of the stakeholders to address, it is common to use a layering scheme (Fig. 2.1).

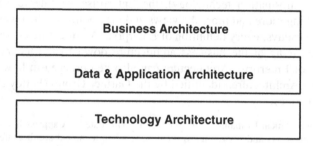

Fig. 2.1 Layers of an enterprise architecture

As stated in the definition given by The Opengroup for the term «Architecture Domains» the layering in (TOGAF) is done as follows:

Business Architecture: As TOGAF states

«In summary, the Business Architecture describes the product and/or service strategy, and the organizational, functional, process, information, and geographic aspects of the business environment.»

This architecture is extremely important, as all the other architectures rely on it. The exact extent to which business-related activities to define this layer will effectively be driven and managed by an Enterprise Architecture program depends on the business environment. For example, in our environment the Enterprise Architecture team had the lead for the definition of an information model and business glossary, but not for the business process architecture itself.

Data Architecture: This architecture deals with all necessary aspects of data management, how applications, services, and business functions utilize enterprise data, how the relationship among data objects are to be modeled, how the transformation of data is to be done, etc. TOGAF provides the following definition:

«A description of the structure and interaction of the enterprise's major types and sources of data, logical data assets, physical data assets, and data management resources.»

Application Architecture: This layer provides all necessary information for the management of the application landscape, how business functions will be realized in terms of applications. The TOGAF definition is as follows:

«A description of the structure and interaction of the applications as groups of capabilities that provide key business functions and manage the data assets.»

TOGAF uses the term «Information Systems Architecture» in its Architecture Development Method (ADM), meaning the combination of the Data Architecture and the Application Architecture, as these two are strongly interrelated.

Technology Architecture: The effective realization of the above-mentioned architecture layers are done in the technology. TOGAF provides the following definition:

«A description of the structure and interaction of the platform services, and logical and physical technology components.»

Depending on the framework you will use for structuring the Enterprise Architecture, different layers may be used (e.g., information layer that contains the business view on data objects, a process layer, an organizational layer, or a solution layer, etc.).

Processes Involved in Enterprise Architecture Management
The processes needed to sustain and deliver a consistent Enterprise Architecture are all part of an overall (IT) Governance process framework. They all make a contribution to the strategic alignment of the enterprise, the value delivery, the risk management, the resource management, and the performance management as stated for example by CGEIT (2012). Processes for the Enterprise Architecture Management (EAM) have been described in different publications (Keller 2007; Dern 2006; TOGAF 2009), but there is no common understanding on this subject. Keller (2007) proposes the following processes:

Strategy and Planning: Deriving the IT strategy from the business strategy, managing the application landscape including the as-is and the to-be architectures.

Modeling and Policies: Definition of the modeling of the different architecture layers and development, enforcement of architecture standards and policies.

Implementation of the Planning: Monitoring of the project portfolio, steering of projects concerning the architecture aspects.

All these processes have one critical success factor in common: It is absolutely mandatory that the top management gives its commitment and support. From our own experience we can testify that you may not have the full necessary support from the beginning, but with the right attitude, enough stamina, seizing the favorable opportunities for your cause and doing a good job, a mind change toward Enterprise Architecture will occur.

2.2 Supporting Frameworks

The discipline of Enterprise Architecture has evolved tremendously in the past few years – and with it the supporting architecture frameworks and methods to help to develop the architectures.

With the evolution of Enterprise Architecture different supporting frameworks and methodologies arose. The best known are the Zachman Framework (Zachman 1987), the Department of Defense architecture framework (DoDAF 2011), the NATO architecture framework (NAF 2011), the Federal Enterprise Architecture Framework (FEAF 1999), and the opengroup architecture framework (TOGAF 2009). All these architecture frameworks have one common goal: To provide the means to structure and govern all the elements pertaining to an enterprise that uses Information Technology resources. Nowadays, the Enterprise Architect will certainly propose to adhere to such a method or framework based on a standard or best practices, before thinking about creating his own way and world of managing the Enterprise Architecture. But there is no secret when adopting any framework, the architects must work their fingers to the bone and adapt the hundreds of pages and bullets to their specific situation.

An architecture framework represents a guideline, sometimes with more emphasis on certain topics (like DoDAF on views or TOGAF on the *Architecture Development Methodology*) and must be adapted to the specific situation of an enterprise. The frameworks provide the architects with good or even best practices on *what*, and seldom on *how*, something should be done.

Sometimes the Enterprise Architecture is prescriptive, but mainly descriptive: A lot of the work to be done involves the description of the architecture in a more or less sustainable way. Drawings must be made, the semantic of the squares and arrows must be defined, and views from different viewpoints of a system have to be designed. Sometimes the architects will work with specialized tools, but often the classic tools of the office palette are still being used.

2.3 The P in EAP

There is still the last word in the title of this book that we did not explain: How are patterns related to Enterprise Architecture?

As we have seen earlier, patterns are a way to describe solutions to recurring problems. Many enterprises and organizations, which took the adventurous path of Enterprise Architecture, have collected valuable experiences, formulated good or even best practices, and have documented solutions to recurring problems. The patterns in this book can be seen as a formalized way to document this kind of knowledge. Of course you will have patterns on different levels in your Enterprise Architecture: As stated earlier, patterns exist in different kinds and forms, in different levels of abstraction. We present here patterns for Enterprise Architecture, meaning that we will motivate each pattern from a business point of view, but showing also the impact on the layers underneath. This is a holistic approach and induces also a certain loss of details.

Patterns in Enterprise Architecture will be established in the next few years, the first initiatives have already been started – so let us take this challenge!

2.4 Your View Depends on Your Viewpoint

If you are reading this book, then we assume that you are a potential stakeholder of the Enterprise Architecture Patterns (EAPs). In this section, we motivate the use of the EAPs by describing the intended readers of this book and the concerns they might have about the things they need to see in an Enterprise Architecture. We first describe the concept of views and viewpoints, as this is fundamental to understand the different notations of patterns presented in this book. The views and viewpoints are closely related to the different stakeholders and their concerns or areas of interests in the architecture domain. We first make an analogy to the «real world» architecture (e.g., buildings and their makers) and then describe the stakeholders and their concerns and how we intend to address them in terms of EAPs.

In order to manage and communicate the artifacts of the Enterprise Architecture it is essential that the most suitable language for the design, communication, and implementation of these results be used. By language we mean the notation for the visualization, the architecture model on which it is based, the choice of words used, the rules, the constraints, modeling techniques, or analytical methods in use. In the concept of Enterprise Architecture this can be summarized with the term «architectural descriptions» (ISO/IEC 42010 2007).

In our understanding a language is suitable, if all involved parties can communicate and understand each other with minimal risk of misunderstandings (you may argue that, although we may all speak the same language, it is by no means a guarantee that we really do understand each other). The Enterprise Architecture can live without formal description, but this makes it rather difficult to communicate any changes or new issues. Moreover, the traceability – the extent to which the proof of how the requirements from the business are met by the underlying infrastructure, and the efficient and effective management of the Enterprise Architecture – may be adversely affected with this approach. Every notation (e.g., description language) that is being introduced to document certain aspects of an Enterprise Architecture must come in conjunction with the appropriate processes to enforce, teach, and further develop the use of this language.

An architect trying to describe the Enterprise Architecture of his company must find a consistent way at different levels of detail. When building a house the (real) architect has a similar problem to solve: He must be able to produce different kinds of blueprints and drawings for the various craftsmen and engineers involved in the construction of the house. These drawings and formal descriptions have certainly a longer tradition than what we use in Enterprise Architecture for the documentation, but nonetheless we have to deal with the same issues: For every viewpoint (sponsor, architects, electrician, craftsmen) the views (drawings, blueprints, level of detail) must be provided and managed, using different kinds of techniques and notations [computer-aided design (CAD) tools, hand drawings, specialized programs to compute insulation values, and so on]. Every stakeholder has his concerns (and hopefully also requirements) that must be met in the language he is able or willing to understand. Every view of the house is equally important as it meets the needs of a specific stakeholder. The sum of all these different perspectives on the house will form the complete description. Even in real architecture it is absolutely normal that no one has a comprehensive understanding of all the details in the different views of the building. We must live with the fact that we will not understand and have a complete grasp of every detail that is to be built.

The concept of views and viewpoints is fundamental in practically every Enterprise Architecture framework. The wording may sometimes be «stakeholder analysis» or «operational view» – the core statement is always that you have to address the concerns of the people participating in your Enterprise Architecture initiative to be successful.

In the chapter «The Role of Architecture Views» (TOGAF 2009) the introduction states:

> «Architecture views are representations of the overall architecture that are meaningful to one or more stakeholders in the system. The architect chooses and develops a set of views that will enable the architecture to be communicated to, and understood by, all the stakeholders, and enable them to verify that the system will address their concerns».[2]

Furthermore ISO/IEC 42010 2007 «Systems and software engineering – Architectural description», as being referenced by TOGAF, defines:

- The architectural view as *«representation of a system from the perspective of an identified set of architecture-related concerns»*, and
- The architecture viewpoint as *«conventions for the construction, interpretation, and use of architectural view and its contributing architectural models»*.

If you follow the ISO standard to the letter, you will notice that the concepts are formulated in a rather abstract way and may be somewhat difficult to communicate to stakeholders who perhaps do not have the same level of abstraction than most Enterprise Architects. We will use a simplified version of these concepts to describe the suitable notation of the EAPs for the different stakeholders of this book.

---

[2] Interesting enough to be mentioned is that the concepts of architectural views and viewpoints in the standard are depicted itself as a class diagram conforming to the UML notation. This narrows the amount of potential readers dramatically…

2.5 Reusability

One of the most important goals of defining patterns is to provide reusability. Reusability itself incorporates different aspects. It should reduce the amount of work, avoid repeating errors other people have made, and generally accelerate the way a solution is planned, developed, and implemented. As many EAPs are only built in one instance in an enterprise, the reusability unfolds its value particularly when developed, refined, and used by the community of enterprise architects. The aspect of applying a common body of knowledge is not only part of the traditional software design patterns but forms the basis of virtually any ICT framework. Thus, the use of Architecture Enterprise Patterns expands the idea of design patterns as well as motivation of frameworks such as TOGAF. In order to be reusable, EAPs need to be formulated in an easily understandable, standardized, and vendor-neutral way, a «pattern language». The definition of 13 EAPs in this book should not be considered as a closing selection of all patterns that are to be used but more as a starting point and we hope that a community emerges that provides additional patterns or modifies existing patterns according to their experience. However, based upon our experience, we are confident that these 13 patterns form a solid base for working with the concept of EAPs.

2.6 Stakeholders and Their Concerns

To understand the patterns presented in this book we first identify the stakeholders and describe their concerns. In terms of Enterprise Architecture development we are talking about the different architectural viewpoints. This gives us the possibility to find the suitable language (architectural descriptions) to meet their expectations. For each stakeholder we describe first his role and then list his possible concerns and how we intend to respond to them in a suitable language in terms of EAPs. The stakeholders will of course use modeling or visualization techniques other than EAPs. By defining how we intend to respond to the diverse concerns with the patterns presented in this book, we are also gathering requirements on what kind of information the EAPs should provide and motivate their use. We mostly deal with four types of stakeholders:

1. Stakeholders whose concerns address the consistency of the overall architecture or the strategic direction to follow in accordance with the business goals. In the context of this book this stakeholder corresponds to the Enterprise Architect.
2. Stakeholders that are mainly involved during an ICT project to build or change a system. These are the Project Sponsor, the Solution Architects, Business Analysts, and Project Leaders.
3. Stakeholders that are charged with strategic planning, decision making. Very often, this is a Chief Information Officer (CIO) or another person who is involved in defining the strategy of how ICT should be used to best support meeting the business goals.

4. Stakeholders that are responsible for the controlling of how efficient ICT is used in an enterprise. This is typically an internal auditor or a controller. By comparing EAPs to the actual ICT landscape he gains an impression of how well ICT is aligned to strategic goals.

The *Project Sponsor* finances an ICT project to change or create a new system. This person will also be the one who formulates the business requirements and gives his approval to go into production (Table 2.1).

Table 2.1 Concerns of a project sponsor

Concerns	The new or changed system must meet the business requirements. Budget and time expectations must be met. He may not be very interested in technical details, but if it comes to the costs of technologies he would be interested in the differences between two solutions
Information in EAP	The business drivers and requirements, the business scenario and the vision depicted in every EAP will help to understand the purpose of a pattern. By means of the holistic view the Project Sponsor can gain an understanding of the impact that a change in the business architecture may have on the underlying layers. Furthermore, the business view of the EAP shows the supported process

The *Enterprise Architect* is in charge of developing and implementing the overall Enterprise Architecture of a company. To achieve the objective of efficiently supporting the business processes a thorough understanding of the business as well as of the ICT architecture are key competences of any Enterprise Architect. Moreover, he must have strong skills in the application of different methodologies, like requirements engineering, Enterprise Architecture, or project management. The Enterprise Architect will certainly have the skills to read and understand different kinds of notations [e.g., (ArchiMate 2011), Unified Modeling Language (UML 2010), network diagrams], although he may not produce documents with all these description languages himself (Table 2.2).

Table 2.2 Concerns of an enterprise architect

Concerns	Getting an overall view, from the business needs down to the technology, but flying high over ground. The level of detail may be coarse, but the dependencies between all architecture layers (e.g., business, data, application, technology) must be visible
	Getting information about a specific pattern consisting of a set of interrelated architecture or solution bricks
	Identify and define new architecture or solution bricks based on new customer requirements and needs
	Identify reusable solutions and architectures. This is directly related to financial issues, like cost optimization and scalability, of the architecture
	Ensure the overall consistency of architecture artifacts
	Identify gaps and «black holes» in the overall enterprise architecture and take the appropriate actions to deal with them
	Ensure the compliance with regulative and legal requirements
	Communicate changes in the enterprise architecture to the different stakeholders
	Cost-efficiency, quality, and feasibility of architectural activities

(continued)

Table 2.2 (continued)

Information in EAP	EAPs fulfill two main goals for the enterprise architect 1. They show a holistic approach to solve reoccurring problems 2. They are a facilitator for finding a common language between all stakeholders in the process of developing and governing an ICT architecture of an enterprise The EAPs must provide an overall view to the Enterprise Architects, from the business layer down to the technology aspects without dealing too much with details. They must be easy to understand—a kind of intuitive Esperanto language. We will therefore use a simplified version of BPMN, UML, and ArchiMate®, using only a subset of the vocabulary provided

The *Solution Architect* is responsible for the resulting architecture of a specific ICT project. He is normally in close contact with the Enterprise Architect(s), the project sponsor or customer, and of course the Project Leader. The solution architect's main task is to develop solutions that meet the customer's needs and integrate seamlessly in the overall architecture of the company. He will certainly have strong knowledge of the conceptual, engineering, or design level, but also skills pertaining to the domain of project management and communication (Table 2.3).

Table 2.3 Concerns of a solution architect

Concerns	Ease of integration through the use of predefined solution bricks and the possible connections between them The solution architect will as much as possible adhere to best practices. He will therefore favor reusable, well-proven solutions Traceability of the requirements through all levels of the architectural descriptions of the solution architecture Ensuring the compliance with the standards, policies, and principles of the Enterprise Architecture Using adequate and efficient tools to document the solution architecture using predefined patterns and shapes Feasibility of the solution (cost, technical aspects, time-budget) Being able to fulfill the customer needs
Information in EAP	The EAPs help the solution architect to understand the overall picture of the ICT architecture in an enterprise (to be more precise, the common, recurring architecture elements of an enterprise). It enables him to examine the pattern catalog and compare the problem descriptions of the various patterns with his own problem he has to solve. As the solution bricks are product-specific and we cannot describe all possible vendor-specific implementations, we give an example of how an EAP can be transformed into a pattern of solution bricks

The *Business Analyst*[3] is the «missing link». He gathers the verbalized requirements from the business, analyses, and transforms them into architecture artifacts like business process diagrams, context diagrams, or use cases. He is

---

[3] This role is sometimes also called *Business Engineer.*

expected to have a strong knowledge of the business and of course well-developed skills in communication and interviewing techniques (Table 2.4).

Table 2.4 Concerns of a business analyst

Concerns	Identify the link between business requirements and the underlying architecture layers and document them in various forms that can be understood by both the business and ICT specialists
	Know which bricks are available and which requirements these bricks address
Information in EAP	As the business analyst must understand the business needs of his customer and provide the necessary information to the solution architect to further define the solution, the EAP must provide input for the business analyst on how a customer request can be implemented and whether there already exists a pattern to fulfill this request. His estimations about time and cost may then become more accurate and the patterns serve as a common understanding between him, the customer, and the solution architect

The *Project Leader* is the coordinator of all activities in a specific project. It is common to distinguish between the project leader on the business side and that on the ICT side. Both types of project leaders have the same goals (satisfying customer needs in time and in budget). Therefore, we will only consider the concerns they have in common (Table 2.5).

Table 2.5 Concerns of a project leader

Concerns	Getting help and support from the enterprise architect to successfully lead the project in time and in budget. The enterprise architect is expected to provide the necessary information and measures to be taken, so that the resulting solution fits into the overall architecture
	Advisory and templates on how to document certain aspects of the architecture (e.g., system layout diagrams, network zoning diagrams)
Information in EAP	The project leader will have to deal with different kinds of description languages, as he has to manage the communication and demand different kinds of documents from the project members. Although he might not be expected to understand all the details, he must be able to lead meetings based on the provided documentation. The EAP will help the project leader to understand the overall architecture of his project and provide him with the possibility to position the different activities and tasks in relation to the architecture. The different views (holistic, business, data and application, technology) are written in the language of the different project members

The *C-level Executive* involved in EAPs is responsible for the strategic alignment of ICT technology with the business goals. In regard to Enterprise Architecture he is often supported by Enterprise Architects. EAPs may be a facilitator and a common language between the Enterprise Architects, the C-level Executive, and the other Board members (Table 2.6).

Table 2.6 Concerns of a C-level executive

Concerns	Align ITC with business goals. He often relies on the expertise of the enterprise architect but has the ultimate responsibility in terms of strategic alignment and investment
Information in EAP	The C-level executive may use EAPs as a valuable resource for keeping oversight of the ICT landscape. Seeing how well EAPs are applied gives him confidence that ICT uses its resources efficiently. The different views (holistic, business, data and application technology) give him the ability to make decisions based on a sound information base

The *Auditor* may use EAPs as a quick indicator where a deviation between the desired state of ICT and the actual state exists. He may demand the use of EAPs as a control objective for the alignment of ICT use with the strategic business goals. The landscape of EAPs used in an enterprise is also a very valuable source for the planning of any audit as the auditor gains a quick overview of the whole ICT landscape (Table 2.7).

Table 2.7 Concerns of an auditor

Concerns	Audit the ICT infrastructure for compliance and alignment
Information in EAP	The use of EAPs may increase the effectiveness, the quality, and the compliance of any ICT environment; the auditor is interested whether and to what extent EAPs are used. The ICT landscape is an important part for planning any audit as it gives an overview of the interdependences of the different applications

We did not list a few other common roles (e.g., Security Architect, Software Architect, Data Architect), which might be also interested in EAPs. This does not mean that they are not welcome to dig with us into the topic, on the contrary.

2.7 Bricks Are the Architect's Best Friends

When designing an EAP you will stumble over the same question as the old Greeks did: «Which is the smallest element that everything is built of?» We will call this element the *architecture brick* (AB), defined as follows:
   The Architecture Brick

- Addresses a set of requirements.
- Is vendor and product-neutral.
- Is attributed to exactly one architecture layer (business, information, application, or technology).
- Provides a well-defined set of interfaces to other ABs.
- Uses interfaces from other ABs.

You can deduce from this definition that an AB has no commercial aspects. It cannot be bought and there are no Service Level Agreements (SLA) associated with it. An AB represents the most abstract form of a basic artifact in an Enterprise Architecture. The AB is the architect's answer to the demand for a certain capability in the Enterprise Architecture that must be provided for the business processes. Of course, an AB actually consists of much smaller components and elements – the coarse definition given here enables us to take the adequate flying altitude to address the concerns of the stakeholders of Sect. 2.5 without going too much into details. The smaller elements, like application components, services, or service-interfaces will be addressed in more detailed views in the description of an EAP. For the understanding of an EAP the granularity of information in an AB is often sufficient.

As stated in the list above, there are no differences for the definition of an AB on the different architecture layers (e.g., business, data and application technology). We do not differentiate a brick that is being used to build a wall on the first floor from the one used on the third floor of a house. They are all described by the same meta-data. The mortar between the bricks is the interface. A brick may use an interface from another brick (even if the brick resides on another architecture layer) and provides some functionality to other bricks through its own interface(s). Starting from the definition of an AB we are now able to write the meta-model for these kinds of bricks. Table 2.8 gives a possible list of parameters you will have to fill in to describe your architecture bricks:

Table 2.8 List of possible parameters to define an architecture brick

Parameter	Description	Example
Name	The name of the AB should be meaningful and unique	Web server brick
Functionality	List of high-level functionalities (the purpose of the brick) provided by the brick	HTML-based pages according to W3C specification
Architecture layer	The name of the layer (Business, Information system, Technology)	Technology
Version	You will have to track the version of all the bricks in the Enterprise Architecture. This implies also that the lifecycle management processes have to be defined and instantiated	1.1
Requirements	A list of requirements that this brick fulfills	Must support PHP-scripting language
Required interfaces	The interfaces from other architecture bricks that this brick requires	Connection to database service
Available interfaces	The interfaces that this brick makes available to other bricks. The description of the interfaces must contain all the relevant parameters so that it can be used	Management Interface for the web server HTTP and HTTPS interfaces according to RFC specification

You may define other parameters to further specify an AB (ownership, creation, and modification date, etc.). The above list should help you to get a start to define a meta-model. Our recommendation is that you should only describe the parameters that are useful to at least one of the stakeholders, because only those will effectively be managed. We will not describe every AB in this book according to the proposed meta-model. We will only describe an AB in more detail if there might arise some ambiguities concerning its functionalities in comparison to another brick.

The architecture bricks are the toys of an Enterprise Architect. They provide a means to structure the overall architecture on a high-level, without having to deal with all the commercial aspects. They are a simplification of the Enterprise Architecture, omitting certain facts. The architecture bricks enable the Enterprise Architects to create specific views without having to deal with all the complexities of the real world.

But how do we address the concerns of a solution architect? He will need a product-specific solution that he can use to design the solution architecture. The answer to this is that one or several *solution bricks* (SB) as shown in Fig. 2.2 will normally realize the AB. The SB is very similar to the architecture brick, with the difference that it is product-specific, and therefore related to commercial aspects as well as to a certain environment. You can put a price tag on it and define an SLA for its usage. For one AB you may have to define one or more SB. Of course the contrary may also be possible: One solution brick can provide the functionality for more than one AB. The meta-model of a solution brick is very similar that of an architecture brick. But the aspects of lifecycle management of a solution brick are extremely important, as the solution brick will be in effective use in a solution within an Enterprise Architecture. This means that such parameters must be taken into consideration when defining the solution brick. For the architects among us using TOGAF this construct of AB and SB is certainly familiar – they are called architecture or solution building blocks.[4]

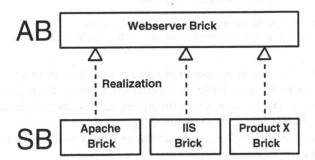

Fig. 2.2 Relationship between architecture brick (*AB*) and solution bricks (*SB*)

In reality, neither the AB nor the SB will be designed from scratch – you will have to analyze your «as–is» Enterprise Architecture, the ongoing projects, the needs from the business, the strategies, etc., in your company to extract the

---

[4] We choose deliberately not to use the same naming as in TOGAF, as we wanted to be independent of any architecture framework.

solution and architecture bricks. The architecture and SB are one way to structure your Enterprise Architecture and are therefore also a contribution to the ICT governance. The same mechanism of deducting an AB from an SB must also be made for the EAP: The effective solution architecture with all the products in place may differ from an EAP, as there will certainly be vendor-specific constraints.

It should be mentioned that it takes a great effort to describe and manage all the bricks in a uniform and consistent way, but this will definitely help to master the Enterprise Architecture. Introducing the notion of architecture and SB in the Enterprise Architecture means that you have to define and instantiate the necessary processes (including roles, performance indicators, etc.,) to manage the lifecycle of these artifacts. The architecture bricks are the basis for the EAPs presented in this book. Essentially, the EAPs are nothing more than a meaningful way of combining these architecture bricks to address a recurring problem. As you will see in Sect. 2.9, where we present the notation(s) for the EAPs, they can be written in different ways to address the concerns of stakeholders.

2.8 How to Make an EAP?

The notion of principles is well established in the Enterprise Architecture world – so why should not we define a few design principles that will guide us when defining and using the EAPs? The following principles have their roots in our own experience – you may well adapt them to your own environment.

Principle 1: Do not invent an Enterprise Architecture Pattern
Gamma et al. (1995) state in their conclusion:

> «Third, look for patterns you use, and write them down. Make them part of your documentation. Show them to other people. You do not have to be in a research lab to find patterns.»

You do recognize them in your environment and then try to extract them to subsequently make them available as generalized solutions for a given problem. You will have to analyze your actual Enterprise Architecture or the actual problems in the different projects and try to recognize a pattern (and the underlying bricks) and address possible upcoming similar problems by defining the pattern in a generalized and reusable form.

Principle 2: Let the patterns evolve
The initial version of a pattern will seldom be the mature one. A pattern will evolve over time. Defining patterns is a process where the different stakeholders will contribute from their experience or point of view. Do not try to grasp every aspect and possible issue in the first version of your pattern. In this case «less is more» is the path to take.

Principle 3: Make the patterns simple and clear
A pattern is not a photographic image of the reality nor shall it ever be. Keep the pattern simple, even knowing that reality would not be that simple. The idea of the pattern is to give the user a clear view of how he can solve a problem. Give them the direction and let them deal with the details, trust them, they will do it well.

Principle 4: Keep the structure
Always keep the structure of the pattern the same, always begin with a meaningful and self-explanatory name and end with the consequences. The structure strengthens the orientation of the reader and helps him to stay focused.

Principle 5: Publish and make the patterns available
Your patterns must be made available. Nobody will ask you for the pattern if you do not take the initiative to «spread the good word». The availability of the patterns does not imply that they in fact will be used. You will have to initiate the discussion, show the benefit, and talk to your stakeholders. You will notice that as soon as you engage the discussion about patterns you will also contribute to a change of mind toward the Enterprise Architecture, as the patterns are a tool to help.

2.9   Notes About Notation

In the sections an overview of what an AB is and who the different stakeholders in our EAP world are, has been given. In this chapter we dig further into the topic of how artifacts can be documented and specify the language in which the patterns are visualized. The chosen notation is derived from the ArchiMate® (ArchiMate 2011) specification, the BPMN standard (BPMN 2011), and a network notation that has been applied in hundreds of ICT-projects at a governmental agency. The notations presented in this chapter deal only with the graphical view of an EAP – the rest of the EAP is described according to Sect. 2.11.

A graphical notation always needs an explanation. You will need to document the semantic, the meaning behind the symbols, and their relationship with English (or your preferred language) words. This can be best done with tables describing the attributes (in UML these attributes are called *tagged values*) that define the content of a symbol. You will find an overview for every view in the following sections and the complete symbols and their meanings in Chap. 6.

We chose the following criteria to define the notation to describe the EAPs:

- Based on standards whenever possible.
- Simple enough, so that a reader can understand the semantic without having to work with the notation everyday. This means that we had to simplify the notations given by the standards without breaking the rules.
- Supported by common design tools used for documenting software or architecture artifacts (e.g., Visual Paradigm, Sparx EA, Bizagi, Visio, and others).

To define the description language in this book, we have taken the stakeholder listed in Sect. 2.6 and defined four different views that address their respective concerns. For every view the suitable graphical notation has been defined.

The diagrams of the different views do not represent the one and only truth –
you may well find other graphical representations or other relationships between
the elements. We believe that they will help to understand the purpose of an EAP
and constitute a consistent and uniform way to allow us to compare the patterns
and keep the same granularity for all views.

2.9.1 Holistic View

This view encompasses all the architectural layers. It consists of the architecture
bricks and their relationships, hiding the details like functions, services, and so on.
It represents the lowest level of detail in the pattern map. This view is well suited to
communicate with stakeholders like project sponsors or the management. To document this view we use a very simple notation, consisting of squares that represent
the architecture bricks (Fig. 2.3) and a symbol that shows whether a brick provides

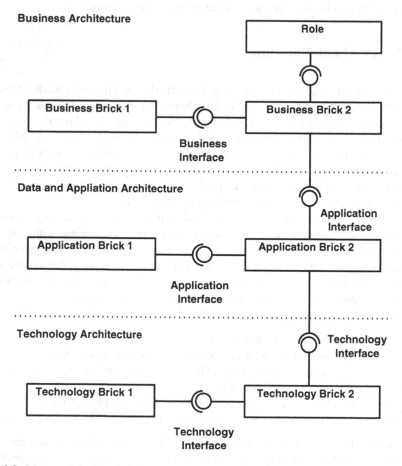

Fig. 2.3 Meta-model of the holistic view

or uses an interface of another brick. The symbol for the interface is the same as what we use for the pattern map. Note that a similar representation with the ArchiMate® shapes could also be made (e.g., process symbols for the Business Architecture, application components for the Data and Application Architecture, and so on). We opted to use only one symbol to represent the bricks in all layers in order to keep a very simple holistic view. A table that provides a description of the most important Architecture Bricks always follows the diagram of the holistic view.

Note that the holistic view can easily be drawn with a UML component diagram or with the ArchiMate® application components and application interface symbols (as we in fact did).

2.9.2 Business View

The BPMN standard is nowadays widely used to document business processes. We will use only a few symbols to document the business layer of the EAPs and provide more insight into the business requirements and drivers of an EAP. As with the holistic view, we will only use a subset of the notation provided by the BPMN standard. We assume that the notation is well known (The symbols used in this book are explained in Chap. 6). Figure 2.4 shows an example.

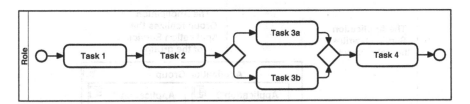

Fig. 2.4 BPMN diagram for the business architecture

2.9.3 Data and Application View

In this view we will look a bit more in detail at the different objects and their relationships to the data and application architecture layers based on a reduced ArchiMate® specification. For the notation we adhere to the same concept of passive, active, and behavioral structure as proposed by the standard. We also use the same symbols, but only a subset of it. The same is true for the different kinds of relationships provided by the specification. We made the following simplifications:

- There is only one element that represents the core of the application. We use the application component and omit the application functions, collaborations, and so on.
- The application component always exposes its functions through an application service. Each service is only accessible through an application interface

(you cannot access a service directly). The service is always responsible for the data it accesses either in write or read mode. This leverages the concept of service orientation.

We also stripped down the number of available connectors: Interfaces are associated to a service or application element, the application service is realized with an application component, an interface is being used by an application component.

Figure 2.5 shows all the symbols and relationships as they are used in this book.

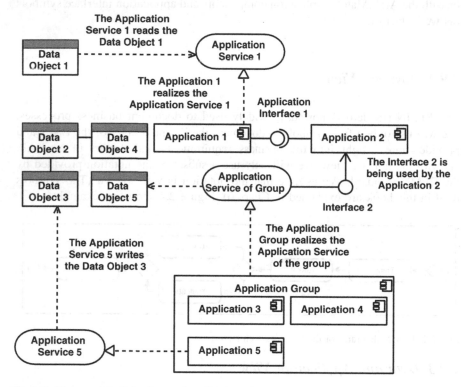

Fig. 2.5 Meta-model of the data and application view

2.9.4 Technology View

In practice not everyone is able (or willing) to read and understand an UML-based notation. Especially when it comes to technical details, networking and hardware issues, a specific notation can be of great help. Figure 2.6 shows the elements we have chosen to deal with these issues. The elements are the servers, clients, directories, gateways, and so on. An arrow visualizes the relationship between two elements. The arrow is annotated with the acronym (e.g., http) of a networking protocol. This view enables us to talk about physical structures, networking policies, redundancy, hardware cost, and so on.

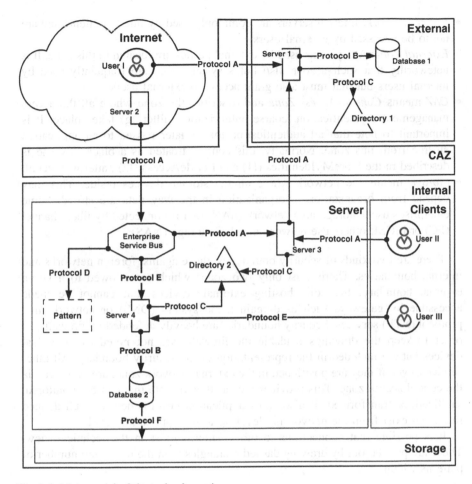

Fig. 2.6 Meta-model of the technology view

We propose this simple notation, which has been used in hundreds of projects and which can be understood by administrators, network engineers, solution architects, or project managers as well.

At the very bottom of this notation lies the networking zone. We propose a universally applicable, very reduced networking structure consisting of the following networking zones:

- *Internal Zone*: This zone is divided into at least two logical zones.
- *Clients Network*: This network consists of internal clients used by employees of the organization. Road warriors are counted to this network zone, as they are normally a part of this network by means of a VPN (Virtual Private Network) connection.

- *Server Network*: Internal servers are commonly used by internal clients and are not to be accessed by external users.
- *External Zone*: All systems used by external parties are located in this zone. It is noteworthy that such a zone also holds systems that are frequently used by internal users but that must also grant access to external users.
- *CAZ* means *Central Access Zone* and describes the zone where all the access management (authentication, coarse authorization, filtering) takes place. It is important to note that all authentication tokens later passed to an application emerge from this zone. Normally, this zone is treated as a black box and is described in the StoreMyIdentities (I1) and LetMeAccess (I2) patterns in detail.
- *Storage* means the network where all the storage devices reside. This may depend from organization to organization in the way data are stored. Some enterprises use a storage area network (SAN) that is connected by fiber channel (FC) or iSCSI; others use network attached storage (NAS).

There are two kinds of security boundaries, those against foreign networks and internal boundaries. There exist only two zones which are allowed to have an external boundary, the zone hosting external services that cannot be made accessible by gateways such as domain name system (DNS) or network time protocol (NTP) services. Security boundaries are heavily defended by firewalls. In order to keep the drawings readable the firewalls are not noted as individual devices but are included in the representation of the security boundary. All other services, even if they are positioned in the external network zone, are accessed via the central access zone. This provides a clear flow of data that can be monitored, sanitized, or transformed. It also eases application development as well-defined interfaces exist from the networking level up to the application level.

It is possible that connections to other patterns exist in the technical view. These are pointed out by drawing dashed rectangles with the name and number of patterns within.

2.10 Pattern Types

We present 13 patterns in this book. We identified them based on our experience when working as architects and discussing with other Enterprise Architects. When putting the patterns together, we had to decide whether we wanted to classify them. One possibility would have been to simply enumerate them as we went along with writing them. To help the reader to be able to choose from the catalog depending on his needs, we came up with a simple categorization scheme: Every company has core business processes and supporting processes like finance or human resources. These two process types gave us the first categories («Business Patterns» and «Support Patterns»). We were still missing a possibility to categorize patterns that work «in the background», meaning that they provided basic services (like security or access management) to the patterns in the two aforementioned categories. We call this category the «Infrastructure Patterns». The differentiation between these three types of patterns reflects the fact that there exists a 1:1 or n:1 relationship between a business process and ICT technology. A 1:1 relationship would indicate that a Business Pattern is needed whereas support and Infrastructure Patterns most often form n:1 relationships, meaning that the ICT infrastructure is needed by different business processes.

Table 2.9 shows the three pattern types with a short explanation.

Table 2.9 Type of a pattern

Type	Explanation
Business	These patterns are directly related to a core business process. The use of these kinds of patterns is dependent on the sector the company or organization makes business. For example, the VendingMachine (B2) pattern will only be implemented by companies selling goods over the Internet. A business pattern uses often far more interfaces from other patterns than it provides
Support	The typical support processes of a company are human resources, financial services, and logistics. We put all patterns in this category that are not directly involved in a core business process, but are nevertheless essential for the direct provision of core business services. We believe that these patterns will be useful in practically all ICT environments. Examples of this type of pattern are FromSupplierToCustomer (S4) or Financials (S1)
Infrastructure	These patterns provide basic services for all patterns. The services are often not directly visible to end users, but are essentials for the effective and efficient functioning of an ICT environment. An infrastructure pattern often provides more interfaces than it requires. Examples are StoreMyIdentities (I1) or UnderControl (I3)

As Infrastructure patterns form the base of all patterns, we recommend having a look at them first (see also Chap. 5 on using patterns). If you have to implement a new selling channel over the Internet, you will certainly first dig into the appropriate Business Pattern and then you will probably be confronted with problems that are being solved using the infrastructure patterns (e.g., Identity Management issues).

2.11 The Structure of a Pattern

We now are ready to define how an EAP should be documented. In the following paragraphs, we will describe the characteristics of a pattern and give some explanations concerning the different parameters common to all patterns. A pattern is described using the following section structure as shown in Table 2.10 (the X is a placeholder for the respective chapter number):

Table 2.10 Structure of a pattern

Section	Subsections
X.11.1 Introduction	
	Name and overview
	Definition
X.11.2 Example	
X.11.3 Context	
X.11.4 Problem	
X.11.5 Solution	
	Vision
	Principles
	Holistic view
	Business view
	Data and application view
	Technology view
X.11.6 Resulting context	
	Interaction
	Consequences
X.11.7 References	

In the following sections, we will dig a little deeper into the structure of a pattern and give a short explanation for every part of a pattern.

2.11.1 Introduction

The introductory chapter must be short and concise. It gives the name and defines the topic of the pattern. Besides the name, a table shows the most important parameters.

Name and Overview
Whereas this chapter is pretty self-explanatory, it should be pointed out that choosing a good name is crucial.

The «gang of four» stated that

> «The pattern name is a handle we can use to describe a design problem, its solutions, and consequences in a word or two. Naming a pattern immediately increases our design vocabulary. It lets us design at a higher level of abstraction. Having a vocabulary for patterns lets us talk about them with our colleagues, in our documentation, and even to ourselves.» (Gamma et al. 1995)

For the notation of the name we use the so-called «camel caps» (or Bumpy-Caps) with the first letter of the word compound capitalized: KnowYourCustomer (B3), VendingMachine (B2), etc. Wherever suitable, we made the word compound with a verb and a noun. The purpose is to show that an EAP is somewhat always related to an activity. A reference to an EAP in this book is always the name of the pattern followed by the abbreviation of the type (first letter, B for Business Pattern)

and the number in parenthesis. This is a similar notation as used by Alexander
et al. (1977) and Gamma et al. (1995), e.g., VendingMachine (B2).

In ICT terminology we know a lot of acronyms like ERP, CRM, IDM, and so
on. When people use these acronyms they often relate them to their experience and
knowledge in their specific field of work. Moreover, vendors leave their mark on
these acronyms and use them in their marketing flavor. In the view of Microsoft a
customer relationship management (CRM) system is not the same as for SAP. You
have to consider these facts when talking to people using acronyms. To avoid
possible misunderstandings or preconceptions, we would not use any of these
abbreviation in the naming of the patterns. Of course we will make, when suitable,
references to these acronyms in the specific patterns. For example, the pattern
KnowYourCustomer (B3) is closely related to CRM (who had thought of this?).

A table such as shown in Table 2.11 is used as an overview of the pattern and
provides hints to architects whether this pattern is suited for their purpose or not.

Table 2.11 Overview of a pattern

Name	The name must be as precise and self-explanatory as possible
Number	Each pattern has a unique number
Type of pattern	Business, support, or infrastructure
Abstract	A short concatenation of the most important facts of the pattern
Capabilities	Capabilities provided by the pattern. This gives a hint, which business requirements are met by the pattern
Referenced patterns	Patterns that provide a service that is going to be used by this pattern
Bricks	Bricks used in this pattern
Impeding Forces	Forces that are working against the implementation of the pattern
Supporting Forces	Forces that support and work towards the implementation of the pattern
Invariance	The degree of confidence we have that this pattern exists in exactly this form in various enterprises
Complexity	The complexity is a measure that gives you a hint of how much effort we think you must put in, to implement the pattern
Connectivity	This parameter measures the strength of interdependence between this pattern and others
Keywords	Keywords help finding and—in case of a database used—indexing the pattern catalog

The «Type of pattern» and the three parameters «Invariance», «Complexity»,
and «Connectivity» need a little bit more explanation:

To differentiate and classify the patterns, we have defined three types as
explained in Sect. 2.10.

The three parameters «Invariance», «Complexity», and «Connectivity» represent a purely qualitative and personal appreciation (and will not withstand any
scientific examinations). They facilitate a comparison between different patterns
and point out possible similarities or differences.

The «Invariance» parameter tries to represent the likelihood that the pattern can be applied in different companies or organizations more or less exactly as described. Alexander et al. (1977) uses a very similar approach: They use the invariance property, marked with two, one, or no asterisks in the pattern. The invariance of a pattern defines whether a problem can be solved as stated in their book.

> «Two asterisks mean that it is not possible to solve the stated problem properly, without shaping the environment in one way or another according to the pattern (…)» (Alexander et al. 1977).

We will use the following metrics to define the invariance of a pattern (Table 2.12):

Table 2.12 Invariance of a pattern

Value	Explanation
Low	The stated problem can be solved in many different ways. The described pattern offers a certain guideline on how you could apply it, but there will certainly be other solutions to solve the problem. These patterns are often highly dependent on the context they are used in. Examples: FromSupplierToCustomer (S4), WorkTogether (B1)
Medium	The proposed pattern has some qualities of invariance, but we strongly recommend that you apply it as described if «in doubt». You may find a solution that suits your needs better than the solution proposed in this book, but the pattern shows you the right direction to take. Examples: Financials (S1), ResourcesAreScarce (S3)
High	We believe that we have found a generic solution to the problem and that the pattern can be applied as described. Examples: VendingMachine (B2), ForYourEyesOnly (S5)

The «Complexity» of a pattern is a hint on the number of elements and relationship between these elements in a pattern. By elements we mean the total number of «things» in all the views: Activities in processes, bricks, applications, servers, and the relationships between these. The complexity is therefore a parameter that reflects how much effort you must put in, to implement the pattern (Table 2.13).

Table 2.13 Complexity of a pattern

Value	Explanation
Low	The pattern consists of only few elements (bricks, applications, servers, and so on) and relationships between these elements. Examples: VendingMachine (B2), ForYourEyesOnly (S5)
Medium	The pattern consists of a moderate number of elements and/or a moderate number of relationships between the elements. Examples: Financials (S1), ResourcesAreScarce (S3)
High	The pattern consists of a high number of elements and relationships between these elements. Examples: WorkTogether (B1), LetMeAccess (I2)

The purpose of the «Connectivity» parameter is to show how highly a pattern is connected to other patterns. It is closely related to the pattern map and gives you a hint how important a pattern may be (It is like in the social communities: the more followers or friends you have, the more important you think you are...) (Table 2.14).

Table 2.14 Connectivity of a pattern

Value	Explanation
Low	The pattern has only little connections with other patterns or systems. It is usually not a core element of an Enterprise Architecture and will normally not be used in every context. It may function in a self-sustaining way and/or serves a highly specialized purpose. Its implementation depends on the nature and maturity of the enterprise. Example: VendingMachine (B2)
Medium	The pattern has a moderate number of connections to other patterns or systems. It is not mandatory to be implemented in every context, but its use is highly recommended. It is often used in companies as an element to support important business processes but we do not consider it to be a core pattern for the underlying infrastructure. Examples: KnowYourCustomers (B3), ResourcesAreScarce (S3)
High	The pattern has a large number of connections to other patterns or systems. It is a core element of any architecture and can be implemented in every context. Patterns with a high degree of interaction, especially when they provide more services than they use, are core patterns. They should be implemented first as the patterns with a lower degree of interaction depend on them. Examples: StoreMyIdentities (I1), LetMeAccess(I2), Financials (S1)

Definition

It is important that the purpose of the pattern is clearly and unambiguously defined. To define a pattern we make references to sources that define the most important terms used. For each pattern we then derive our own definition.

2.11.2 Example

The motivation of a pattern should be introduced by telling a story from real life. This conforms to the statement of Gamma et al. (1995) that a pattern should not be invented but found.

> Bob works at the company TheWineBottle as a key account manager. During his sales tours he often has to contact the sales department over phone to get possible changes in prices and stock information. It would be more efficient if Bob could have all these information in time and online without having to call over phone.

2.11.3 Context

The context describes under what circumstances the pattern is applicable and what the preconditions are that an enterprise must fulfill in order to use this pattern.

2.11.4 Problem

This section describes the problem that should be solved in greater detail and emphasizes the forces that must be taken into account. As Harrison states:

> The notion of «forces» equates in many ways to the «qualities» that architects seek to optimize, and the concerns they seek to address, in designing architectures. (Harrison 2007)

Forces should be taken into account before implementing the pattern as this alleviates the planning and project marketing. In nearly every circumstance there exist forces that help in promoting the pattern (called supporting forces) as well as forces that stand against a successful implementation (impeding forces). The goal of anyone trying to implement a pattern must be to correctly identify the relevant stakeholders and their concerns. The opposing stakeholders should be convinced of the beneficial effect to transform them into supporting forces or at least to keep them neutral so as not to endanger the successful use of the pattern. The supporting forces should be fostered to gain momentum during the planning, implementation, and use of the pattern.

The problem description features three views, the organization's view, the Enterprise Architect's view, and the end-user's view. The first view represents the problem as the organization sees it, meaning why and where deficits exist that hinder the organization to use its ICT infrastructure efficiently. It is the overall problem description. The Enterprise Architect's view describes the situation as it is perceived by the Enterprise Architect. Often this description makes a relation to the organization's view and how this must be changed. Last but not least is the end-user's view that shows if and how the end-user is affected by the problem. The end-user may be an employee as well as a customer depending on the pattern. It is noteworthy that most patterns solve more than one problem. However, it may be possible that a problem mentioned in the description is not solvable in its entirety by one pattern alone but more likely by a combination of different patterns.

2.11.5 Solution

The solution consists of a vision, principles, and the different views as described in Sect. 2.9.

Vision and Principles

The vision describes the desired state a pattern should enable. It should be used as guidance for governing the infrastructure and processes affected by the pattern.

The principles are derived from the vision and state high-level targets that must be adhered to in order to reach the goal of the pattern.

The vision and the principles taken together describe, in fact, the core of a possible strategy. They define the «to be» architecture on a very high level and are suitable to communicate with the management. We described some of the principles in the EAPs, you may well add further ones which reflect the situation of your company.

Holistic View

The Holistic View gives an oversight of the pattern and helps to link together the various views and concerns of the different architecture, business, and ICT levels. Having a holistic view is important as otherwise the successful and sustainable implementation is endangered. If you «forget» about the business processes it may well be that a pattern is perfectly realized at the infrastructure level but no one is going to use it or people use it in a way it has not been made for.

Business View

The Business Architecture represents the view of the business toward a pattern. Therefore, the main focus lies within the description of the business case and the business processes that are going to be supported or enabled by this pattern.

It must be formulated in a way that makes no reference to the technical solution but should give the frame for ICT support. Therefore, the Business View should be as abstract as necessary in order to be applicable in any environment trying to implement the pattern but as precise as possible so that it is unambiguous. The Business View could be seen as derivative of a business scenario concentrating on the business level form the architect's point of view.

The Business View must include the following elements:

- BPMN-based diagram showing the whole process.
- Short description of the business process.

As already explained in Sect. 2.9, the BPMN-based diagram defines the flow of information throughout the business process and points out the most important steps and decisions that are made by the participants of the process. The description of the business process and the actors strengthens and refines the BPMN diagram in a way that enables the reader to fully understand the intent and outcome of the Business Architecture layer. The main purpose of the Business View is not to show the detailed activities, but to set the context of the pattern.

Data and Application View

The Data and Application View is the glue between the Business View and the Technology View. While the business architecture is driven by the business needs

and constraints, the technological architecture must take the technological possibilities and restrictions into account. The data and application architecture is where both layers meet and it is important that this layer is fully understood and agreed upon by the business architects as well as by the technology architects. The Data and Application View is described in a notation based on ArchiMate®.
Following the diagram is a short description.

Technology View
The Technology View describes the pattern in a technical way. The notation is kept very simple and should give a good overview of every component needed to implement the pattern. The notation has been in use in the Federal Administration of Switzerland for several years and has been proved as well-defined and comprehensible by all participants.

Basically, it consists of the following elements:

- The technological bricks (being a logical aggregation physical or virtual systems, such as a database system or a web server).
- Different networking zones with different levels of security.
- Connecting or dividing elements between these zones (firewalls, gateways).
- Information and connection flows between the bricks.

The network layout may be seen as the map on which the technological architecture is built. It roughly shows the flow of connection and information. The main components being used («the buildings») are the technological bricks we utilize. It is important that this is done in a vendor-neutral way as the pattern should be applicable regardless of any vendor decisions an enterprise has made.

2.11.6 Resulting Context

The resulting context describes what the architect has to expect when implementing the pattern. It consists of an interaction diagram and the consequences arising from the pattern.

Interaction
The interaction between patterns is one of the most important points to consider. The notation chosen is similar to the way Gamma et al. (1995) described the Design Pattern relationships. The pattern being described is in the center, as shown in Fig. 2.7, whereas relationships and interactions with other patterns are referenced through the use of or through providing interfaces.

In the context of interaction, the *use* of an interface from another pattern is most interesting, as it shows how (in-) dependent a pattern is from its environment. The less interfaces a pattern uses in relation to the interfaces it provides, the more it can

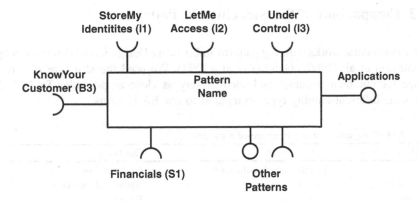

Fig. 2.7 Interaction of an EAP with other patterns

be considered as «standalone». This is typically true for an infrastructure pattern: StoreMyIdentities (I1) or LetMeAccess (I2) are being highly used by every other pattern, but they need practically no external interfaces.

As we did certainly not describe every possible pattern that may exist, we cannot show the full picture of every imaginable interaction of a pattern with its surrounding environment. For example, the number of business applications that use the Financials (S1), WorkTogether (B1), or InformationChest (S2) will vary greatly depending on the business of an enterprise. We therefore chose to use a placeholder for the name of a provided or used interface in the case where the number of patterns that use this interface will not be in our list of described patterns (e.g., «External Financial Applications» or «Applications»).

The complete EAP map consists of all interaction diagrams of the EAPs in this book.

Consequences
The section about consequences describes what the advantages and disadvantages, the risks and chances are that an enterprise has to expect when using this pattern. The architect implementing a pattern should have a clear notion of the advantages and disadvantages of a pattern as well as the possible conflicts. It must be said that patterns – although helpful – can have side effects, for example, decreasing the degree of freedom for certain projects.

2.11.7 References

This section contains further information related to patterns. These are references to publications like books, journals, or Internet links.

2.12 Comparison of the Structure of Patterns

Two fundamental works defining patterns in Software Design have been written by
Buschmann et al. (2000), Gamma et al. (1995). We used the structure as a reference for our own structure and tried to stay as close as possible. Table 2.15
shows the different naming types compared to our EA Patterns.

Table 2.15 Comparison of the structure of a pattern

Buschmann et al.	Gamma et al.	Our book
Name	Pattern and classification	Name and overview
Also known as	Also known as	Name and overview
Example	Motivation	Example
Context	Applicability	Context
Problem	Intent	Problem
Solution	N/A	Solution
Structure	Structure and participants	Resulting context/structure
Dynamics	Collaborations	Resulting context/interaction
Implementation	Implementation and sample code	N/A, case study
Solved example	N/A	N/A
Variants	N/A	N/A
Consequences	Consequences	Resulting context/consequences
See also	Related patterns	Resulting context/interaction

References

ArchiMate (2011) The Open Group: ArchiMate® version 2.0. https://www2.opengroup.org/
  ogsys/catalog/C118. Accessed 21 June 2013
Alexander C, Ishikawa S, Silverstein M (1977) Pattern language: towns, buildings constructions.
  Oxford University Press, New York
BPMN (2011) Business process model and notation version 2.0 (BPMN 2.0). http://www.bpmn.
  org/. Accessed 28 July 2011
Buschmann F, Meunier R, Rohnert H, Sommerlad P, Stal M (2000) Pattern-oriented software
  architecture. Wiley, New York
CGEIT (2012) Certified in the Governance of Enterprise IT (CGEIT). http://www.isaca.org/
  Certification/CGEIT-Certified-in-the-Governance-of-Enterprise-IT/Prepare-for-the-Exam/
  Job-Practice-Areas/Pages/default.aspx. Accessed 5 Dec 2012
Dern G (2006) Management von IT-Architekturen. Vieweg
DoDAF (2011) The DoDAF architecture framework version 2.02. http://dodcio.defense.gov/
  Portals/0/Documents/DODAF/DoDAF_v2-02_web.pdf. Accessed 28 July 2011
FEAF (1999) Federal Enterprise Architecture (FEA). http://www.whitehouse.gov/omb/e-gov/fea/.
  Accessed 28 July 2011
Gamma E, Helm R, Johnson R, Vlissides J (1995) Design patterns. Elements of reusable object-
  oriented software. Addison-Wesley, USA
Harrison R (2007) TOGAF 8.1.1 study guide. Van Haren Publishing, Zaltbommel

ISO/IEC 42010 (2007) JTC 1/SC 7: ISO/IEC 42010:2007 systems and software engineering: recommended practice for architectural description of software-intensive systems. International Organization for Standardization, Geneva

Keller W (2007) IT-Unternehmensarchitektur, dpunkt

Lankhorst M (2005) Enterprise architecture at work modelling, communication, and analysis. Springer, New York

NAF (2011) NATO architecture framework. http://www.nhqc3s.nato.int/HomePage.asp?session= 295712985. Accessed 28 July 2011

NIH: National Institute of Health Enterprise Architecture (2008) What is enterprise architecture? https://enterprisearchitecture.nih.gov/Pages/what.aspx. Accessed 21 June 2013

Perks C, Beveridge T (2003) Guide to enterprise IT architecture. Springer, Berlin

Pettey C, Stevens H (2009) Gartner identifies ten enterprise architecture pitfalls. http://www.gartner.com/it/page.jsp?id=1159617. Accessed 28 July 2011

TOGAF (2009) The Open Group architecture framework. http://pubs.opengroup.org/architecture/togaf9-doc/arch/. Accessed 28 July 2011

UML (2010) The Object Management Group: unified modelling language version 2.3. http://www.omg.org/spec/UML/2.3/Infrastructure/PDF/. Accessed 28 July 2011

Wikipedia EA (2011) Enterprise architecture. http://en.wikipedia.org/wiki/Enterprise_architecture. Accessed 28 July 2011

Zachman J (1987) A framework for information systems architecture. IBM Syst J. http://old.zachmaninternational.com/images/stories/ibmsj2603e.pdf

Chapter 3
The Catalog and the Map

> «All fixed set patterns are incapable of adaptability or
> pliability. The truth is outside of all fixed patterns.»
>
> Bruce Lee

Abstract In this chapter we first give an overview of the pattern catalog with a
short description of every EAP. The first view shows the pattern map from high
above. We then dig into the pattern map and show all dependencies.

3.1 The Pattern Catalog

The pattern catalog contains 13 patterns, divided into three types. Their names and
purposes are listed below to give you an overview. We do not describe all the
possible Enterprise Architecture Patterns – in our understanding there is no
comprehensive list of EAPs. We defined in the catalog the most important patterns
from our point of view and our personal experience.

3.1.1 Business Patterns

We have defined three patterns of the business type. A Business Pattern directly
refers to the business process of an enterprise and its architectural representation.
Of course there may be numerous other patterns in this category. We can easily
imagine that the catalog may be extended with industry-specific patterns, like
patterns for health care, finance, or the automotive industry. We think that we have
found three generic patterns that can be applied in different industries.

WorkTogether (B1) is a pattern that unifies different communication and collaboration functionalities. Internal or external users to the company can join
groups of discussion, share knowledge, and work together on documents to
achieve a common consensus.

VendingMachine (B2) describes how an electronic vending channel (e.g., a web
shop) can be realized. The pattern shows the customer side as well as the organization side that wants to sell goods. The main elements (catalog, order, customer

T. Perroud and R. Inversini, *Enterprise Architecture Patterns*,
DOI: 10.1007/978-3-642-37561-3_3, © Springer-Verlag Berlin Heidelberg 2013

database) are shown in relation to the backend (owner) and frontend (customer) views.

KnowYourCustomer (B3) describes the various ways of interacting and communicating with the customer.

3.1.2 Support Patterns

We have defined five patterns in this category. They are directly related to the typical support processes such as financials, human resources, and logistics.

Financials (S1) provides all necessary services to manage the financial supply chain. It supports the financial performance analysis, the management of accounts, and assets.

InformationChest (S2) deals with the management of structured and semi-structured information. It describes how information can be acquired, transformed, delivered, stored, and archived.

ResourcesAreScarce (S3) provides a solution for an electronic-enabled human resource management («e-HRM»).

FromSupplierToCustomer (S4) encompasses the planning and management of all activities involved in sourcing and procurement, conversion, and all logistics management activities.

ForYourEyesOnly (S5) supports the manual and automatic exchange of files between internal and external persons or systems in an asynchronous way. The pattern provides the necessary mechanisms to protect the files during transport and storage.

3.1.3 Infrastructure Patterns

This category contains five patterns that provide services for all the other patterns. It is certainly a good start to begin to leaf through these patterns first, as all others refer to them.

StoreMyIdentities (I1) describes how electronic identities are created, stored, managed, and used. Identities may refer to internal or external collaborators, customers, suppliers, or other persons, or entities that have a relationship to the enterprise. Tightly connected to the management of identities are credentials and authorization rights, which are also covered by this pattern.

LetMeAccess (I2) provides a solution to grant access to resources, how the requester is authenticated, and how the traffic is transported between different security zones.

UnderControl (I3) is a pattern that gives you a solution for basic security services like logging, network security, or monitoring.

YouHaveMail (I4) deals with all aspects of sending and receiving electronic mails.

TalkToMe (I5) provides a solution for synchronous communication with audio and visual capabilities.

3.2 The Pattern Map

The pattern map gives you an overview of all the patterns and their relationship. The first view as described in Sect. 3.2.1 («Flying High») shows the relation between the types of patterns without looking at the individual patterns. The next view in Sect. 3.2.2 («A Look Inside») shows in detail the relationship between all the patterns in this book. Figure 3.1 shows the organization of the patterns with the three main types, *Business Patterns, Support Patterns,* and *Infrastructure Patterns* with their respective patterns.

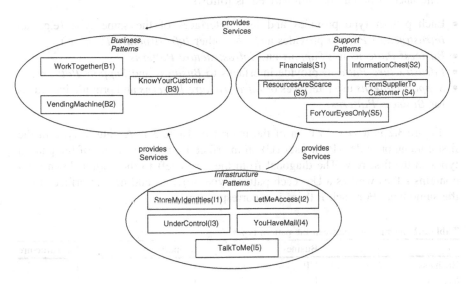

Fig. 3.1 Pattern map

3.2.1 Flying High

The high-level view in Fig. 3.2 shows the generic structure of how these pattern types interact. The components «Business Pattern», «Support Pattern», and «Infrastructure Pattern» are connected through interfaces. The O-shaped connectors («lollipops») represent the provided interfaces and the U-shaped connectors use an interface.

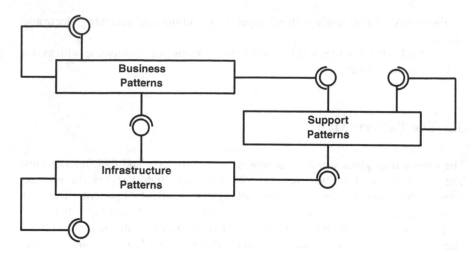

Fig. 3.2 High-level view of the pattern map

The interaction can be summarized as follows:

- Each pattern type provides and uses interfaces of the same type (e.g., an *Infrastructure Pattern* provides and uses other *Infrastructure Patterns*).
- *Business Patterns* use *Support* and *Infrastructure Patterns*.
- *Infrastructure Patterns* provide interfaces to *Business* and *Support Patterns*.
- *Support Patterns* use interfaces of *Infrastructure Patterns* and provide interfaces for *Business Patterns*.

Figure 3.2 is a visualization of the matrix in Table 3.1. A pattern type in the first column provides (P) or uses (U) an interface from one or more of the pattern types in the first row. The diagonal from the upper left to the corner down right contains a P as well as a U – each pattern type provides and uses interfaces from the same type. For each P there is a corresponding U.

Table 3.1 Interactions between the pattern types

	Business	Support	Infrastructure
Business	UP	U	U
Support	P	UP	U
Infrastructure	P	P	UP

This high-level view enables us to better understand the differences between the pattern types. *Business Patterns* mainly use interfaces from the other types, *Infrastructure Patterns* provide interfaces, and the *Support Patterns* use and provide interfaces. Note that there are no blank cells in the table. This means that all the pattern types are related to each other. This is not true on the level of the individual patterns, as we will see in the next section.

3.2.2 A Look Inside

Every pattern in this book contains an interaction diagram (see Sect. 2.9) that shows the connections of a pattern with its surrounding patterns. The sum of all these interaction diagrams forms the base of the detailed pattern map. As it would be quite confusing to visualize all the interactions between all the patterns on one page, we provide only the complete matrix of all interfaces and interactions between the patterns as shown in Table 3.2. Each row corresponds to exactly one interaction diagram in the descriptions of the patterns. This means that you will find in the interaction diagram of the pattern VendingMachine (B2) that this pattern uses interfaces of KnowYourCustomer (B3), Financials (S1), InformationChest (S2), FromSupplierToCustomer (S3), StoreMyIdentities (I1), LetMeAccess (I2), UnderControl (I3), and YouHaveMail (I4).

Table 3.2 Interaction matrix of all the patterns

	B1	B2	B3	S1	S2	S3	S4	S5	I1	I2	I3	I4	I5
WorkTogether (B1)	–	–	–	–	U	U	U	U	U	U	U	U	U
VendingMachine (B2)	–	–	U	U	U	–	U	–	U	U	U	U	–
KnowYourCustomer (B3)	–	P	–	–	U	–	U	–	U	U	U	U	U
Financials (S1)	–	P	–	–	P	P	P	U	U	U	U	U	–
InformationChest (S2)	P	P	P	U		P	P	U	U	U	U	U	
ResourcesAreScarce (S3)	P	–	–	U	U	–	P	U	U	U	U	U	–
FromSupplierToCustomer (S4)	P	P	P	U	U	U	–	–	U	U	U	U	–
ForYourEyesOnly (S5)	P	–	–	P	P	P	–	–	U	U	U	U	–
StoreMyIdentities (I1)	P	P	P	P	P	P	P	P	–	UP	U	P	P
LetMeAccess (I2)	P	P	P	P	P	P	P	P	UP	–	U	P	P
UnderControl (I3)	P	P	P	P	P	P	P	P	P	P	–	P	P
YouHaveMail (I4)	P	P	P	P	P	P	P	P	U	U	U	–	–
TalkToMe (I5)	P	–	P	–	–	–	–	–	U	U	U	–	–

Table 3.2 shows only the interaction between the patterns described in this book. When looking at the interaction diagrams in the patterns, you will notice that almost all patterns can also use interfaces from external applications. (e.g., Financials (S1) uses external banking services). We do not mention these interfaces in Table 3.2, as they are not part of the provided patterns.

The diagonal from the upper left to the down right corner is empty, because a pattern does not provide or use interfaces of its own. The matrix is subdivided into nine rectangles – every rectangle corresponds to one field of the matrix entry in Table 3.1.

Chapter 4
More About EAP

«Finally, in conclusion, let me say just this.»
Peter Sellers

Abstract The first part deals with how EAPs can help in structuring the Enterprise Architecture. The second section deals with the application of the patterns and how they evolve over time. In the last two sections, we take a look into the future and motivate the use of EAPs in upcoming trends in ICT.

4.1 More Reasons for Using EAPs

In Chap. 2, we described how EAPs might help in structuring the overall Enterprise Architecture and consolidate existing environments. In the following sections, we give some thoughts about further reasons for using EAPs.

4.1.1 Identifying Fields of Action

We expect that the one who reads the most about EA patterns is the Enterprise Architect. He who defines, plans, aligns, and pushes forward the architecture of his enterprise may use the pattern catalog as an inspiration as well as a comparison to find «his» patterns in his enterprise. There may already be many patterns in place, but also multiple instances of a pattern might be a helpful indicator that work needs to be done. How does your Enterprise Architecture compare to patterns? This may be used as a guidance on where action is needed; for instance, if you observe reoccurring installations all resembling a certain pattern. A typical case may be found with the occurrences of different access management installations.

T. Perroud and R. Inversini, *Enterprise Architecture Patterns*,
DOI: 10.1007/978-3-642-37561-3_4, © Springer-Verlag Berlin Heidelberg 2013

4.1.2 Facilitating Discussions

The noblest purpose of a pattern is to facilitate the discussion between the various stakeholders. The Enterprise Architect finds himself often in the role of a mediator between various requirements and expectations. In order to guide the discussion toward meeting the various requirements, he may use the pattern catalog first to find suitable patterns. Then he discusses the chosen pattern with the various stakeholders. To do this, he focuses on the architectural layer where the discussion partner is most likely to be at ease. He uses the business architecture layer to talk to the stakeholders representing the business and the technical architecture layer for the network or system engineer who has to build the system. The layer in between, the information system layer, should be the glue between these two.

   Whenever a problem needs to be solved that can be described with one of the following questions, the use of patterns may be helpful:

- We want to implement a new ICT strategy, how do we start? Patterns may help by getting a quick overview of the action needed and by providing glue between the business processes and the ICT infrastructure.
- The various stakeholders, especially the business oriented and the infrastructure oriented, do not talk the same language. If you hear repeatedly the sentence «this solution does not meet my requirements» and the answer of ICT is something like «you did not specify this requirement», patterns are a wonderful means to provide a common understanding of needs, requirements, and infrastructure.
- A long-term program to implement a business process is established. Patterns help in every phase of the program to gain oversight and direction and to stay focused.

4.1.3 Working in Projects

While patterns are helpful at a strategic or governance level, the use of Enterprise Architecture Patterns also alleviates the dire everyday work, consulting and guiding projects and trying to fulfill their needs in an ordered and foresighted way without negatively impacting the blueprint of the Enterprise Architecture. As with every project, you should be clear about the requirements of the various stakeholders. Therefore, it is necessary to conduct a stakeholder analysis right at the start. The patterns may serve as a catalog where the Enterprise Architect can show various examples to the stakeholder asking him «did you mean something like this?» When starting the process of clarifying the requirements and proposing solutions, the catalog is very helpful to locate interesting patterns. By looking at the interfaces provided at the three architectural levels, the architect is able to identify and propose promising patterns. As the project progresses, he may use the patterns as a guideline to check whether the project stays focused and is likely to accomplish its goals.

4.2 It Depends…

As every company is unique, with its own identity, communication culture, governance, and business, there is no magic formula we can give you on how to
implement the patterns. It depends on many factors that may even be unique for
your enterprise. But reading and trying to understand the purpose and goals of the
pattern may already be the first steps to leverage your Enterprise Architecture –
independently of the current maturity. Your own debate with the patterns and the
mental mapping with your environment may already help you to structure things in
a better way.

We introduced a language to describe the patterns that we think may be helpful
for the common understanding. This does not mean that the terms we use may be
the right one for your specific environment. You may want to map our terms to
your glossary and definitions. This will first help you to better understand the
patterns (and to question them) and second enable the discussion with your
colleagues.

Even if the patterns are not implemented, they may nevertheless help you in
gaining more insight into a certain topic. The patterns provide a «tour d'horizon»
on a certain topic. This may help you to first gain an oversight and then find the
starting end of the golden thread on how to get into the topic. Take for example
ResourcesAreScarce (S3): The Business View and the Data and Application View
gives you a list of possible tasks and related applications and services that may be
of interest in human resource management. Depending on your environment, you
may already have some elements in place. Perhaps you did not have a structured
overview, as described in the pattern, or some of the elements may be missing. In
this case, the pattern can serve as a reference, an information source, or a possible
to-be architecture, even if you do not implement it.

4.3 Patterns Within Patterns

Several patterns within Enterprise Architecture Patterns seem to exist. We are not
going to discuss these in deeper detail but would like to point them out nevertheless as they give a strong indication of the importance of some of the Enterprise
Architecture patterns or show commonly known and applied paradigms of ICT.

A high-level pattern that characterizes a type of business is the «Acquire-
Transform-Publish» sequence. This pattern is for example shown in Fig. 8.8 of the
InformationChest (S2) pattern. This is a typical sequence found in many business
processes. Examples are governmental agencies gathering statistical data, companies performing customer surveys, or a search engine provider.

At the business level, a frequently occurring schema is the process of login/
logout that surrounds the actual business action. This typical structure that can be
observed as soon as privileges for an operation are slightly elevated, is shown in

Fig. 4.1. This fact emphasizes the importance of the StoreMyIdentities (I1) and LetMeAccess (I2) patterns.

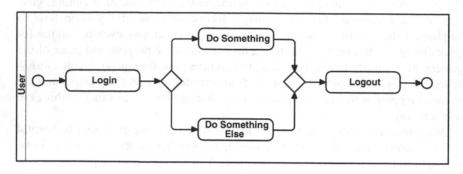

Fig. 4.1   Login/logout structure

Another pattern within patterns at the business level is the search and selection of information that afterwards is modified, enriched, or simply worked upon, see Fig. 4.2. As this pattern is used by all other patterns dealing with information (and we are talking about Information Technology, so it is ubiquitous), it is defined as a business process in the InformationChest (S1) pattern and implicitly used in all other patterns or applications.

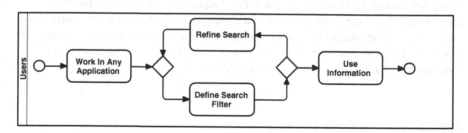

Fig. 4.2   Search pattern

One commonly encountered archetype within patterns is the distinction between frontend and backend at the application level. Often, the frontend is facing the customer whereas the backend is facing internal applications and business logic as well as the further processing of the request that has been placed by the customer. This characteristic has its origins at the business level and can also impact the technical level. It is common that both tiers access the same datasets sometimes with equal rights, but very often users in the backend have more rights as they process the data entered in the frontend. The separation between frontend and backend not only has advantages by simplifying deployment but also in terms of security (Fig. 4.3).

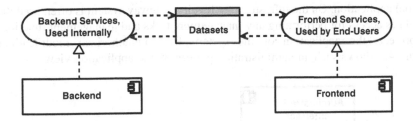

Fig. 4.3   Frontend/backend pattern

At the technical level, the combination of a web server that stores the data in a database, which in turn has access to a storage system, can be seen in nearly every pattern. It is most common but has many implications on various levels. A distinction between these elements decouples the elements and improves manageability, security, and robustness. Changes at any element can be done more easily than in a tightly coupled environment (Fig. 4.4).

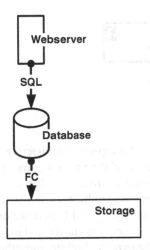

Fig. 4.4   Web server/database pattern

Through all levels of most patterns an administration schema can be seen. As most applications need to be managed, a management or administration interface with the necessary technology must be defined. At a relatively high abstraction level, these have many similarities and, in fact, they can be implemented in a uniform way by defining specially protected administration systems that are accessible for administrators only and that are restricted to the management of systems. This pattern exists on all levels, from the business layer view to the application view down to the technology view. Basically an actor, e.g., a system administrator or an application administrator has to fulfill administration tasks such as modifying configuration parameters. This is done using a management application that can be standalone or embedded into the functionality of the normal application. On the infrastructure level, a gateway system is often used that regulates access for performing any management tasks and management functions. It protects the application or the system from unauthorized modifications. Figure 4.5 shows such an administration pattern on the application view.

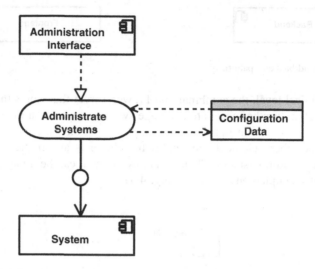

Fig. 4.5   Administration pattern

4.4 (De-)composition

Understanding the nature of Enterprise Architecture is an ongoing process of decomposition and composition of the various parts. At first glance, it is a nearly impenetrable jungle of business processes depending upon applications and infrastructure elements. After having observed the architecture, different recurring patterns are emerging. First, they may be diffused and unclear and this is where the pattern catalog may help out. It helps to clarify and identify different key elements in the infrastructure of the Enterprise Architecture, thus enabling you to decompose the jungle into understandable and manageable bits (and bytes). By having identified the patterns in your own Enterprise Architecture and comparing them to the proposed pattern, you should now be able to compose the new infrastructure by adopting the patterns and changing the Enterprise Architecture into something that is well understood and maintainable and that serves the business best.

4.5 The Life Cycle of a Pattern

EAPs and the real-world architecture evolve and change over time. This may be, for example due to technological advancement (who does nowadays acquire a fax to use them in a business process?) or changes in business processes («it was common to do it that way, the best practice are nowadays to do it this way»). The patterns are the blueprints to transform the Enterprise Architecture but are only useful when taking the real-world situation into account. New facts in the real world influence the patterns and the patterns will lead to a re-Architecting of the real world. The first application of the patterns will probably have the largest impact on re-Architecting efforts, but the more the Enterprise Architecture matures, the less re-Architecting efforts will be necessary.

The life cycle of a pattern begins with the identification in the «as-is» architecture. Identifying means to look out for similarities. A prerequisite to be able to identify patterns is certainly that one must have a description of the «as-is» architecture.

The similarities could be found on every architecture level – be it the business, data and application, or technology level. There are patterns that are obvious, take for example the StoreMyIdentities (I1) or LetMeAccess (I2) patterns. Others may occur only in a certain industry, like a stock exchange application.

The next step consists in documenting the pattern. You may do that according to our proposal in this book or develop an own documentation scheme that suits you best. The important thing in documenting the patterns is to know who will read it and what objectives you want to reach. As described in Sect. 2.8, we recommend beginning with a simple version of the pattern and then refining it over time.

The pattern will help you to define the scope of a project to realize it. It represents, therefore, a part of the to-be architecture and will serve you as a guideline for the implementation. During the implementation you will probably gain new insights. This can lead to modifications of the pattern – and you may make it available to the Enterprise Architecture community.

4.6   Where to Begin: A Question of Maturity

We believe that two ways of applying these patterns exist:

- You have a project to implement and want to help the project leader or solution architect by giving some guidance from the point of view of Enterprise Architecture. We will describe this approach in Chap. 5: The patterns are being applied to solve the problems arising in a project.
- You want to structure your overall Enterprise Architecture, consolidating existing environments, reduce costs, streamline your different architectures, etc. In short: do your job as an Enterprise Architect. This is what we describe in the following:

So, where to begin? For every pattern the three parameters, *Complexity*, *Connectivity*, and *Invariance* are defined according to our opinion. Each parameter can be set with one out of three possible values: Low, Medium, and High. The exact meaning of these parameters and values are defined in Sect. 2.11. This leads to the following Table 4.1:

Table 4.1 Invariance, complexity, and connectivity for every pattern

	Complexity	Connectivity	Invariance
FromSupplierToCustomer (S4)	High	High	Low
StoreMyIdentities (I1)	High	High	Medium
LetMeAccess (I2)	High	High	Medium
InfoChest (S2)	High	High	Medium
WorkTogether (B1)	High	Medium	Low
UnderControl (I3)	Medium	High	Low
Financials (S1)	Medium	High	Medium
KnowYourCustomer (B3)	Medium	Medium	High
ResourcesAreScarce (S3)	Medium	Medium	Medium
TalkToMe (B5)	Low	Medium	Medium
ForYourEyesOnly (S5)	Low	Medium	High
YouHaveMail (B4)	Low	Medium	High
VendingMachine (B2)	Low	Low	High

In Table 4.1, the patterns are sorted according to their complexity and connectivity and not according to the type and number of the pattern. This is due to the fact that there is no correlation or causality between the type of the pattern and the three parameters taken together.

The *Invariance* parameter is the measure for our confidence in having found a generic pattern. The higher the value, the more confident we are. When looking at the last row we can see a tendency: The higher the complexity and connectivity, the less generic the pattern is to our understanding. This is quite obvious as an increasing connectivity and a high complexity makes different implementations of a pattern much more likely. Another tendency that can be deduced is that the simpler the business layer, the lower the complexity.

Using patterns to consolidate your Enterprise Architecture means that you need an overall view of the topic of patterns you want to implement: As the green-field approach in most cases is not an option, you first have to gain an understanding of what is already in place. Take for example the StoreMyIdentities (I2) pattern: Chances are high that there are already many different instantiations in your architecture. To be able to document the «as-is» architecture of your identity management environment, you will need to get the necessary resources and management commitment. If the Enterprise Architecture function is not yet well established, you will encounter many obstacles that are not directly related to the implementation of the pattern. The justification of the existence and goals of the Enterprise Architecture will be questioned and you will have to do a lot of lobbying for your cause. The less mature the Enterprise Architecture, the more difficult it is to handle architecture topics that affect the overall architecture. In relation to Table 4.1 this means that it is certainly easier to start with the patterns at the bottom of the list, if the Enterprise Architecture function is still in its infancy. If the maturity of the Enterprise Architecture is low, you should do the following: Begin with patterns where you do not need a high commitment from upper management. This can be done for patterns with a low to medium complexity and connectivity. VendingMachine (B2) and ForYourEyesOnly (S5) are in our opinion the most easy patterns to implement and do not represent a large risk. If you do not need these patterns, take the first one that suits you, beginning at the bottom of the list. Doing so allows you not only to implement patterns successfully, but also to gain broad acceptance for the Enterprise Architecture. This finding correlates also to our rating of the invariance of a pattern. In other words, when choosing first a pattern with a high invariance and therefore a low complexity and connectivity you are on the safe side. However, if your Enterprise Architecture has already gained some level of maturity and you have at least partial support by top management, the gain of implementing a pattern with high complexity and connectivity such as StoreMyIdentities (I1) or LetMeAccess (I2) may be of greatest benefit for the enterprise as many applications profit and as many other patterns can unleash their full potential. If you want to measure the maturity of your Enterprise Architecture, take for example (NASCIO 2007) or (ACMM 2007) as a guideline.

There is certainly no magic formula that will tell you which pattern you should implement first. Every environment is different and has its own specificities to consider. Assessing the maturity of the Enterprise Architecture is one way of getting into the topic. Another possibility is shown in Chap. 5.

4.7 Less Is More

While writing this book and carrying on our jobs, we observed an interesting phenomenon that may give a hint on how the «as-is» landscape of an Enterprise Architecture evolves. We believe that the evolutionary stage gives an indication of the maturity level an enterprise has concerning Enterprise Architecture in general and of the use of EA patterns.

What can often be observed is that for many of the patterns, especially Infrastructure and Support Patterns, a variety of unconnected instances may exist. In the first stage; the instances multiply as every project is confronted with such requirements and is forced to find a solution on its own. It may seem to be an unsolvable task to introduce some organization into this jungle. In the next stage, the instances within one pattern begin to harmonize and one after the other is given up or integrated in the instance with the highest potential. This process can be unguided, driven by the pressure of cost saving and complexity or it can be guided by a strategy, which of course is the preferable way. After some time, a form that is often very likely to these presented in this book has evolved. Simultaneously with the reduction of instances within one pattern, links between different instances of the same pattern begin to form and are getting more and more important. Figure 4.6 shows such an evolution. At the initial stage, two different Business Patterns have their own instance of the same support and the same Infrastructure Patterns. For example, the VendingMachine (B1) pattern (or an application resembling this pattern) and the KnowYourCustomer (B3) pattern both use their own instances (named *a*, *b*, *c*) of the InformationChest (S2) and the StoreMyIdentities (I1) pattern. In fact, there exist three StoreMyIdentities (I1) instances as the identities are fragmented into internal and external users. During the transitional phase, a consolidation of the various instances can be observed. While the instances of the Support Pattern are migrated into a new application, the identity management is concentrated into one of the existing instances (I1c). When a level of maturity is reached, the connections are well-defined and simple. The new Support Pattern has evolved and is being used by both Business Patterns; the same applies for the Infrastructure Pattern, from which only one instance exists that is being used by all patterns.

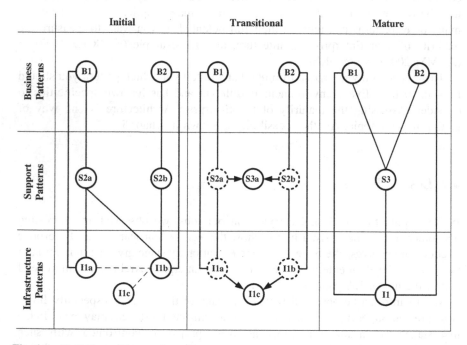

Fig. 4.6   Evolution of the number of instances

4.8 EAPs and Actual Trends in ICT

During the writing of the book, we were asked several times, whether the patterns would become obsolete with the upcoming of *cloud computing*. We are convinced that even in a cloud computing environment, be it software-as-a-service (SaaS), platform-as-a-service (PaaS), infrastructure-as-a-service (IaaS), or even business-as-a-service (BaaS), the patterns can be applied. Identity and access management, collaboration, or customer management outcomes must be solved even in a cloud computing environment. Moreover, we think that new patterns may arise. On-demand capacity management and pay-per-use services are two examples that could be investigated further. The just-in-time provisioning of computing resources can even be leveraged by the use of EAPs: The patterns will not only help in provisioning single computing resources, but entire solutions with networks of resources according to a pattern.

The announced demise of Services-Oriented Architecture (SOA) in 2009 by Anne Thomas Manes (Manes 2009) and her call to concentrate on *services* is still valid. Service orientation is still a topic, but perhaps with less euphoria and more (economic) realism. The EAPs support the paradigm of service orientation: Architecture bricks are decoupled through the use of interfaces, and applications communicate using services. The services are coarse grained and have a high degree of reusability.

Mobility is one of the major trends in ICT: The access to business information on the road, concepts like Bring Your Own Device (BYOD) or the convergence of data and telephony on the smartphone are now radically changing our ways of communicating together. People are constantly online, checking their e-mails, organizing meetings, or approving application when outside of the company. We tried to take this trend into account when describing EAPs: You will find for example references to mobility in all Business Patterns.

The upcoming of *social media* within companies will open new communication and information paths. The first companies have already begun – for example, by formulating policies that will ban e-mails and substitute it with social media technologies (wikis, blogs, electronic pin boards, etc.). WorkTogether (B1), KnowYourCustomer (B3), or ResourcesAreScarce (S3) are all EAPs that refer to the communication between persons, be they employees, partners, or customers. You will find in all these patterns references to the use of social medias as possible means of communication.

The promises of the hype called *big data* to unveil new insights in the ever-growing amount of data will be put to test in the next few years. Besides the mastering of the necessary technologies to cope with real-time analysis of huge amounts of data, we will probably also need new skills of experts who are able to investigate these data. This may lead to new processes and ways of dealing with information and subsequently to new Enterprise Architecture Patterns.

4.9 The Future

We are convinced that Enterprise Architecture is one of the most important fields for most enterprises as otherwise they risk losing control over cost and orientation in the field of Information Technology and data architecture. In order to reduce the complexity and to have a common understanding between the various stakeholders, the concept of patterns may be of high value.

If you have come this far in the book, we would like to encourage you to follow the path of working with patterns and to share new or derived patterns with the community.

References

ACMM (2007) United States Department of Commerce: enterprise architecture capability maturity model. http://ocio.os.doc.gov/ITPolicyandPrograms/Enterprise_Architecture/PROD01_004935. Accessed 28 Feb 2012

NASCIO (2007) National Association of the State Chief Information Officers. http://www.nascio.org/publications/documents/nascio-eamm.pdf. Accessed 21 June 2013

Manes A (2009) SOA is dead; long live services. Burton Group blogs. http://apsblog.burtongroup.com/2009/01/soa-is-dead-long-live-services.html. Accessed 4 Mar 2012

Chapter 5
Using Patterns

«*Good wine needs no bush.*»
Saying

Abstract In this chapter we show how patterns can be identified and applied in a real-life scenario. The fictive company, TheWineBottle, is used in all the examples and in the description of the patterns as well.

5.1 Phil: The ICT Enterprise Architect of TheWineBottle

TheWineBottle is a small to medium enterprise selling high quality Italian wine. The company started 10 years ago with wine packages being solely delivered to customers who took out a subscription, receiving every two months three equal bottles of wine. Meanwhile, the activities evolved and TheWineBottle became one of the largest wine delivery companies in the country. Nowadays, the company delivers wine not only directly to private customers (B2C), but also to business customers (B2B). The product catalog has been vastly expanded, including also articles related to wine in general (wine glasses, corkscrews, and so on).

May we introduce Phil, the ICT architect of the company called TheWine-Bottle. Phil is in charge of the overall architecture and is confronted with an increasing need for information and communication services. This is mostly due to the flourishing activities of the company and its strategy to acquire new customers and markets.

To fulfill its business, the company relies now heavily on Information Technology:

- Sales representatives need up-to-date information anytime, everywhere.
- Electronic identities and related attributes of customers and company personnel must be managed.
- The access to information for field agents and customers must be possible with any kind of electronic device (workstation, handhelds, and electronic tablets) used to navigate on the Internet.
- In order to stay competitive, new sales channels provided by modern Internet technologies must be incorporated into the overall architecture.

T. Perroud and R. Inversini, *Enterprise Architecture Patterns*,
DOI: 10.1007/978-3-642-37561-3_5, © Springer-Verlag Berlin Heidelberg 2013

- Critical business information must be securely exchanged with partners, customers, and supporting companies.
- The delivery chain and all the logistics processes must be supported within the whole information and communication environment.
- Accurate and up-to-date financial information must be provided to the management.

TheWineBottle has actually only a rudimentary web-shop in production. The customers can fill-in their orders on a web page with an integrated product catalog, but the order is then sent as a structured e-mail to the backend systems. Currently, there is no option to pay by credit card. The customers always receive an invoice by e-mail. In the past, the current solution proved to be prone to errors, mainly due to the many gaps in the electronic end-to-end processing of an order. One issue is that the delivery process is not as effective as the management would like it.

These facts were well known to Phil and his crew of ICT specialists, so they decided to remedy these problems. Besides the goal of improving the efficiency and effectiveness of the delivery process, the new solution must also integrate a state-of-the-art web-shop into the existing environment. An expected side effect of this initiative is that the basis for a better customer relationship management and the ability to gain new customers is laid. Phil got the necessary attention from the management (meaning support, money, and resources) to define the «as-is» as well as the effective solution architecture that is going to be built. Subsequently, the implementation of the solution architecture will be handled by a project.

To achieve his goals, Phil remembers having read a book on Enterprise Architecture Patterns with a catalog of predefined solutions to recurring problems (Ok, now we are in a recursive loop...).

5.2 Identification of Patterns

The first thing Phil is going to do is to *identify* the relevant patterns for him to use. There are different ways how to identify patterns, each Enterprise Architect is going to have his own «magical formula» that is very often based on a mixture of personal experience and best practice. We do not advise at all to change this: The following way, how Phil tries to extract important elements, is just a suggestion.

Having worked as a software engineer, Phil uses a technique often used in object-oriented programming: He uses a highlighter and marks every relevant noun in the strategic documents, the requirements description, and in the project descriptions, identifying possible candidates. These are likely to be indicators for «things» which are also referenced in a pattern.

Doing so, Phil produces the following keywords: Electronic devices, electronic identities and related attributes, web-shop, customer relationship management, delivery chain, financial information.

When working with our book, Phil can use these nouns to identify the following patterns as being possible candidates to dig further into: StoreMyIdentities (I1), LetMeAccess (I2), Financials (S1), KnowYourCustomer (B3), and VendingMachine (B2).

Having also worked as a requirements engineer, Phil is used to another technique well suited to identify the patterns: He compares the list of requirements he got during the requirements engineering phase, with the ones described in the patterns. Each pattern comes with a list of capabilities, so the task for Phil to find a possible (or suitable) pattern is in fact comparing his set of requirements with the provided capabilities. Phil will probably have to categorize or sort the requirements slightly differently, so that he may be able to match them to the capabilities in the patterns.

In most cases, the choice of the pattern is obvious as the requirements will often contain keywords that can rapidly be matched to a capability provided by a pattern. So Phil is able to identify the following requirements and the suitable patterns (Table 5.1):

Table 5.1 Requirements and capabilities—first iteration

Requirements	Capabilities in EAP	EAP
Sales representatives need up-to-date information anytime, everywhere	Enabling mobile users to access internal resources	InformationChest (S2)
(…) electronic identities and related attributes of customers and company personnel must be managed	Managing information of partners and customers	KnowYourCustomer (B3)
The project must also integrate a state-of-the-art web-shop	Offering products and services on the Internet (web-shop)	VendingMachine (B2)
(…) the delivery chain and all the logistics processes must be supported	Supporting the delivery chain and planning the internal resources	From SupplierToCustomer (S4)

To be sure that Phil got all the relevant patterns he then consults the provided map of EAP, which shows the relationship between the patterns in the catalog. The «Connectivity» (the number of connections to other patterns) is a parameter that helps Phil to identify possible other patterns he may apply (Fig. 5.1).

Phil takes then a closer look at the interaction view of the pattern VendingMachine (B2):

The pattern is, for example, in direct relation with StoreMyIdentities (I1), LetMeAccess (I2), and Financials (S1). Depending on the requirements and the «as-is» architecture, Phil must decide how many branches (relationships) he wants to follow and take the related patterns into his list. Of course, Phil must decide how deep the recursion may go. From the analysis of the relationships, Phil adds the following patterns to his list (Table 5.2):

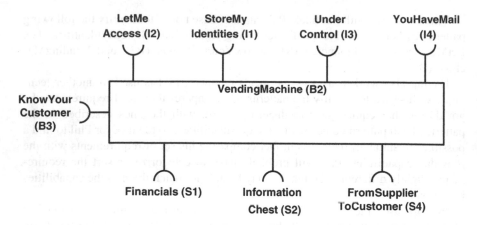

Fig. 5.1 Interaction of VendingMachine (B2) with other patterns

Table 5.2 Requirements and capabilities—second iteration

Requirements	Capabilities in EAP	EAP
Managing identities of internal and external users	Create and manage identities	StoreMyIdentities (I1)
The access to information for field agents and customers must be possible with any kind of electronic device (workstation, handhelds, electronic pads) used to navigate on the Internet	Manage access to resources	LetMeAccess (I2)
Accurate and up-to-date financial information must be provided to the management.	Management of the overall financial supply chain	Financials (S1)

5.3 Getting Clear Views

In most cases, the architect will not be able to start from scratch – the green-field approach is often not an option. So Phil is confronted with a more or less well documented «as-is» architecture. From this point of view, the application of the patterns is actually the definition of a «to-be» architecture based on the identified patterns from the catalog. Phil must decide which patterns are most suitable for his needs. In order to gain a first impression of which patterns are really suitable he examines the introduction, especially the supporting and impeding forces, the context, and the problem description and compares the information found to his current situation. The patterns found suitable give Phil some guidance on how he is subsequently going to define his solution architecture.

Phil takes all the patterns he found suitable to the different stakeholders in order to start a discussion and to verify if his selection of pattern matches the expectations of the stakeholders. This discussion can be extremely useful as the pattern language allows Phil to talk to the stakeholders in an easily understandable yet concise and hopefully unambiguous way. If necessary, Phil is going to adapt his selection of patterns or reorder their priority based upon the feedback he receives. This first meeting with the stakeholders also enables Phil to promote his endeavor and to prepare the following discussions on the solution architecture. The usage of patterns through the whole process of the design of the new application provides continuity and a certain effect of recognition. The early involvement of the stakeholders is very important and gives them confidence that their requirements are understood and taken seriously. On the other hand, Phil gets input at a very early stage that helps him plan and improve the overall Enterprise Architecture Landscape as well as design an appropriate solution architecture.

Phil is now able to produce different views of his «to-be» architecture using the descriptions of the EAPs. Let us see how he produces a view of the combination of the three patterns StoreMyIdentities (I1), LetMeAccess (I2), and VendingMachine (B2). Phil decides to produce two different views of the concatenation of these three patterns.[1]

The Holistic View shows the chosen patterns in relationship. In most of the cases, the two patterns StoreMyIdentities (I1) and LetMeAccess (I2) will come as a pair – to provide access to resources that Phil will need to authenticate and authorize subjects in his overall architecture. He now gets an idea of how he could combine the web-shop with a centralized identity and access management solution that provides single-sign on capabilities and secure access to the resources. This Holistic View enables Phil to have a sight on his «to-be» architecture from high above.

The second view deals with the technological aspects of the VendingMachine (B2) and the related patterns. Phil wants to show his networking team which components will possibly be added to the network layout and how they will communicate. Phil does not yet deal with product-specific issues; this will be the task of designing the solution architecture.

A VendingMachine (B2) pattern is typically a service where different types of persons will want to access the resource: The customer who will often go through a process of self-registration before buying goods (material or immaterial) from the web-shop, the administrator of the product catalog will issue new versions, the administrator of the system will want to manage the overall system, and so on. Phil can show these different stakeholders in the technological view to his fellow technicians with an appropriate description language.

As a next step, Phil is going to incorporate all relevant patterns using the same methodology as for the VendingMachine (B2).

---

[1] We do not show these views here, as they take too much place.

5.4 Defining a Strategy

We assume that Phil has already documented the as-is architecture – preferably over all architecture layers (business, data, application, and technology). We know that this task is always an endeavor in itself. Many stakeholders must be interviewed and a sustainable documentation must be put in place and kept up-to-date. But this is the daily business of the Enterprise Architect – isn't it?

Phil is now able to draw a big picture and define with the business an overall strategy to implement the chosen patterns. The Holistic View of the concatenation of all relevant patterns for TheWineBottle is in fact a representation of the to-be architecture. With the visions and principles defined in the patterns, Phil and the management are now able to formulate an overall strategy encompassing all architecture layers. The to-be architecture constructed from the EAPs does not show any products or commercial aspects. The mapping of this big picture to the processes, applications, and technologies already in place must then be performed. This allows Phil to conduct a gap analysis as a basis for the next steps.

5.5 Deriving the Solution Architecture

Based on the strategy and the gap analysis, the management will then ask Phil to plan the next steps: A plan with implementation projects and the financing, staffing, and roadmap must be written and be approved. The effective solution architecture will then emerge in the project and the necessary adjustments due to financial or resourcing reasons can be made.

5.6 Governance of the Architectural Landscape

After successful implementation of one or more patterns, the work of Phil is not finished; in fact, the work of TheWineBottle's Enterprise Architect is never finished. The Architectural Landscape must be closely monitored; any strategy, project, or change in the ICT environment must be evaluated against the desired state of the Architectural Landscape. Phil uses EAPs to have a simple way of measuring the gap between what he considers a preferable Architectural Landscape with the actual as-is landscape. He compares the strategy and the projects at TheWineBottle with EAPs and decides whether a strategy or a project helps in getting nearer to the desired state of Enterprise Architecture. During discussions with management, project leaders, and other stakeholders, Phil uses the EAPs and the pattern language as an efficient way of facilitating communication between persons with different background, technical understanding, and viewpoints.

5.7 Extending the Pattern Catalog

While analyzing the Architectural Landscape of TheWineBottle, he noticed that there must be more patterns out there that are waiting to be described. So one evening Phil opens a good bottle of TheWineBottle's best wine (he got it from his boss as a reward for his outstanding work with implementing a new web-shop by using the VendingMachine (B2) pattern) and begins to think about reoccurring problems and their associated solution schemes. The authors of this book are looking forward to hear about Phil's newly described patterns at the ea-patterns.com web page.

Chapter 6
Symbols and Their Meanings

«My yachts were, I suppose, outstanding status symbols.»
Paul Getty

Abstract This chapter serves as a reference for the different diagrams in this book. We describe the symbols and their meaning for the Holistic View (component diagram), the Business View (BPMN diagram), the Data and Application (ArchiMate®), and Technology View.

6.1 Holistic View

The Holistic View consists of a simple component diagram as specified in Table 6.1 (UML 2010).

Table 6.1 Elements of the Holistic View

Element	Description	Notation
Architecture Brick	This component is being used on the three architecture layers (business, data and application, technology) as a placeholder for the different elements in the detailed notations (role, process, application, or technology)	**Architecture Brick**
Providing an interface	An Architecture Brick may provide an interface that can be used by other Architecture Bricks. An Architecture Brick may provide an interface to the same architecture layer or to a layer above. The provided interface is being realized by the Architecture Brick that provides it	
Using an interface	An Architecture Brick may use an interface that is being provided by another Architecture Brick. An Architecture Brick may use an interface from the same architecture layer or from a layer below	
Layer divider	A horizontal dashed line divides the three architecture layers (business, data and application, technology)	

T. Perroud and R. Inversini, *Enterprise Architecture Patterns*,
DOI: 10.1007/978-3-642-37561-3_6, © Springer-Verlag Berlin Heidelberg 2013

6.2 Business View

The Business View is made of BPMN diagrams. We use only a small subset as shown in Table 6.2. The descriptions of the elements are based on the wordings in the BPMN 2.0 specification (BPMN 2011).

Table 6.2 Elements of the Business View

Element	Description	Notation
Start or End Event	As the name implies, the Start Event indicates where a particular process will start and the End Event where it ends. We use the same symbol for both events, although in BPMN the line thickness would be larger	
Activity	An Activity is a generic term for work that company performs. A synonym is task	**Activity**
Collapsed subprocess	The details of the subprocess are not visible in the diagram. A "plus" sign in the lower center of the shape indicates that the activity is a subprocess and has a lower level of detail	**Sub-Process**
Gateway	A gateway is used to control the divergence and convergence of sequence flows in a process. It will determine branching, forking, merging, and joining of paths. We use only the exclusive or (XOR) gateway	
Sequence Flow	A Sequence Flow is used to show the order that activities will be performed in a process. We use only the simple arrow to model the sequence flow	
Exclusive decision, Branching point	This decision represents a branching point where alternatives are based on conditional expressions contained within the outgoing sequence flows. Only one of the alternatives are chosen	Activity 1 / Activity 2
Lane	A lane is the graphical representation of a participant in a process and contains the process	Lane

6.3 Data and Application View

The Data and Application View uses a subset of the ArchiMate (2011) specification (Table 6.3).

Table 6.3 Elements of the Data and Application View

Element	Description	Notation
Application	A modular, deployable, and replaceable part of a software system that encapsulates its behavior and data and exposes these through a set of interfaces. The Application unifies the Application Component and Application Function as defined by ArchiMate	Application
Application group	An application group is an Application that consists of two or more sub-applications. This corresponds to example 17 in (ArchiMate 2011)	Application Group — Application 1 — Application 2
Application Interface	A point of access where an application service is made available to a user or to another Application	
Application Service	A service that exposes automated behavior	Application Service
Used by	The "Used by" relationship can be drawn with two kinds of symbols: The interface symbol, as used in the Holistic View, and an arrow pointing from the Application Interface to the Application that uses it	
Interface, Application Service, and Application Interface	An Application Service is always being accessed through an associated Application Interface. The association is a simple line. An Application realizes an Application Service. The realization relationship is an arrow with a dashed line pointing to the Application Service. The name contains, whenever possible, a verb	Application Service — Application Interface — Application
Data Object	A Data Object is defined as a passive element suitable for automated processing. The name is always a noun	Data Object

(continued)

Table 6.3 (continued)

Element	Description	Notation
Read Data Object and Write Data Object	A Data Object is always being accessed through an Application Service. An arrow with a dashed line pointing to the Data Object is a write access, when pointing to the Application Service it is a read access	Data Object 1 — write — Application Service — read — Data Object 2
Data Object to Data Object	The relationship between two Data Objects is a simple line	Data Object 1 — Data Object 2

6.4 Technology View

The Technology View consists of a diagram type that uses a few shapes to model the servers, clients, and networks (Table 6.4).

Table 6.4 Elements of the Technology View

Element	Description	Notation
User	The User interacts with the environment using a client machine	User
Server	The Server is a generic shape for physical machines that hold applications	Server
Database	Server for database software	Database
ESB	The Enterprise Service Bus (ESB) is a server that can be used to integrate different services	Enterprise Service Bus

(continued)

Table 6.4 (continued)

Element	Description	Notation
Directory	A Directory server is used in the context of Identity and Access Management and holds electronic identities and attributes	Directory (triangle)
Network	The Network defines the boundary of a security perimeter. The perimeter is delimited by firewalls. We defined five types of networks that an organization may have: External Zone, Internal Zone divided into the Server and Client Zones, Central Access Zone	External (rectangle)
Internet	The Internet	Internet (cloud)
Connection	A connection is a TCP/IP communication path. The arrow starts at the client and ends at the server providing the service. The arrow is labeled with the corresponding protocol	●——HTTPs——▶
Pattern	We need sometimes to make a reference to other patterns within the Technology View. This is done with a square with a dashed line and the name of the referenced pattern within	Pattern (dashed box)

References

ArchiMate (2011) The Open Group: ArchiMate® Version 2.0. https://www2.opengroup.org/ogsys/catalog/C118. Accessed 21 June 2013

BPMN (2011) Business process model and notation Version 2.0 (BPMN 2.0). http://www.bpmn.org/. Accessed 28 July 2011

UML (2010) The Object Management Group: unified modeling language Version 2.3. http://www.omg.org/spec/UML/2.3/Infrastructure/PDF/. Accessed 28 July 2011

Part II
Pattern Catalog

Chapter 7
Business Patterns

Abstract This chapter contains three Business Patterns. The first deals with collaboration issues, the second presents a web-based vending channel, and the third provides a solution for managing customer-related information.

7.1 WorkTogether (B1)

«You can help me. Whatever comes out of these gates, we've got a better chance of survival if we work together. Do you understand? If we stay together we survive.»

Maximus to Cassius in the Movie «Gladiator»

7.1.1 Introduction

Name and Overview

Name	Work Together
Number	B1
Type of pattern	Business
Abstract	WorkTogether (B1) is a pattern that unifies different communication and collaboration functionalities. Internal or external users to the company can join groups of discussion, share knowledge, and work together on documents to achieve a common consensus
Capabilities	Collaboration using different medias
	Sharing of documents
	Communication with external partners
	Meetings in collaboration space
	Managing collaboration groups and profiles

(continued)

T. Perroud and R. Inversini, *Enterprise Architecture Patterns*,
DOI: 10.1007/978-3-642-37561-3_7, © Springer-Verlag Berlin Heidelberg 2013

(continued)

Name	Work Together
Referenced patterns	StoreMyIdentities (I1), LetMeAccess (I2), UnderControl (I3), YouHaveMail (I4), TalkToMe (I5), InformationChest (S2), ResourcesAreScarce (S3), FromSupplierToCustomer (S4), ForYourEyesOnly (S5)
Bricks	Collaboration portal, telephony application, video application, document sharing, calendar mail, telephony infrastructure, video infrastructure, document management infrastructure, calendar mail infrastructure
Impeding forces	Communication culture Organizational inertia Complexity of a project to unify different existing systems, data and applications No business data model with clear responsibilities for the business objects Lack of governance
Supporting forces	Effort to unify and instantiate a standardized collaboration environment. Emerging social community applications also for use within the companies. Constant pressure to minimize costs
Invariance	Low: The invariance of this pattern is per se very low, as the term collaboration may vary in interpretation depending on the context. When introducing a collaboration platform not all possible communication channels (synchronous or asynchronous as well) will be necessary. The implementation may therefore vary greatly
Complexity	Medium: The pattern is modular and parts can be left out
Connectivity	Medium: This pattern is connected to other patterns that provide communication capabilities
Keywords	Collaboration, information sharing, team work, consensus

Definition

The WorkTogether (B1) pattern deals with different aspects of collaboration. The understanding of collaboration has tremendously changed since the upcoming of electronic information and communication technologies. From a world of publishers we have evolved to participants in an electronic dialog, content is being edited and enhanced by online users (wikis, tagging of information, comments in blogs and forums, etc.) and people can join working or interests groups with a few mouse clicks. In the last 5 years a huge amount of books concerning electronic collaboration have been written, ranging from innovation and e-collaboration (Davila 2006), to new user experiences (Kolfschoten et al. 2010) up to Web 2.0 technologies and collaboration (Coleman and Stewart 2008 or Governor 2009). Patterns for collaboration in different shades and levels of detail have been published. See for example the patterns published by the National Institutes of Health (US agency), one of them being a web collaboration platform pattern (NIH 2011) or the patterns described by (Schümmer and Lukosch 2007).

It is not easy to narrow down the term «collaboration» to a comprehensive, widely accepted definition. We will therefore shed some light from different viewpoints on the topic to formulate our own definition.

According to Merriam-Webster:

1. To work jointly with others or together, especially in an intellectual endeavor;
2. To cooperate with or willingly assist an enemy of one's country and especially an occupying force;
3. To cooperate with an agency or instrumentality with which one is not immediately connected.

Teresa Hogue (see Hogue 1994) defines the way in which people (or communities) work together at five different levels. This happened in 1994 – long before collaboration became also an IT terminus. The weakest form of working together is networking; a bit stronger is cooperation or alliance that goes over into coordination or partnership. The second strongest form is coalition whereas collaboration is the strongest form and has the following key parameters:

The purpose:

- Accomplish shared vision and impact benchmarks.
- Build interdependent system to address issues and opportunities.

The structure:

- Consensus used in shared decision making.
- Roles, time, and evaluation formalized.
- Links are formal and written in work assignments.

The process:

- Leadership high, trust level high, productivity high.
- Ideas and decisions equally shared.
- Highly developed communication.

Although Hogue is very clear about the various levels, we postulate that collaboration in the context of this pattern may act at all levels that Hogue defined.

Coleman and Stewart (2008) identified the three critical success factors for a holistic approach to a successful collaboration:

- People (behaviors, attitudes, culture).
- Process (critical business processes with collaborative leverage).
- Technology (offers good user experience, integrated and connected to many data sources).

Derived from these definitions, we can see that collaboration is a process where two or more persons, teams, or organizations work together to achieve common goals sharing knowledge, learning, and building consensus. In our understanding, collaboration goes beyond the obvious activities of working together. To collaborate also means to solve problems in *the future* more easily. Every collaboration initiative must induce a *lessons learned* aspect, so that the organization can evolve toward a collaborative culture with benefits for the business goals. Many artifacts that are being generated in the collaboration process have the quality of blueprints, graphical or verbalized explanations, attempt to clarify one's position, and enable a common understanding and learning.

Collaboration in Information Technology is enabled by collaborative platforms (a.k.a. groupware), which provide the functionality to transform the way documents and rich media are shared. The collaboration platforms offer a set of software functionalities and services that enables the user to find each other and the information they need to achieve the business goals. Some common features of most collaboration platforms and tools are synchronous (real-time) communication through voice or video conferencing, simultaneous editing of documents, chat, web-conferencing, desktop sharing, and others. Asynchronous information exchange takes place through messaging (E-mail, calendaring, scheduling, contacts, instant messaging), blog, wiki, forums tagging, RSS, shared bookmarks, file synchronization, and task management. This may be defined as «store and retrieve» functionalities, where the users can collaborate without being online at the same time.

Besides these typical functions there exist specialized collaboration platforms for voting, ranking, learning environments, and social communities (Twitter, Facebook, etc.). Collaboration platforms are often part of an overall solution and enhance the functions by integrating them into a single, uniform application for end-users.

To summarize, we use the following definitions in the context of Work-Together (B1):

> Electronic collaboration is the process that involves different people or organizations in order to reach common goals. They accomplish this by sharing information, discussing, learning from each other, making decisions and creating new information. These processes are supported by an ICT infrastructure such as a portal, unifying the various technical components.

7.1.2 Example

To extend their business activities, TheWineBottle collaborates with external project staff, consultants, and partners. This is often done on a project basis, where documents, memos, or audio information (e.g., phone conferences) are shared and worked upon together. As the company sells products from abroad, the collaboration partners are often outside of the country. The management of TheWineBottle has decided to implement an electronic collaboration platform to facilitate the exchange of information and the process of working together.

7.1.3 Context

WorkTogether (B1) can be used in every enterprise or governmental organization irrespective of its size, business area, or technological background. Differentiations that can be made result from the degree and type of interaction between the collaboration partners, and from the type of communication media used (e.g., video, document sharing, audio).

The borders of this pattern are difficult to draw, as it may be considered as a concatenation of different communication capabilities to work together. Similar elements can be found in InformationChest (S2), YouHaveMail (I4), or TalkToMe (I5).

The following preconditions must be met to successfully implement this pattern:

- The enterprise must be aware that the pattern may require a change of communication culture. A company that wants to introduce a collaboration environment faces a lot of challenges. New ways of working together with the support of collaborative platforms may change the way we are used to communicate. Before introducing such a platform we strongly recommend to assess the way the communication works now and how it could be affected in future.
- One of the biggest hurdles in the typical medium- to large-sized enterprise is the desire to standardize knowledge practices across the enterprise and to implement tools and processes to support that goal. These issues are directly related to the InformationChest (S2) pattern.

It is important to note that having well-defined data model, interface descriptions, and networking policies are crucial elements when implementing this pattern. The reason is simple: binding together information sources and elements of communications can only be successful if it is done in a holistic way.

7.1.4 Problem

WorkTogether (B1) addresses the business processes where individual users or groups of users work together to achieve common goals. The users may be in the same location or dispersed geographically across the world. They may work together in a synchronous way or the collaboration may be completely asynchronous.

The need for collaboration through means of Information Technology is not new. Before the up-coming of wikis, blogs, etc., tools and protocols like file transfer (ftp), telnet sessions, or E-mail were and are still being broadly used for this kind of interaction. The term «Groupware» has been replaced with electronic collaboration. Collaboration is important for any organization regardless of its size or business model. The business need for collaboration can be stated as follows:

- The need to collaborate and access shared resources across institutions and trusted networks in industry, education, and government sectors is rapidly growing.
- Sharing of acquired knowledge, improving knowledge in a certain business area, and building consensus among different users. The users may even be mobile and accessing information or participating in collaborative tasks with mobile devices.
- Enabling project management with internal and external stakeholders. This encompasses all the typical project management tasks (calendaring, mailing, document sharing, planning, etc.).
- Reducing costs (travel) and latency of business events by using conferencing tools (video, telephony, conjoint editing of documents).
- Acquiring new customers by giving the opportunity to participate in a virtual group of persons with the same interests. Enabling participation is an emerging need: Examples are all the social communities' portals or initiative from political associations or governments to encourage citizens to participate in a political dialogue or open data initiatives where citizens play an active role in providing data.

John is a project leader of TheWineBottle and is in charge to implement a new campaign to sell organic wine. He hired an external marketing consultant to support him during the writing of the concept. John writes a first draft and emails it to the consultant. The consultant writes remarks and sends them back. John distributes the comments in the project team. Some team members answer by E-mail, some comment on the text directly in the original document, and others create a new document. By this time the documents have been multiplied and a versioning control has become difficult, not to say, impossible. If John forgets someone in the project team, this person will never know about the consultant's comments on the documents.

Organization's View

In order to reach the aforementioned business goals the organization has to solve the following problems:

- Providing a platform that enables collaboration within and crossing organizational borders.
- Having one portal for all the different methods of collaboration (ranging from Document Sharing, over Calendar, E-mail to Voice and Video communication).
- Enabling the use from any device and any place at any time.

- Channeling and securing the flow of information in order to avoid data leakage.
- Convincing users to adapt the newly created platform and to avoid unofficial methods of collaboration such as free cloud services that may violate data protection regulations.

Enterprise Architect's View

The Enterprise Architect must accompany the planning and implementation of any collaboration solution very closely. There are important decisions to be made that very often are only reversible with a high amount of time and money. Such a decision is whether to unify the different elements of collaboration under one portal but to stay with independent single solutions or to move toward a more integrated approach where the whole collaboration comes from one vendor. The first approach integrates existing elements into one portal. The second approach has a deep impact on the overall architecture and may be very costly but has a good integration of the individual elements. It is important to define the interfaces and protocols to be used between the single components and between the collaboration platform and other elements of the Enterprise Architecture. Another important thing to note is the marketing of the new platform in order to convince projects and end-users to solely use the new collaboration platform and to set aside the former methods of collaboration. A cultural change must take place in terms of collaboration and in terms of changing to a more centralized form of collaboration. The requirement that nowadays is very common with many applications is of great importance to any collaboration platform: it must be accessible from anywhere with any device. As social networks are on the rise and often offer some kind of collaboration tools as well, the Enterprise Architect should leverage the discussion about the need for integrating social network functions into the collaboration platform. In conclusion it can be said that good architectural governance is needed in order to solve the problem area of collaboration in an efficient and sustainable way.

End-User's View

The end-user needs to work closely together with other people – be they internal or external. Very often he uses different, unconnected channels, such as sending a document by E-mail and making a phone call 5 min after in order to discuss this document. This is neither efficient nor user-friendly. A platform that unifies collaboration into one portal and offers the user to choose different means of collaboration can have high acceptance and reputation if it fulfills the expectations of ease of use, reliability, and is accessible from everywhere with any device. But as in most enterprises collaboration took place long before any platform had been established, the new platform must be actively promoted in order to gain the end-user to work on this platform and to abandon his old means of collaborating with others.

7.1.5 Solution

Vision

TheWineBottle enables the seamless collaboration of employees, project teams, customers, and partners. The collaboration must be possible regardless of the actual geographic location, time, and ICT technology used by the collaborative groups. The collaboration environment ensures that information is readily available for all participants based on their needs. Decisions can be taken or prepared electronically in a way that ensures full accountability and visibility to all stakeholders. The collaboration reinforces communication between all stakeholders. It supports the active participation of external persons, be they customers, citizens, or partners.

Principles

1. *Principle*	*Leveraging a new communication culture*
Statement	The use of collaborative platforms will enable new ways of communications within the company and with external persons, like business partners and customers
Reasoning	New collaboration mechanisms enables TheWineBottle to have a more direct link to our customers, provide them with new user experiences and let them participate more actively in the product design. Partners can be involved easier in the processes where information must be exchanged or created together. The active participation of customers and partners in the evolution of TheWineBottle helps us to sell better products
	Facilitating a virtual face-to-face collaboration will support the employee's need for mobility and geographical independence of work place. This allows a better integration of home-working places and may contribute to a better work-life balance
Consequences	The company must make itself ready for the use of new collaborative platforms. The management is solicited to play an active role to lead by good example
2. *Principle*	*Collaboration must be user-friendly, simple, effective, and efficient*
Statement	The introduction of new forms of collaboration must be an enabler for easy and user-friendly communication. No tool has priority, but the effective and efficient collaboration
Reasoning	The user acceptance is a critical success factor when introducing communication platforms. Users do not accept technologies that are cumbersome to handle, inefficient, or not suited to their needs
	An effective and efficient collaboration environment increases the productivity. Collaborative scheduling functionalities help organizing meetings and events, video conferencing will decrease costs for traveling (traveling time, fees, and stay)
Consequences	It is imperative that the requirements must be specified together with the users

(continued)

(continued)

3. Principle	Collaboration takes place without endangering the intellectual property or the security of the enterprise
Statement	Collaboration means exchanging information of all kinds, especially when collaborating with external partners TheWineBottle must define which information should be accessible under which circumstances to avoid unwanted loss of intellectual property
Reasoning	Not all information of TheWineBottle is intended to be shared with everyone. There are business critical documents and information that should not be disseminated and made accessible for external partners
Consequences	Strong governance of the collaboration efforts ensures the aligning of people, processes, and technical means in order to reach the business goals in an effective and efficient way. TheWineBottle must integrate the collaboration efforts into the overall governance strategy Information must be classified and cleared for external use before releasing it for collaboration. The collaboration environment must support the users in defining and granting the correct access rights and privileges as appropriate to their business roles The security of access to resources provided by the collaboration platform must be well balanced between ease of access and protection of the information The employees of TheWineBottle must be trained and made aware of information leakage issues related to collaboration
4. Principle Statement	The number of different collaboration platforms and tools must be limited The market for collaborative platform is huge and hundreds of tools exist in this category. TheWineBottle must therefore restrict the number of platforms for collaboration to use them in a cost-efficient manner
Reasoning	The more platforms the company uses, the more complex the technology and application landscape gets
Consequences	The management of TheWineBottle (e.g., the CIO) must define which platforms and tools are to be used for collaboration. The management must approve the introduction of new platforms and tools. Old platforms must be decommissioned

Holistic View

The Holistic View in Fig. 7.1 typifies the core of electronic collaboration: WorkTogether (B1) provides the integration of different communication and collaboration capabilities provided by other patterns.

The business layer shows the three main actors: The internal and the external users (partner, customer) and an administrator, who is managing the collaboration space. In our definition of collaboration we have defined two core processes for collaboration:

- Collaboration must be organized.
- Information must be shared and the topic must be discussed in a collaborative manner.

The data and application layer is a typical picture of what collaboration means when using electronic communication capabilities. Depending on the business needs of the company, applications for synchronous (video, telephony, desktop web sharing) and asynchronous (E-mail, document sharing) communication and collaboration are used together. To organize a collaboration meeting, scheduling (e.g., calendar) functionalities must be provided. All these components may be integrated into a single application. This can also be realized by building internal and external collaboration portals (Table 7.1).

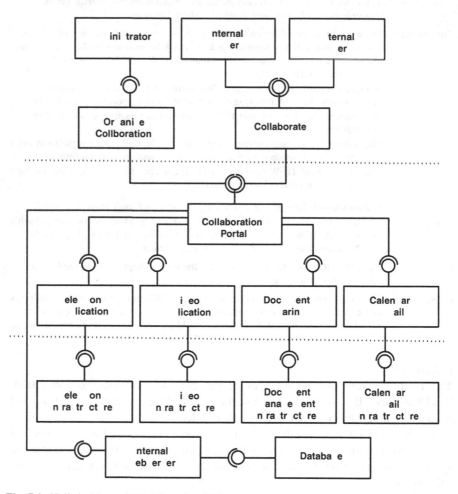

Fig. 7.1 Holistic View of WorkTogether (B1)

Table 7.1 Architecture bricks of WorkTogether (B1)

Brick	Description
Collaboration portal	Portal that unifies different collaboration applications
Document sharing	Document management application
Calendar and mail	Application for handling E-mail and calendar
Telephony application	Integration of telephony capabilities into the portal
Video application	Integration of video capabilities into the portal

The technology layer regroups the different infrastructures needed to provide audio, video, calendar, E-mail, and document sharing infrastructures.

Business View

The design and implementation of a new collaboration process is a challenging task, as conflicting requirements must be taken into consideration. Besides the existing skills and communication culture, the new process must fulfill requirements for more efficiency or improved productivity (see Kolfschoten et al. 2010).

Before beginning a collaborative session, meeting or project, the participants must be able to join the virtual team. This means that the collaboration room must be set up, the access rights defined, and the invitations sent. Of course the synchronous collaboration by means of video or audio tools, online chats, or simultaneous editing of documents demands the participants to take part at the same time at the meetings. Asynchronous tasks are done at the time chosen by the user. After he logs in, the portal should inform about new tasks, documents, and scheduled meetings.

The first activity in Fig. 7.2 consists of setting up a collaboration space. This can be a website with documents, a video or audio-conference configuration, a blog or a wiki environment. The next step is to create the user accounts [see StoreMyIdentities (I1) for more details] and the associated access rights. Depending on the collaboration that has been set up, a (self-) registration may be supported or the user can use his existing electronic identity and credentials (e.g., in a single-sign on environment). The participants must then be invited and can

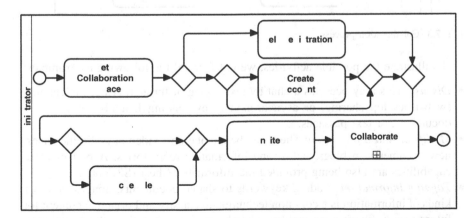

Fig. 7.2 Organize collaboration process

afterwards share their knowledge and discuss the business matter. Sometimes a self-organized collaboration with no moderation is required. We associated the pool with the role of the administrator, but this can in fact be an internal or external user to the company as well.

The second business process, as shown in Fig. 7.3, describes the actual collaboration. The participants first have to join the collaboration space. As collaboration has many different facets, the user will then perform different activities, depending on the capabilities provided by the collaboration environment.

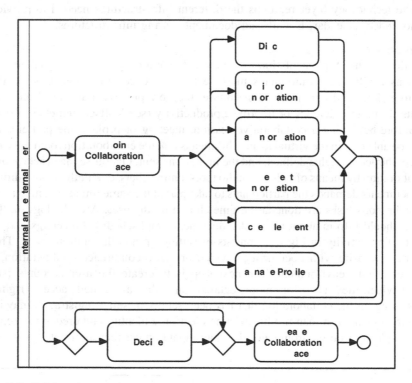

Fig. 7.3 Collaboration process

To illustrate the possible activities, we put forward the following as examples:

- *Discuss*: This may occur as a chat by text typing or through (video) telephony, (web-) desktop sharing, or asynchronously by sending E-mails, commenting documents, or text passages.
- *Modify or Add Information*: These can be annotations, video or audio messages, new documents in blogs, wikis, and information repositories. A part of these capabilities are also being provided the InformationChest (S2) pattern.
- *Tagging Information*: Adding keywords to shared documents, images, or other kinds of information is a common technique to classify and organize content for future search, filtering, or analysis. Collaborative tagging gives the participants

the possibility to define the importance of information items. See (Governor 2009) for further details described in the «Collaborative Tagging» pattern.

- *Request Information*: This is an important activity when collaborating – participants need information from other participants. Request encompasses search and find capabilities.
- *Schedule Event*: To be able to meet in a collaboration space at a specific time, the users can schedule events and manage (group-) calendars.
- *Manage Profile*: The user can modify his or her profile, adding a picture, interests, etc.

These activities may be done more than once in order to find consensus or come to a decision. The last activity is to leave the collaboration space.

Data and Application View
Figure 7.4 shows the Data and Application View. The centerpiece is the collaboration portal (external or internal) that provides different collaboration services. Notice that most of the services may also be provided directly by core applications like video, telephony, or document management applications.

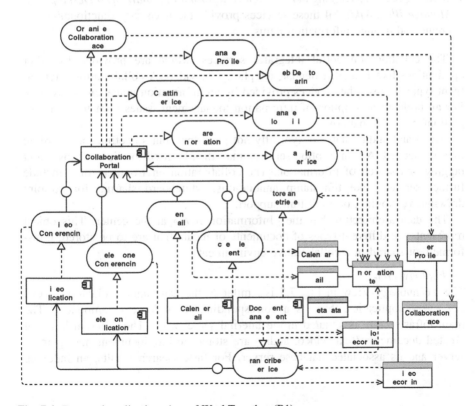

Fig. 7.4 Data and application view of WorkTogether (B1)

Collaboration applications are often client software integrated in the office automation packages (e.g., scheduling functionalities are provided by the calendar application or computer integrated telephony are part of the address book software). We chose to show the full integration of different collaboration applications into a single portal. The portal may be internal or external, depending on the type and groups of users accessing the applications.

The portal offers the following collaboration services:

- *Organize Collaboration Space*: This service is used to set up a collaboration environment, define which type of collaboration tools will be used, and who can access the applications under which circumstances.
- *Schedule Event*: Depending on the type of collaboration (e.g., synchronous working on the same information items), the participants must be invited to a session or event. This means to find a common time slot in the calendars of the participants, send invitations, and receive acknowledgements for their participation.
- *Manage My Profile*: Users can manage their own profile (e.g., nickname, picture, skills, etc.) to customize their presence in a collaboration space.
- *Chatting Service, Tagging Service, Share Information, Share Web Desktop, and Manage Blog/Wiki*: All these services provide the necessary functionalities to create and change information items.

The collaboration portal integrates services, which are provided by other applications like E-mail, calendar, telephony, or video. A collaboration environment typically uses the services provided by an information management system. For an in-depth description of information management issues refer to the InformationChest (S2) pattern.

Video and audio chats are typically not persistent, but sometimes a recording may be needed. A transcription services may then be used to allow a subsequent tagging and search of information. The collaboration environment may include further services like timestamp annotations, whiteboard sharing for co-joint drawing, versioning, or audit trail support.

The data architecture has the «Information Item» at the center. This object represents the different types of documents or media that are to be stored, transformed, or shared in a collaborative environment.

Technology View

The Technology View in Fig. 7.5 is similar to the Data and Application View. For every application there is a corresponding technological component. The main infrastructure is situated in the internal server zone. The different kinds of created documents (text, video, audio) are stored on the document management server and its associated database server. For faster search results, an indexing

server can be used. The external partners access the collaboration portal in the
external zone, whereas the internal users may use both the internal and the
external portals.

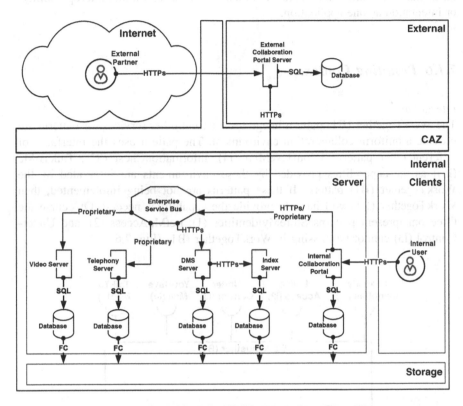

Fig. 7.5   Technology View of WorkTogether (B1)

Communication between the external collaboration portal and the internal
infrastructure is routed through a gateway in the *central access zone* (CAZ). Note that
depending on the business requirements, the whole infrastructure could be placed
completely in the external zone, without internal portal. All participants would then
use the external portal. Another possibility would be to have a similar backend
infrastructure [video, telephony, document management system (DMS)] in the
external zone as in the internal. The decision to place which part of the infrastructure
in the internal or/and internal zone must be taken by weighing the advantages and
disadvantages of security, business, and financial issues. Information can be stored on
the DMS infrastructure or when implemented, via the InformationChest (S2) pattern.

Although there exists first initiatives for interoperability in a collaborative environment [see OSCAF (2011) or COA (2011) from the Jericho Forum], the market for collaboration software is still very proprietary. Often, collaboration takes place with different tools (a lot of them client based) without interoperability[1] or integration as one application.

7.1.6 Resulting Context

Interaction
The WorkTogether (B1) pattern integrates different other services (or patterns) to provide a uniform collaboration environment. The pattern uses the interfaces of different other patterns [YouHaveMail (I4), InformationChest (S2), TalkToMe (I5)] as the capabilities provided by these environments are integrated by the WorkTogether (B1) pattern. If these patterns are not being implemented, then WorkTogether (B1) will have to provide the capabilities needed. Of course the three omnipresent patterns StoreMyIdentities (1), LetMeAccess (2), and Under-Control (I3) cannot be missing in WorkTogether (B1) (Fig. 7.6).

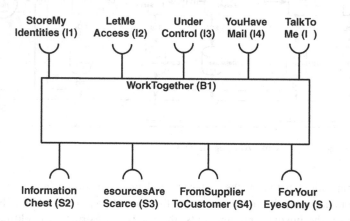

Fig. 7.6 Interaction of WorkTogether (B1) with other patterns

---

[1] As an example: for the writing of this book we used subethaedit, facetime, and dropbox for collaboration. These tools are totally independent of one another but provide complementary functionalities.

Consequences

WorkTogether (B1) presents different communication capabilities in a uniform way to the end-user. It enables sharing of information and working across geographically dispersed locations on the same topic.

A collaboration platform does not replace any face-to-face communication and human interaction. The introduction of collaborative tools may change the way people communicate (see Amyris 2008) – and some may not be able or be ready to follow that new path.

The implementation of WorkTogether (B1) is certainly also impeded by certain risks. Users may have information objects in different locations during transition. As the new platform may have to be accepted by persons who are not ready to work in a new environment, information may still be held in the old locations (e.g., intranet shares versus web-based document management platform with access from outside users). This may pose problems such as document redundancy and integrity of information. Another risk is the leakage of information: If the data owner does not specify the roles and their access rights properly, unauthorized users may access information.

As WorkTogether (B1) may be seen as a conglomeration of different communication bricks, there may arise some conflicts: A functionality to share documents with the means of a web platform can be stated as a DMS or a video-conferencing may be a standalone solution. At the end it really boils down to your definition of the term collaboration and which functionalities must be supported in your environment. There is no common definition.

Unified communication and collaboration (UCC) is one of the top trends in the ICT discussion of the past few years. As the pattern shows, implementing a unified environment for internal and external communications means also instantiating strong governance on (meta-) data management. Closely related to unified communications and the information assets of a company are of course the social community applications: They are means to share, comment, and sharpen the understanding and store the knowledge (or intellectual property) and information on the company's systems.

We dare to predict that the way we work together will dramatically change in the future. The use of social media technologies for collaborative tasks paired with the digital native generation (see Prensky 2001) will have a huge impact on collaborative activities. When analyzing how social media platforms are being used and which services are provided, we may well assume that, for example, the use of E-mail will no longer be the preferred way of communication – perhaps E-mail will suffer the same fate as fax technology?

7.2 VendingMachine (B2)

«I like vending machines, because snacks are better when they fall. If I buy a candy bar at the store, oftentimes I will drop it so that is achieves its maximum flavour potential.»

Mitch Hedberg

7.2.1 Introduction

Name and Overview

Name	VendingMachine
Number	B2
Type of pattern	Business
Abstract	This pattern describes how an electronic vending channel (e.g., a web shop) can be realized. The pattern shows the customer side as well as the organization side that wants to sell goods. The main elements (catalog, order, customer database) are shown in relation to the backend (owner) and the frontend view (customer)
Capabilities	Managing and presenting a catalog of articles with features to the customers
	Offering products and services on the Internet (web-shop)
	Any kind of sellable goods or services may be bought (including downloadable articles like software or electronic documents)
	Gives the customer the possibility to put items/articles into a virtual basket
	Guides the customer through the checkout process according to shipping and payment conditions defined by the business needs
	Gives the customer to manage their profiles and orders
	Supports the order and payment management
	Gives the VendingMachine (B2) owner the means to analyze and track the activities on the online platform
Referenced patterns	StoreMyIdentities (I1), LetMeAccess (I2), UnderControl (I3), YouHaveMail (I4), Financials (S1), InformationChest (S2), FromSupplierToCustomer (S4), KnowYourCustomer (B3)
Bricks	VendingMachine Backend, VendingMachine Frontend, Catalog, Orders, Customers, Webserver, Database
Impeding forces	A new channel for selling goods will induce changes to business processes, contractual matters, and to the organization
	Some elements like the customer brick containing the information pertaining to the customers may be realized in the KnowYourCustomer (B3) pattern
	Because of existing regulations (i.e., network policies, financial regulations), the integration of a VendingMachine (B2) with internal systems like financial or human resources applications may be difficult to realize

(continued)

(continued)

Supporting forces	New business opportunities may arise
	A new channel for selling goods can be established
	The web presence is intensified
	Communications with business partners in the sourcing and delivery processes are facilitated (less media breaks)
Invariance	High: The pattern can be applied as described
Complexity	Low: The pattern consists of only a few bricks and is not very difficult to implement
Connectivity	Low: The pattern is not connected to many other patterns
Keywords	Web-shop, selling, customer, goods, online ordering

Definition

The VendingMachine (B2) pattern solves the problem of presenting goods or services from a catalog for selling over an Internet platform (web shop/online shop). It is used for Business-to-Consumer (B2C) or Business-to-Business (B2B) processes. A customer can browse the online catalog, get information about price, features of the articles, and put them into a basket. The customer is guided through the checkout process and may, depending on the vendor's policies, choose the shipping and payment methods. The following definitions describe what an online shop/store or web-shop is:

«The Web shop allows you to define which products you want to sell in the Business-to-Business and Business-to-Consumer scenarios of SAP Internet Sales (R/3 Edition). You specify the contents in the product catalog, which also forms the basis of the Web shop» (SAP 2011).

In the book «Managing The Digital Value Chain» the authors define what electronic business is and what an electronic shop is:

«An electronic shop (often also called a web shop or an online shop) is a Web based software system that offers goods and services, generates bids/offers, accepts orders, and handles delivery and modes of payment» (Meier et al. 2009, p. 4).

Derived from these statements, we define the VendingMachine (B2) as follows:

The VendingMachine (B2) is an online selling channel for Business-to-Consumer (B2C) or Business-to-Business (B2B) processes. It has the following capabilities:

- Managing and presenting a catalog of articles with features to the customer.
- Any kind of sellable goods or services may be bought (including downloadable articles like software or electronic documents).
- Gives the customer the possibility to put items/articles into a virtual basket.
- Guides the customer through the checkout process according to shipping and payment conditions defined by the business needs.
- Gives the customer the ability to manage their profiles and orders.

- Supports the order and payment management.
- Gives the VendingMachine (B2) owner the means to analyze and track the activities on the online platform.

7.2.2 Example

The company TheWineBottle sells fine Italian wines in different physical stores. The company wants to open a new selling channel over the Internet and expand its business to the Internet. The goal is to reach new markets and acquire new customers. The customers should be able to browse the same catalog as the existing catalog on paper and buy articles online. The use of credit cards and the possibility to either pick-up the goods at a local store or have them sent by postal mail must be possible.

7.2.3 Context

This pattern can be used for every kind of business and for any size of company that sells goods. The pattern provides an online channel for selling goods of any kind and is not mandatory to be implemented in every company.

The two main actors are the company itself, represented by the administrator of the VendingMachine (B2) (by the term administrator we mean the persons in charge of managing the VendingMachine (B2) from the business point of view) and the persons who use the VendingMachine (B2) to buy articles and profit from the online services.

It is difficult to draw an exact separating line to other patterns. For example, patterns like KnowYourCustomer (B3), FromSupplierToCustomer (S4) or Financials (S1) may provide some functionalities or architecture bricks that are also contained in the VendingMachine (B2).

7.2.4 Problem

A company wants to intensify their web presence or acquire new customers by providing the possibility to buy goods over the Internet. To do so, it needs to expand its ICT and business capabilities to integrate this new channel.

TheWineBottle has acquired its actual customers by classical marketing activities, e.g., flyers, advertisements in print media, and mouth-to-mouth advertising. If a customer wants to order or re-order a wine, he has to fill in a printed form and send it to TheWineBottle by classical mail. This is nowadays extremely laborious and customers relinquish to order this way as it is too cumbersome. This means that the company cannot easily acquire new customers and existing customers often do not re-order, due to the time-consuming process.

Organization's View
The organization wants to sell goods or services over the Internet. This must be done in a secure and user-friendly way. While the organization has experience in selling goods or services, using the Internet as a sales channel is new. Many important systems and services such as financial backend systems, databases containing customer information, or order management systems already exist and must be integrated. These systems are often located in isolated networks that are not open to the Internet and their security is strongly based upon this fact. Changing this has an impact on interfaces and their security. Therefore, these systems, services, and interfaces need to be adapted in order to support the new channel.

In order to build the new sales channel, existing systems and services like financial backend systems, databases containing customer information, or order management systems must be adapted in order to support the new channel. Besides having an impact on existing business processes, the new vending channel will hopefully lead to an increase in sales. This must be taken into account when implementing the new processes. It may have an impact on the existing organizational structure and working mentality as well as on the capacity of the fulfillment processes.

Security and compliance considerations play an important role in the implementation of this pattern. Having a security breach can be very costly and damages the reputation of the organization. Therefore, the VendingMachine (B2) should be integrated into existing security and monitoring environments. If necessary, additional measures should be planned and implemented. All systems used must be hardened and ready to be exposed at least partially to the dangers of the Internet.

Enterprise Architect's View
Planning and integrating a new sales channel such as VendingMachine (B2) is an interesting task for any Enterprise Architect. He must have a close look at the necessary adaptations to the business processes and the organizational structure.

As it is stated above, most often many infrastructure elements do already exist but are not designed for being linked to an Internet-based sales channel. The Enterprise Architect must have a close look that the necessary adaptations are done in a secure and policy compliant way in order to safeguard the existing infrastructure. He must plan and ensure that the new interfaces and the crossing of network borders are created in a secure way in order to help keeping the protection level adequate. Another important task is to integrate the new channel with other systems, especially the financial backend systems and the systems that store customer information. Data redundancies should be avoided and care should be taken that all data are in the same form and exchangeable between the different applications. Regarding processes and information flows, discontinuities, media breaks, and generally any interruption must be eliminated and the new sales channel should be integrated in the existing environment as seamlessly as possible. As the platform is accessible from the Internet, it is important to avoid proprietary protocols and plugins. When sticking to official standards changes are good to avoid incompatibility problems and vendor lock-ins.

End-User's View
There are basically two types of end-users, the internal employees that work with the backend of the Web shop and the customers that are buying goods or services via the Internet. The first group has the expectation that they can work with the necessary functions and information, as they are used to from the hitherto existing system. New employees that have experience with such a sales channel expect additional and Internet-specific functionality such as how a customer moved through the web site. The customers have high expectations from Web-shop solutions in terms of usability, security, and payment options. One often heard requirement is that access to the platform should be possible from any device, especially from smartphones and tablets.

7.2.5 Solution

Vision

To stay competitive in the wine selling market, the TheWineBottle must integrate an online selling platform. The platform must support all the services and functionalities according to the definition given in this pattern. The new selling channel must fully integrate with the existing business processes and supporting services.

Principles

1. *Principle*	*Seamless integration with existing processes and services*
Statement	The VendingMachine (B2) must fully integrate with existing processes and services. Any new media breaks or redundant information sources are not allowed
Reasoning	Media breaks (e.g., manually copying customer information from the VendingMachine (B2) to internal systems or vice versa) may lead to inaccurate and out-of-time information about the performance of the selling process. This may lead to wrong management decisions
Consequences	A thorough analysis of the existing interfaces and information bases must be performed. The master (business responsibility) for every information item (e.g., customer data, order management information) and the information flow from and to the VendingMachine (B2) must be described and where needed adapted

2. *Principle*	*Support devices commonly used to access online services*
Statement	The online services must be accessible through any kind of commonly used devices to access the Internet (smartphones, workstation, laptops, tablets, etc.)
Reasoning	Customers use, depending on their mobility and activities, different kinds of devices to access online services. The customers use more and more mobile devices to shop over the Internet (Stanley 2009). We don't want to lose any customer because he cannot access the VendingMachine (B2) with a commonly used device
Consequences	This is a mandatory requirement for the evaluation of the VendingMachine (B2) platform
	The VendingMachine (B2) must be accessible through platform independent technologies

3. *Principle*	*Implementation of Web standards*
Statement	The VendingMachine (B2) must support the use of well-known and accepted standards like the guidelines from the web accessibility initiative (WAI 2011), the W3C standards in general, common transport and communication protocols (HTTP, SOAP, SFTP, and so on)
Reasoning	The use of well-known, widely used standards will support a better interoperability with existing systems and an easier integration with external B2B environments
Consequences	This is a mandatory requirement for the evaluation of the VendingMachine (B2) platform

4. *Principle*	*Secure implementation*
Statement	The online services must be designed with security in mind
Reasoning	Reasoning: Any breach of customer's privacy or attack against the financial transaction system can result in a loss of money and reputation
Consequences	This is a mandatory requirement for the evaluation of the VendingMachine (B2) platform. The risks of the new channel must be regularly assessed and measures against new threats must be implemented at short notice
	No credit card information should be stored in the VendingMachine (B2). This means that the services of an external partner for credit card transactions must be integrated

Holistic View
Figure 7.7 shows the main bricks in the middle (Catalog, Orders and Payments, Customers, Conditions) of the data and application layer. The VendingMachine's administrator accesses these bricks through the VendingMachine (B2) *Backend* brick, whereas the Customers do this by using the *VendingMachine Frontend* brick. Each of these bricks provides specific interfaces and services that are accessible through the frontend and backend bricks (Table 7.2).

Business View
The Business View consists of two core processes. Further, more in-depth examples may be found in (Pinterits 2009, pp. 104–106).

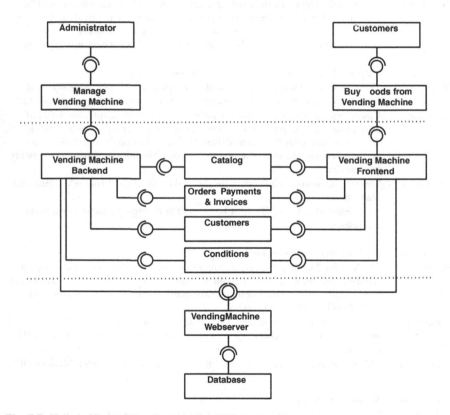

Fig. 7.7 Holistic View of VendingMachine (B2)

The *Manage Vending Machine* process as shown in Fig. 7.8 encompasses all the activities needed to manage the content of the VendingMachine (B2). The process itself is rather simply drawn. In reality, an activity like changing the terms

Table 7.2 Architecture bricks of VendingMachine (B2)

Brick	Description
Vending machine backend	Allows the administrator to manage the catalog, invoices, payments, customers, and conditions
Vending machine frontend	Provides the main functionality for customers. It allows the customers to search and browse the catalog, to manage wish lists, their profile, orders, etc.
Catalog	This brick is the heart of the VendingMachine (B2) and contains all the articles in a (hierarchical) structure. All the articles are described with a set of attributes (price, color, weight, picture, and so on)
Orders, payments, and invoices	Contains all the orders and their states (pending, closed, on hold, etc.), the ordered articles and the chosen shipping and payment conditions for the specific order. Functionalities to manage invoices sent to the customers are also supported
Customers	Application to manage customer information and let customers modify their profile
Conditions	Contains everything pertaining to the commercial terms and conditions of the VendingMachine—e.g., shipping, payment, price rules, disclaimers, and so on

and conditions is certainly more complex; as different stakeholders must be involved, the alignment with the business requirements must be assured or the legal aspects must be investigated. We only show the operative activities on the VendingMachine (B2) as performed by the administrator.

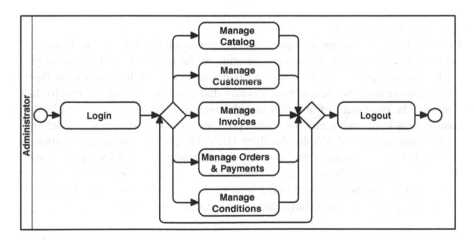

Fig. 7.8 Manage VendingMachine (B2) process

The second business process as shown in Fig. 7.9 is associated with the customer that uses the online services of the VendingMachine (B2). This process may differ depending on the functionalities provided. Typically, the customer will browse the catalog and put articles into the virtual basket. The VendingMachine (B2) supports search functionalities, so that the customer can quickly find an article depending on a feature like category, color, price, or size. Depending on the terms and conditions the customer can checkout without having to register, or he can do this as a «guest» [no personal profile will be saved for subsequent visits to the VendingMachine (B2)]. A registered customer can access his orders and profile after login in (*Manage Profile* subprocess not shown in detail in the pattern).

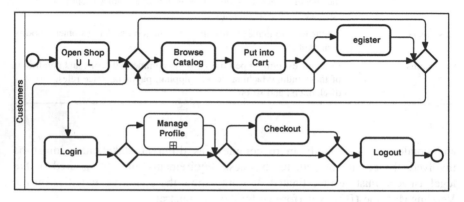

Fig. 7.9 Buy goods from VendingMachine (B2) process

Data and Application View

Figure 7.10 shows the most important data objects on the left side and the connections between the application components on the right side. For every activity in the business process there is a corresponding service in the application layer. The customer can only access two services that allow writing operations to data objects: The placement of an order and the management of the customer profile (address book, password and username, preferences like receiving a newsletter).

The managing of the VendingMachine (B2) includes also the service *Configure Pages* that allows creating and changing web content, like information pages, disclaimers, opening hours, contact information, etc. The administrator can get statistics about the performance of the VendingMachine (B2) (e.g., number of sold goods in a period, financial information, etc.) using the service *Get Statistics*.

The data architecture shows that a catalog is often structured in categories: A product category is a view of the overall catalog. A product may be in different categories, i.e., a red wine may be in a region category and a price category.

The conditions are split into shipping and payment methods, which the customer can choose from in the checkout process.

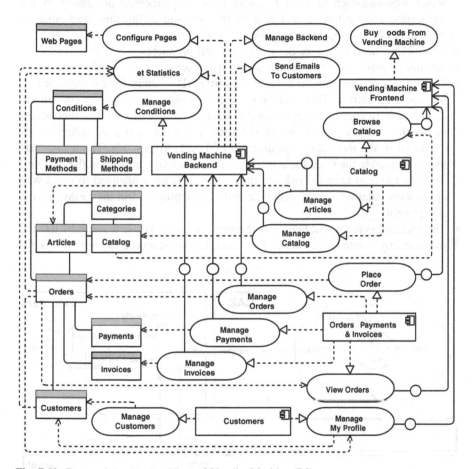

Fig. 7.10 Data and Application View of VendingMachine (B2)

Technology View

The Technology View as shown in Fig. 7.11 is spread over four different networking zones.

The customer connects over the *Internet* with any kind of device that is commonly used to access online services (e.g., desktop, smartphone, tablet, etc.).

The VendingMachine (B2) is located in the *External Zone* of the company (aka Demilitarized Zone, DMZ). The different services may be separated on more than one physical or virtual server, depending on the size and frequency of use of the VendingMachine (B2):

- The *VendingMachine Webserver* for the presentation of the content and with the actual VendingMachine (B2) business logic implemented according to the application architecture. Depending on the solution architecture, the business logic may be on a separate application server.
- A *Database Server* to store the webpages and products.
- An *Index Server* for a fast search and find service.
- We strongly recommend the StoreMyIdentities (I1) pattern for the managing of the user credentials. This will help to get answers to questions concerning identity federation or self-registration processes of customers. Communications across the security boundaries of the networking zones use the gateways as described in the technology architecture of LetMeAccess (I2). The access service is located in the *CAZ*, the directory service for external users in the *External Zone*. In order to keep the risk of attacks low, it is recommended to use a web application gateway with filtering capabilities as proposed in the LetMeAccess (I2) pattern.
- The backend systems that belong to the surrounding EAPs will partly be located in the internal zone (e.g., financial systems, human resources systems, etc.). Of

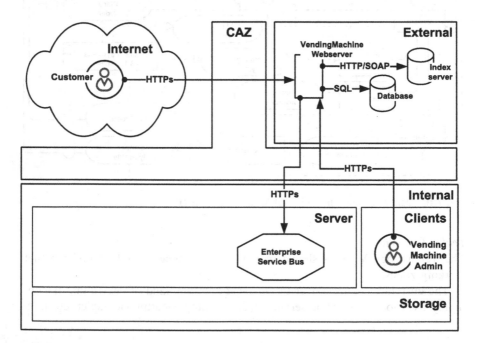

Fig. 7.11 Technology View of VendingMachine (B2)

course the network policy must explicitly allow the communication from systems in the external zone to these internal systems.

- We recommend implementing an *Enterprise Service Bus* (ESB) [see Chappel (2004) or Fowler (2002) for patterns] to decouple the communication between all the involved systems. The communication should take place using only standardized protocols like (S)FTP, hypertext transfer protocol HTTP(S), or simple object access protocol (SOAP). We put the ESB as an integration component in the *Internal Zone*. Patterns like KnowYourCustomer (B3), Financials (S1), InformationChest (S2), or FromSupplierToCustomer (S4) can be connected through this component.

7.2.6 Resulting Context

Interaction
Figure 7.12 shows the interaction of the pattern with the surrounding EAPs. Note that the VendingMachine (B2) itself does not provide any interfaces for other patterns. This is mainly due to the fact that the pattern only provides an additional channel for selling goods, but does not provide any services to other patterns.

The VendingMachine (B2) uses the following EAPs:

- StoreMyIdentities (I1), LetMeAccess (I2), and UnderControl (I3): These EAPs are referenced practically in all patterns as the implementation of these central services is of great benefit for the Enterprise Architecture as a whole. Using an existing service for storing identities and authentication and authorization quickens the development of the VendingMachine (B2) and makes its implementation more secure.

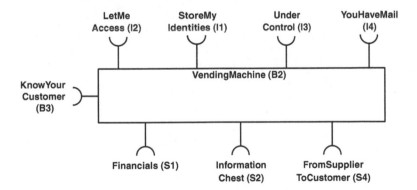

Fig. 7.12 Interaction of VendingMachine (B2) with other patterns

- Financials (S1): Financial transactions must all appear in the main ledger. Therefore, the *Invoices* and *Orders and Payments* will use the financial services.
- YouHaveMail (I4): Communication with the customers is done via messaging capabilities. A relaying SMTP host for sending E-mails from the VendingMachine (B2) is located in the external zone and the mailbox infrastructure is in the Intranet Zone.
- KnowYourCustomer (B3): All information related to partners and customers is managed within this pattern.
- InformationChest (S2): The VendingMachine (S2) may use information from the overall information management landscape of the company.
- FromSupplierToCustomer (S4): The VendingMachine (B2) is an additional channel in the source and delivery processes.

Consequences

By using this pattern the company is able to add a new channel to sell goods. Doing so, the company enhances its presence on the Internet, acquires new customers, or facilitates the communication with business partners by eliminating media breaks in the source and delivery processes. The implementation of the pattern has an impact on the business processes and demands new skills in the organization.

It is absolutely mandatory that a master data concept be in place: The VendingMachine (B2) produces order numbers, invoices, payment data, or customer information records. The company must define which are the leading systems, and how the import and export of information from the VendingMachine (B2) to the surrounding EAP may take place. The naming convention for data modeling must be developed and implemented. This leverages the principle of avoiding unwanted data redundancies, inconsistencies, and integrity issues. It is also crucial that a comprehensive risk assessment, that is regularly repeated, takes place in order to manage the additional risks that may arise by an Internet facing sales channel.

7.3 KnowYourCustomer (B3)

«The consumer isn't a moron; she is your wife. You insult her intelligence if you assume that a mere slogan and a few vapid adjectives will persuade her to buy anything. She wants all the information you can give her.»

(David Ogilvy, Confessions of an Advertising Man).

7.3.1 Introduction

Name and Overview

Name	KnowYourCustomer
Number	B3
Type of pattern	Business
Abstract	This pattern describes the various ways of interacting and communicating with the customer
Capabilities	Management of customers
	Storing and retrieving information regarding customer communication
	Enhancing business opportunities by offering the customer what is interesting to him
	Knowing the customer and his needs better by analyzing all information available
Referenced patterns	StoreMyIdentities (I1), LetMeAccess (I2), UnderControl (I3), InformationChest (S2), VendingMachine (B2)
Bricks	Customer portal, sales portal, marketing portal, support portal, admin interface
Impeding forces	Decentralized and unlinked customer information storage, information is often considered as a professional secret by different account managers
	Security and privacy considerations as a KnowYourCustomer (B3) can contain security sensitive information
Supporting forces	Generating new business opportunities
	Customer experience and expectations
	Reducing costs of maintaining multiple similar systems
Invariance	High
Complexity	Medium
Connectivity	Medium
Keywords	Customer, interaction, information, communication, management

Definition

Nowadays, customer orientation is one of the most often spoken terms in a highly competitive and globalized business environment. Enterprises should withstand the temptation to try to manipulate its clients. It is a fact that customer are getting more and more informed and are willing to quickly switch their supplier if they do not feel well served or if a competitor makes a better offer. Therefore, understanding the customer and serving him/her well is crucial to every business. The recent rise of social networks and the implication on the relationship between the different customers and an enterprise increases the necessity of knowing your customer as any slight lapse of understanding may result in a loss of market share as social media tend to be an amplifier.

But who is this interesting species we call customer? Richard C. Reizenstein defines the term customer as an

> «individual or entity that is the recipient of a good or service made available by a supplier or provider, usually in exchange for something of value that is generally but not always monetary in nature. A customer may or may not be the end user of the good or service» (Reizenstein 2004).

The relationship between supplier and customer is a fragile one and keeping a customer is getting increasingly difficult and is strongly dependent on the customer experience an enterprise is able to deliver. Kostojohn et al. describe it very precisely as follows:

> «Providing customers with the most satisfying and effective interactions possible is an increasingly important competitive differentiator. Customers are not nearly as loyal today – they can often simply search the web and find a «better» alternative to your product or service within minutes. In addition, technology tools such as blogs, ratings sites, and social networks have increased the scale and impact of the consumer's "word-of-mouth", making positive customer experiences even more important.»

Goldenberg (2002) defines customer relationship management (CRM) as follows:

> «CRM» integrates people, process, and technology to maximize relationships with all customers. CRM is a comprehensive approach that provides seamless coordination between all customer-facing functions. CRM increasingly leverages the Internet.

Expanding this definition, we postulate that CRM represents all people, processes, and technology needed in order to provide the best customer experience to its customers for reaching the highest possible customer loyalty and being able to identify new customer expectations as soon as possible.

In the context of this book we do not differentiate between customers as individuals (B2C customers) or organizations (B2B customers) as the differences are not so big on the abstraction level of an Enterprise Architecture Pattern.

7.3.2 Example

> TheWineBottle is planning to present a gift to its most loyal customers that should be chosen based on their time being a customer, on the money spent, and on their interest besides wine. The gift should be free attendance at the opening night of the new product called Wine and Dine. But who exactly is to invite? Such an event must be carefully planned and the participants must be carefully selected. A well-structured and cultivated CRM is crucial for this event to succeed.

7.3.3 Context

Every company has customers, but the kind of relationship strongly differs. Some have many customers that just do not want any more service than just the cheapest price and fastest delivery; other enterprises have just a few customers but will do virtually anything for them. However, it is a fact that every satisfied customer is invaluable in terms of word-of-mouth recommendation. As the pattern does not favor any type of relationship or type of customer it can be implemented by any enterprise planning to foster the relationship to its customer base.

7.3.4 Problem

The problem to address seems easy, but is complex in reality. As this patterns deals with a relationship between a customer and an enterprise, which implies the relationship between human beings, it is most likely that the success or failure of having a prospering relationship decides on the business process level and not on the IT level.

In order to emphasize the problem that needs to be solved, we would like to tell a little story of the chief sales representative of TheWineBottle:

> After having visited many customers personally, the chief sales representative of TheWineBottle returns to his office and takes a look at a pile of sheets of paper where he did write down many things he found interesting while talking to some of his best customers. He has many ideas and suggestions for new products, services, and also some complaints. He is starting up his computer and begins to write all these things in a Word document. From time to time he shares his thoughts with co-workers by sending them an E-mail and suggesting the launch of a new product. One year later he returns to his office with an even more impressive stack of papers and to his disappointment the complaints have nearly doubled and the suggestions mostly were the same as last year.

Organization's View

Having a well-planned and productive CRM application and infrastructure enables employees to impact the relationship with their customers in a way that the customer feels at ease with the enterprise. Unfortunately, many implementations of CRMs do not follow the path of first talking about culture, business processes, needs, and experience of the customer facing employees, but are trying to put them in a more or less tight frame defined by the software. Any organization implementing a new CRM or trying to improve the existing CRM should first talk about business processes, about culture and expectations, both on the side of the employees as well as on the customer's side in order to understand the requirements better. Knowing the customer and serving him in an individual and convenient manner gets more and more important, as customers are willing to change a supplier very quickly if it docs not measure up to their expectations.

Enterprise Architect's View

A good Enterprise Architect can influence the successful implementation of a CRM system greatly. He has a good overall view of the various data sources and data sinks that need to be considered in order to provide all necessary data to the customer service representatives. He must avoid any solution that is isolated and lacks the view of the organization as a whole. Not only the obvious data flows must be observed, but all, e.g., not only should the contacts between customer service representative be logged but also any support ticket opened by the customer and its resolution time. Having exact information about what the customer thinks and feels at this moment enables the customer service representative to anticipate the customer's requirements, expectation, and his current attitude toward the organization and thus to serve him better. Having access to all information means to integrate different systems into the CRM environment such as customer portals, marketing platforms, ticketing/support systems, and sales portals. The process of integrating the scattered and often incompatible account may be time-consuming and challenging but offers great reward. During this integration process not only technical obstacles must be overcome, but cultural problems as well as valuable information about customers sometimes is not voluntarily shared between competing divisions within the organization. As a CRM solution contains often valuable and sensitive information, the Enterprise Architect must ensure that adequate protection measures are planned and implemented.

End-User's View

There are different types of end-users. The customer is the most important one, even though he is going to have contact only with a very limited part of the CRM system, mainly with the support and customer portals. Yet he is the one in focus, as he should benefit from the CRM. His requirement is not that a CRM is in place but that he is served well by all employees from the organization. He expects that he needs to talk about his requests and concerns only once and that in any follow-up this information is known to his counterpart. The other end-user types consist of customer service representatives, account manager, sales staff, and support people. Their expectation is that they can access correct and up-to-date information whenever they need it, but especially when they are going to be in contact with a customer. They need information in an easy and quick way so that they can focus on the customer and are not distracted by the handling of the application. This leads to the conclusion that usability is an important area that must be handled with care.

7.3.5 Solution

The proposed solution tries to focus on the business processes, applications, and the interaction with other patterns instead of promoting a technical solution. Basically, it should be possible to implement the pattern with any CRM system available on the market. What is much more important is how the organization adopts and integrates different technologies into its business processes and lets them support and enhance the interaction of a customer with the enterprise. This includes many patterns proposed in this book as well as the integration of social media but does not end with that. It is at least as important that the customer representatives have a simple to use interface that provides them with all the necessary information about a customer or a customer group in order to understand them and thus to serve them in a friendly and competent way. Kostojohn et al. (2011) describe the value of a CRM solution as follows:

> «The marriage of a set of well-documented, consistently executed processes, with a business application that supports, monitors, and reports on them provides the foundation for an agile organization that learns and evolves. This agility can help you stay one step ahead of your competition».

In order to provide this value, the pattern needs to provide the following overall capabilities:

- It must support the workflow over all interactions with a customer. It may do so by providing its own capabilities or by integrating capabilities of other applications such as InformationChest (S2).
- It must store and provide all information regarding a customer in an easily accessible way.
- It should integrate social networks and media not only as a channel to reach the customer, but also as much as an interaction platform and as a source of information in order to understand the customers' expectations. In fact a next generation of CRM systems seem to evolve called social customer relationship management (SCRM) that goes far beyond Social Media but in fact is a new kind of CRM toolset.
- Every interaction with a customer should cause a trail of information in the system. This information is used to understand and serve the next customer in a better way.

In order to achieve these goals, KnowYourCustomer (B3) has to take into account the business processes, the actors, and the information before defining the underlying technical infrastructure. Unfortunately, the approach is often contrary and a CRM technology is chosen and the processes are adapted to the technology. Even if some success is possible by introducing a new tool for managing customer data, it rarely unleashes the full potential. This is why we chose to name the pattern KnowYourCustomer (B3).

Vision

> During his travels the sales representative of TheWineBottle starts up his tablet pc and checks the latest orders and conversations with his customer that he is going to meet in a few moments. During the meeting he makes notes that can easily be uploaded onto the customer's profile as well as linked into the idea database for future product enhancements. Complaints can be handled on-site by checking order status, giving discounts, or granting vouchers. After having returned to TheWineBottle some of his new ideas have already emerged into formal proposals for new products and have been discussed internally among his colleagues. Before leaving his office he checks the order forecast and is pleased to see a continuous rise since the adaption of the KnowYourCustomer (B3) pattern.

Principles

1. *Principle*	*Electronic-based workflows for all customer contacts*
Statement	Every contact with a customer—be it a phone call or an order—is embedded into a workflow that ensures that all information is gathered, processed, and stored in order to be at hand for the next customer contact
Reasoning	Every customer is a human being who likes to be treated in an individual, personal way, and values it if his requests and suggestions are taken seriously
Consequences	The KnowYourCustomer (B3) pattern must be tightly integrated in any communication platform as well as in every document management system. It must provide simple and quick-to-use workflows that are customizable to the enterprise needs
2. *Principle*	*Mobility*
Statement	Any information about a customer must be readily available regardless of the geographic location and the device used to access the information
Reasoning	Access to customer information must be possible from everywhere. Especially as this information may change quickly and frequently, it is mandatory that anyone on the road has access to current and correct information. The same must be possible for customers changing their profile. This must be available on a broad choice of devices
Consequences	Access must be possible from everywhere with any device suitable for working on the road such as smartphones, tablets, and laptops

(continued)

(continued)

3. *Principle*	*Accurate information*
Statement	Information must be correct and authentic
Reasoning	As decisions are based upon the information regarding a customer, care must be taken that all information entered is correct
Consequences	Plausibility checks and validation of all information must ensure that all information entered is correct. A mixture of technical and organizational measures must achieve this
4. *Principle*	*Customer centric*
Statement	The CRM must serve the customer
Reasoning	It is all about the customer. If he is satisfied by the service he gets, he is willing to return as well as recommend the enterprise to other potential customers
Consequences	The system must be designed in a way that serves the customer best. If he is required to enter information he should be aware of the purpose why he is requested to fill in a form
5. *Principle*	*Security and privacy*
Statement	Information must be protected according to privacy laws. There must exist a privacy statement that is adhered to
Reasoning	The collection of all information about a customer may cause uneasy feelings on behalf of the customer or of privacy and consumer organizations. Theft or loss of information may result in reputation damage
Consequences	Information stored must be strongly protected in its integrity, confidentiality, and authenticity. The customer must know what information is stored and must agree. He must have the possibility to revoke his consent

Holistic View

Figure 7.13 shows that there exist five groups of main actors with their own services. The main actors are either directly involved with the customer (*Sales*, *Support*, and the *Customer* himself) or work based on data of the customer and feed him with information (*Marketing*). As such an infrastructure can become quite complex, the administration is drawn as its own service. Overall, it can be said that the most important part of KnowYourCustomer (B3) is on the business layer with the different actors that are connected together on the application layer.

The business processes are roughly sketched as they can be much more complicated in reality. But they represent the main interaction between enterprise and customer:

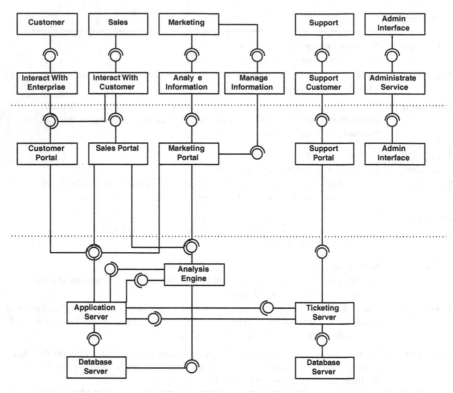

Fig. 7.13 Holistic View of KnowYourCustomer (B3)

- *Customer*: The customer is the most important actor in this pattern. He is the one who should be understood and to whose wishes the enterprise should have an answer. Information about the customer–be it former orders, the path he follows on the web site, or the whole communication between him and the enterprise–is tracked by the KnowYourCustomer (B3) pattern. He directly interacts with the customer portal and indirectly by other patterns such as VendingMachine (B2).
- *Sales*: Sales personnel are one of the most important players as they sell the services or goods the customer requests. If selling performance is above average, it is crucial that the sales team understands the customer well and that it proposes the right products to the customer. If selling is done automatically through Information Technology, such as by using the VendingMachine (B2) pattern, interfaces between both patterns should be established. VendingMachine (B2) is one of the most important data suppliers for KnowYourCustomer (B3), while KnowYourCustomer (B3) can provide invaluable information to the

VendingMachine (B2) and therefore directly to the customer who is buying goods. One good example of such a coupling is products that are presented based on former purchases of a customer and by goods other customers with a similar profile have bought.

- *Support*: Supporting the customer in an efficient way is one of the most important parts for retaining customers. On the other hand, it can be very expensive for an enterprise. If customer support can be alleviated by the sensible use of Information Technology, an enterprise is most likely to have a competitive advantage. Supporting by the means of IT often includes having a support portal where the customer places his requests, a ticketing system for tracking the requests and support personnel trying to solve the pending problems.
- *Marketing*: Marketing primarily uses the CRM system as an information source for preparing new campaigns and to derive trends. The second part is customer communication in order to promote new services. The customer data is the mine marketing digging for gold–the more accurate and detailed the information, the more targeted a marketing campaign can be made.

On the application level several portals exist, serving as a melting point for the different business processes. It is noteworthy that these portals can form one big application or a rather loosely coupled assembly of different applications. It is often observed that each of these applications has an underlying technology that is dominating the business processes which always results in interface problems. In a typical situation a *Customer Portal* exists, often a web application, sometimes coupled with a web-shop [remember the VendingMachine (B2) pattern]. The *Support Portal* is realized by a specialized ticketing application, whereas the actual CRM is an application itself that is only used by account management and sales. This approach leads to the situation that there is always information that is lacking. For example, it would be crucial for an account manager to see whether a customer has many pending or unsuccessful service requests, whereas it would be important that the service level agreements are visible in the ticketing application.

The technical view represents a mixture of the desired state and realistic assumptions. It is one application server for both *Marketing Portal* and *Customer Portal*. For the ticketing system, a dedicated server is assumed that provides/uses interfaces with the application server that runs the customer relationship application. This application comprises the *Customer Portal* as well as the *Marketing Portal* and provides/uses interfaces of the *Analysis Engine*. The administration is done by an *Admin Interface*. The connections needed are omitted to keep the diagram readable.

The following bricks are used in this pattern: (Table 7.3).

Business View

The main actors, customer, sales personnel, marketing personnel, supporters, and administrators are the core of the following business processes.

Table 7.3 Patterns in relationship with KnowYourCustomer (B3)

Brick	Description
Customer portal	Access for the customer to his profile and for sales and account management to customer information
Marketing portal	Provides information to the marketing and uses as an interface to various marketing channels
Support portal	Allows the customer to place support requests that are handled by support personnel
Sales portal	Provides aggregated information for the sales people and connects them to the customer
Admin interface	The admin interface is for the application administrator's use to manage the systems
Analysis engine	The analysis engine provides various analysis methods to perform data mining on the customer data
Ticketing server	Handles the support workflow
Application server	Provides the runtime environment for the actual CRM System
Database server	Stores data. There are two database servers: one for the application server and the other for the ticketing system

Figure 7.14 shows the most important process, how the customer interacts with the enterprise, which results in a trail of information that can be used by the customers' contacts within the enterprise. One typical interaction is the request for support, which includes every kind of demand that is handled by the enterprise, such as information requests, complaints, and questions. Other processes of the customer are the use of the VendingMachine (B2) pattern that leaves a trail in the KnowYourCustomer (B3) pattern.

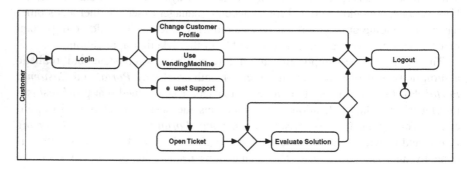

Fig. 7.14 Customer business process

Figure 7.15 shows how a typical support requests is tracked. This is often done by a ticketing system. Often, the supporter makes use of another pattern when answering support requests–the InformationChest (S2). After taking a customer's ticket, the supporter proposes a solution that can be accepted or not by the customer (see Fig. 7.14, *Evaluate Solution*).

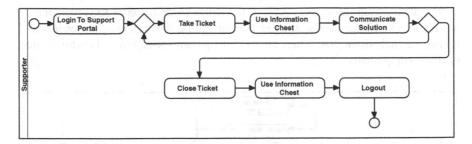

Fig. 7.15 Business process for the support case

Figure 7.16 shows the work of a sales person in terms of the KnowYourCustomer (B3) pattern. Data are analyzed or entered. According to the data of a customer, the sales person can decide about different options such as granting a discount, contacting a customer, or making changes to the selling strategy.

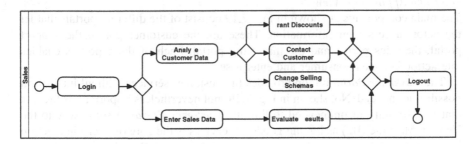

Fig. 7.16 Business process of sales people

Another important stakeholder of the KnowYourCustomer (B3) pattern is the marketing personnel. Typically, marketing personnel plans campaigns and surveys or analyzes customer data to suggest actions to promote the products of the enterprise (see Fig. 7.17). When doing so, the use of InformationChest (S2) often comes in handy.

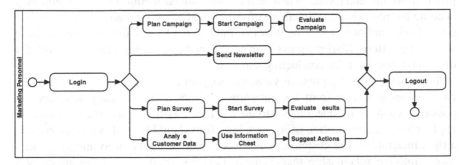

Fig. 7.17 Business process of marketing personnel

The administration (see Fig. 7.18) of the KnowYourCustomer (B3) pattern may have a lot of different tasks, such as administrating the various components and tuning the analysis engine. It may also include parameterization and customization of these components.

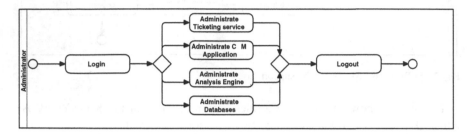

Fig. 7.18 Business process of administrating the KnowYourCustomer (B3) pattern

Data and Application View
The main components as shown in Fig. 7.19 consist of the different portals that let the actors access their information. These are the customer portal, the support portal, the sales portal, and the marketing portal. Each of these portals enables interaction between consumer and enterprise.

The *Customer Portal* on top provides the customer services with all interaction possibilities needed. Not shown in Fig. 7.19, but nevertheless important, is the fact that it is strongly recommended to link the *Customer Portal* in some way to the VendingMachine (B2) as buying goods or services is the core of every interaction between the customer and the enterprise. The *Customer Portal* features services for the interaction such as updating the own profile and consuming information. The customer portal uses interfaces from all the other portals, thus concatenating the information that the customer is interested in. How this is technically done depends upon the actual software used. This can be achieved by content syndication, by providing different direct links, or by a completely seamless integration in a way that all the systems are connected by the use of web services. The customer can manage its own information (his profile) and consume information provided by the enterprise. When dealing with social media this distinction may become blurred however. Speaking of social media, we treat social media as one possible channel of information flow that may be fed by any information available within the pattern. Marketing may use social media for doing campaign work for distributing news or for conducting surveys.

From the customer's point of view, the *Support Portal* is very important in the case he needs advice from the enterprise. It should be as easily reachable as possible, ideally fully integrated into the *Customer Portal*. Very often the support application is an application of its own, but effort should be undertaken to provide a tight integration. The customer portal would also be the point to integrate social media into the relationship management. One possibility is to integrate content from social networks or to integrate content from the customer portal (based upon the discretion of the user) into a social network.

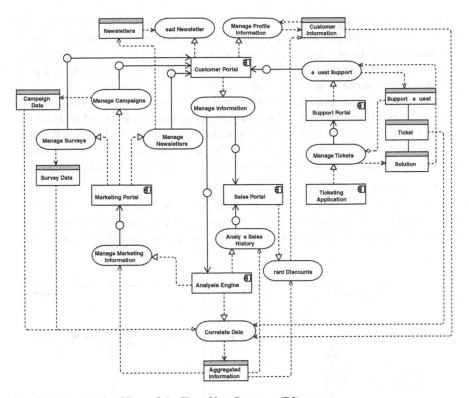

Fig. 7.19 Application View of the KnowYourCustomer (B3) pattern

The support portal provides two services, one for the customer who is requesting support and the other for the supporters providing support. In order to do so, they need to accept the customer's support ticket. All tickets and the path to the solution are handled by the ticketing application. Not in the graphic, but nonetheless very desirable, is the integration of the InformationChest (S2) to provide solutions in a fast and coherent way. The data objects that are worked with are all handled in the form of tickets that are composed of the support request and – hopefully – a solution to this request.

From the point of view of the enterprise, equally important are the *Sales* and the *Marketing Portals*, as these connect sales people and marketing people to the customer and give them all the information needed such as the buying profile of a certain customer as well as statistically analyzed data about a certain customer segment. The sales portal lets the sales people interact with the customer in regard to granting discounts, making special offers, and learning from the behavior of a typical customer segment. It does not produce data of its own as the information is either stored in the customer profile or in the VendingMachine (B2) pattern.

The *Marketing Portal* is the direct frontend for pushing out information to the customer such as newsletters, surveys, or campaigns. These also form the data objects that are written by the *Marketing Portal*. In order to have these as targeted as possible, marketing people need information. All information – for marketing, or for sales – is prepared by an analysis engine that connects all the sources together and produces aggregated information as a data object. If a strong integration into social networks is demanded, the marketing portal should have a push functionality in order to serve content directly into social networks.

To summarize, the application view mainly consists of different portals that can be coupled to different extents and an analysis engine that connects and analyzes the various data objects. This view on the application is deliberately chosen as it leaves enough room for different philosophies by the different vendors of CRM systems, but sets a direction to a customer and business process centric point of view.

Technology View
The technology view (Fig. 7.20) spots the different portals with the web servers belonging to it. It is important to note that the actual implementation and the distribution of the different systems in the network may change with the vendor chosen.

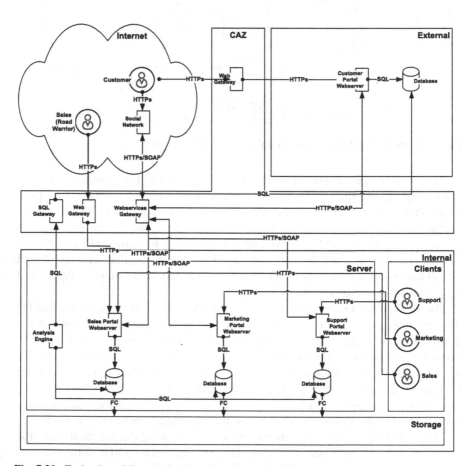

Fig. 7.20 Technology View of the KnowYourCustomer (B3) Pattern

The *Customer Portal Webserver* is in the external network, whereas the other parts are in the internal network. It gives the customer one application that may implement different parts from different patterns. It consists of the web server hosting the web application and a database. Depending upon the nature of the data stored, it may be wise to place the database in a specially protected environment. If a tight integration of social media is desired, a connection between the customer portal and one or more different social networks must exist. Using a web service traversing the web services gateway is the favorable solution. However, as the social network decides upon the interfaces available one must be open to adopt other solutions.

The various systems interact by the use of the web services gateway implementing a web services protocol. The SOAP protocol serves as an exemplary and widely used protocol but any other implementation of a web service can be used, e.g., REST. The interaction done by the web services is crucial for the functioning of the KnowYourCustomer (B3) pattern, as the different aspects of a customer relationship must be linked together. Even if you use one product for all or a suite of products from the same supplier it is likely that some parts of the systems must be positioned in an externally reachable zone (the customer portal), whereas other parts remain in the highly protected internal network. The pattern requests that all communication between different service elements of the pattern is done by web services. All connections should pass the web services gateway in order to filter and control information flow and thus reduce risks.

The *Marketing Portal Webserver* is accessed by HTTPs and is connected to the *Customer Portal Webserver* and to the *Analysis Engine*. It consists–just as the other portals–of a web server and a database that stores marketing data. Not drawn in the technical view, because it belongs to another pattern, are the connections to the communication patterns such as YouHaveMail (I4). If marketing is targeted at social media, the marketing portal should be connected to social networks, ideally using a web service that is controlled by a web services gateway in the CAZ.

The *Support Portal* is often a system of its own, as there exist many different ticketing applications. It should interact as tightly as possible with the other systems as often the support and how he interacts with customers decides whether a customer is becoming a loyal long-term customer or not. For sales and marketing people it is crucial that they know about escalations of unresolved support cases. In order to present the customer with just one interface to the enterprise, opening and tracking a support request should be integrated into the customer portal in an optical and logically coherent way so that no rupture between the different interactions of a customer with the enterprise exists.

Users access the different portals by using a browser and HTTPs. As sales people are often on the road, it is important that they can use the sales portal from anywhere using different mobile devices. For the marketing and support portals this is not as important. Whether internal users are allowed to access the portals directly or via a web application gateway depends on the security requirements of the enterprise.

The *Analysis Engine* collects and correlates data by directly accessing the databases. This access is done in a read-only mode and – like the access of the internal users – can be done using a gateway, in this case an SQL gateway. Depending upon the integration of the analysis engine it is thinkable or even advisable to use a web service for gathering data from the various data stores throughout the KnowYourCustomer (B3) pattern. An *Analysis Engine* may be technically spoken as a set of rules for retrieving and analyzing data of different sources, but can also take the shape of a Data Warehouse and its associated tools (Business Intelligence tools) that are used to retrieve, transform, and analyze the data in the different Data Marts.

7.3.6 Resulting Context

Interaction

As a typical Business Pattern KnowYourCustomer (B3) uses many interfaces of other patterns, mainly of Infrastructure Patterns, as shown in Fig. 7.21.

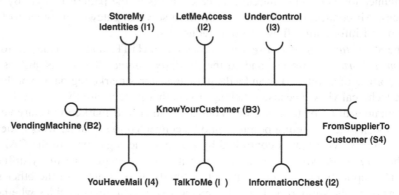

Fig. 7.21 Interaction of the KnowYourCustomer (B3) pattern

As selling goods strongly depends on knowing the customer, there is an interface offered to VendingMachine (B2). The same is valid for the FromSup-plierToCustomer (S4) pattern. Because of these strong relationships it is crucial to define which of the patterns has the lead over the other two. The KnowYour-Customer (B3) is rather demanding when it comes to use interfaces from Infra-structure Patterns. It can make use of all defined Infrastructure Patterns. However, even if not all Infrastructure Patterns are in place, KnowYourCustomer (B3) can be realized nevertheless. The implementation may be slightly more demanding as all interfaces must be either realized inside the KnowYourCustomer (B3) pattern or some of the interfaces must be requested in the enterprise and used as a service.

Consequences

Using this pattern can be a strong signal to focus on customer satisfaction as this pattern puts the customer and the related business processes in the center. It is key that the implementation of this pattern is guided by business needs and not by a technological view. Every implementer should regularly ask himself the question whether an element really does serve the customer, and if yes, to what extent. It is perfectly normal that an enterprise wants to sell more items or services to a customer but whether this desire is going to be successful or not depends upon the customer's perception that the additional sale proposal serves him well or if he figures out that someone is trying to trick him into a purchase.

One should be clear about the fact that implementing the KnowYourCustomer (B3) pattern influences some core business processes of an enterprise and therefore must be undertaken carefully. The implementation should be watched closely and regularly checked. Customers should be integrated in the process by using surveys and by taking any feedback seriously.

Similar to the VendingMachine (B2) pattern, a master data concept must be in place to work efficiently with the data acquired. Data should not be collected unless they really serve a purpose in order to avoid privacy issues and to keep the information stack manageable.

The actual implementation of this pattern may vary from enterprise to enterprise as not only the sector influences the relationship between enterprise and customer, but the strategy of an enterprise as well and the culture associated with it. This may change emphasis on the different elements and their interaction but the authors are confident that the pattern is likely to exist in many different enterprises with different cultures.

References

Amyris F (2008) Cultural influences on virtual teamwork collaboration in the Encyclopedia of e-collaboration. Information Science Reference, Hershey

Chappell D (2004) Enterprise service bus. O'Reilly, USA

COA (2011) COA framework standard. https://www.opengroup.org/projects/security/coafwk/. Last accessed 20 Sep 2011

Coleman D, Stewart L (2008) Collaboration 2.0: technology and best practices for successful collaboration in a web 2.0 world. Happy About, California

Davila T (2006) Making innovation work: how to manage it, measure it, and profit from it. Wharton School Pub, Upper Saddle River

Fowler M (2002) Patterns of enterprise application architecture. Addison -Wesley, USA

Goldenberg B (2002) CRM automation. Prentice Hall PTR, Upper Saddle River

Governor J (2009) Web 2.0 architectures. O'Reilly Media Inc., Sebastopol

Hogue T (1994) Community based collaborations – wellness multiplied, Oregon center for community leadership. http://crs.uvm.edu/nnco/collab/wellness.html. Last accessed 20 Sep 2011

Kolfschoten G, Briggs R, Vreede G (2010) A technology for pattern-based process design and its application to collaboration engineering in collaborative technologies and applications for interactive information design: emerging trends in user experiences. Information Science Reference, Hershey

Kostojohn S, Johnson M, Paulen B (2011) CRM fundamentals. APress, Berkeley

Meier A, Stormer H, Gosselin E (2009) eBusiness & eCommerce: managing the digital value chain. Springer, Berlin

NIH (2011) Web collaboration solution pattern. https://enterprisearchitecture.nih.gov/Pages/webcollaboration.aspx. Last accessed 20 June 2013

OSCAF (2011) Open Semantic Collaboration Architecture Foundation. http://www.oscaf.org/. Last accessed 20 Sep 2011

Pinterits A (2009) Coordinating internet sales with other channels. Gabler, Wiesbaden

Prensky M (2001) Digital natives, digital immigrants – on the horizon, vol 9, Nr 5, MCB University Press

Reizenstein RC (2004) Encyclopedia of health care management. Sage Publications, Thousand Oaks

SAP (2011) Managing the web shop. http://help.sap.com/saphelp_crm40/helpdata/en/9d/0c054e48a04b44a08c7d15f966a900/content.htm. Accessed 29 July 2011

Schümmer T, Lukosch S (2007) Patterns for computer-mediated interaction. Wiley, England Hoboken

Stanley M (2009) The mobile internet report. http://www.morganstanley.com/about/press/articles/4659e2f5-ea51-11de-aec2-33992aa82cc2.html. Accessed 21 June 2013

WAI (2011) Web accessibility initiative (WAI) http://www.w3.org/WAI/. Accessed 7 Aug 2011

Chapter 8
Support Patterns

Abstract This chapter contains five Support Patterns with solutions for financials, information management, human resources, supply chain management, and secure information exchange.

8.1 Financials (S1)

«I work all night, I work all day, to pay the bills I have to pay.»

(ABBA «Money, money, money»)

8.1.1 Introduction

Name and Overview

Name	Financials
Number	S1
Type of pattern	Support
Abstract	This pattern provides all necessary services to manage the financial supply chain. It supports the financial performance analysis, the management of accounts, and assets
Capabilities	Management of the overall financial supply chain
	Financial performance management (controlling, consolidation, financial statements)
	Management of assets (cash, payroll, etc.)
	Accounts management (ledger, payables, receivables, invoices)

(continued)

T. Perroud and R. Inversini, *Enterprise Architecture Patterns*,
DOI: 10.1007/978-3-642-37561-3_8, © Springer-Verlag Berlin Heidelberg 2013

(continued)

Referenced patterns	StoreMyIdentities (I1), LetMeAccess (I2), UnderControl (I3), YouHaveMail (I4), InformationChest (S2), ResourcesAreScarce (S3), FromSupplierToCustomer (S4), ForYourEyesOnly (S5), VendingMachine (B2)
Bricks	Asset and treasury, accounts management, financial performance, application server, database server
Impeding forces	Missing or only informal financial processes
	Missing resources to implement the pattern
Supporting forces	Comprehensive view over the full financial supply chain
	High business criticality
	High management attention
Invariance	Medium: the pattern may differ from business to business and may therefore vary in the implementation
Complexity	Medium
Connectivity	High: the pattern will be used by many other patterns, especially business patterns
Keywords	Financial processes, assets, accounts management, financial performance, e-finance, banking

Definition

The world of financial management is well described, as it is the foundation of every business since hundreds of years. We will therefore restrict our definition to a generally accepted description without going too much into details.

«Finance is the study of concepts, applications and systems that affect the value (or wealth) of individuals, companies and countries over the short and long term. The study is both qualitative and quantitative (...)» (Banks 2010).

The following definition for finance is given in the Merriam-Webster dictionary:

«Finance

1. plural: money or other liquid resources of a government, business, group, or individual
2. the system that includes the circulation of money, the granting of credit, the making of investments, and the provision of banking facilities
3. the science or study of the management of funds» (Merriam-Webster 2005)

In the context of the Financials (S1) EAP we will use the following definition:

«Financials (S1) encompasses all the activities in a company or organization that are related to the transfer of money (in cash or electronic), the planning of investments and the management of transactions.»

8.1.2 Example

The Chief Financial Officer (CFO) of TheWineBottle needs accurate and up-to-date financial information about the status of sold articles, pending orders, open bills, the value of the wine in stock, and the salary sum of all internal and external employees for the weekly meeting with the CEO. He wants to be sure that his forecasts of the development of the financial supply chain are as accurate as possible and that the annual accounts are correct and may be taken directly from the accumulated financial data. Another problem he would like to solve is that the revenue from the new Online Shop is directly recorded in the financial backend system.

8.1.3 Context

The Financials (S1) pattern can be implemented in every company of any size. Financial processes are typical support processes that are present in every company or organization. The use of the pattern may help to improve the business processes for effective budgeting and financial reporting. Depending on the business of the company applying the pattern, it may be extended with specialized financial applications.

8.1.4 Problem

Many companies face the problem that they do not have accurate and up-to-date financial information as a basis for business decisions.

The CFO of TheWineBottle tries hard to have an accurate view of all the financial flows and information in the organization, but the circumstances are quite difficult: Employees send the wrong invoices to customers, the company gets regularly reminders for not having paid bills in due time, or wine bottles are sold without being recorded in the financial system. So, every end of the year, the CFO tries to straighten up things by collecting all financial information in the different departments to be able to present at least once a year a more or less accurate financial report.

Organization's View

From the organization's point of view, several different problems exist:

- Bills are being paid too late (missing early payment discounts).
- Invoices are not issued or sent to the wrong organizations or persons.
- Financial information must be copied manually from one system to another due to data and interface incompatibilities.
- Financial processes costs are too high.
- An end-to-end view over the whole financial chain is not possible and a consolidation of financial performance data is prone to a lot of errors.
- Financial data is lost or stolen.

In Basware (2010) the following statements underpin the problem:

«Costly finance errors

- Weaknesses in finance processes are resulting in additional costs in some cases – 30 % of respondents state having missed early payment discounts and 27 % have incurred late payment fees in the past 12 months.
- 24 % of respondents know of instances where their organization has not been paid due customer/external finance department errors and 35 % know of suppliers who have not been paid due to internal finance department errors.
- Respondents also state that 7 % of purchase invoices contain errors, equating to more than 6,000 erroneous invoices per year in a typical enterprise from the study.

    Lost in Process

- Invoice scanning/data entry is identified as both the most time-consuming (38 %) and the most error-prone (41 %) element of inbound invoice processing.
- 4 in 10 invoices are not based on purchase orders (POs) and one-third (32 %) of finance departments have difficulty reconciling invoices with POs.
- 61 % of respondents think invoice processing could be speeded up and 56 % think it could be more accurate».

The organization must have processes that form a financial system that supports an end-to-end view and that deliver accurate financial information in real-time. As the financial process supports many other processes it is crucial that appropriate and well-defined interfaces exist. Both flow directions are equally important, information about finances and financial assets entering and leaving the financial system. As financial information has high requirements for confidentiality and integrity, the system must support an adequate protection of this information.

Enterprise Architect's View

An Enterprise Architect must not only ensure that the financial system chosen suits the enterprise as good as possible and delivers the expected performance, he must also be concerned about interfaces to other applications and must govern its implementation and operation in a way that only in the official financial system information is stored and worked with. During the initial phase focus should be set upon defining the necessary processes and deciding which and to what extent these processes should be underpinned by ICT technology. This leads to the definition and the redesign of processes and of the necessary interfaces. During the operation, projects must be kept aligned with the financial system in order to avoid interrupts in the financial flows. The Enterprise Architect should have a close look that media breaks are avoided: No one should transcribe financial information by hand as this is error-prone and leads to inaccurate and delayed information. In order to guarantee an adequate level of integrity and confidentiality to financial information, security is a concern for the Enterprise Architect. The financial system must not only protect itself against unauthorized access but must be integrated into the security services of the organization. Often, the implementation of a consistent and overall financial system is, although a vital core capability of an enterprise, hindered by forces like the lack of the necessary resources or the habit to stick to informal processes without too much administrative tasks.

End-User's View
The end-user can be divided into two main categories, the power-user who mainly works with the financial system, e.g., an accountant, and the end-users that need financial information in order to make sound decisions. Both expect that the financial system delivers accurate and real-time information and that work can be done in an efficient way. If the system is able to aggregate information in a way that is easily read such as by the means of a dashboard, it is most welcome to the users that use financial information regularly. Another important expectation is that the system must support fine-grained reporting functions that allow the end-user to retrieve the information needed and to provide a view of the current financial situation.

8.1.5 Solution

Vision

> The financial supply chain of TheWineBottle supports the end-to-end view over all financial activities. All communication involving financial transactions will be made electronically (billing in and out, payments) without any media breaks. Accurate financial reports can be delivered according to the business needs.

Principles

---

1. *Principle*	*Accurate and up-to-date financial information*
Statement	Accurate and up-to-date financial information is crucial for the management to be able to take the right decisions
Reasoning	It is absolutely mandatory that all financial information reflects the reality of the business situation as accurately as possible. Lost or falsified information will have a negative impact on business decisions. False financial information may also lead to conflicts with legal requirements
Consequences	Documentation of all financial processes is mandatory
	Control objectives for all financial transactions must be put in place
	The Financials (S1) pattern must support the reporting and planning of all financial activities
2. *Principle*	*Reduced costs of financial transactions*
Statement	The implementation of an end-to-end financial system must lead to lower costs of financial transactions
Reasoning	In the past, TheWineBottle has lost a significant amount of money due to loss of track of invoices and bills. The internal costs of a transaction, from the order to the delivery of the wine to the customer, are too high because of manual activities (copying manually financial information from one system to the other). Early payment discounts have been missed in the past
Consequences	Any media breaks must be avoided in the financial transactions and automation of most of the activities must be supported by the Financials (S1) pattern
3. *Principle*	*Security of financial transactions*
Statement	Financial transactions are an interesting target for unauthorized people (e.g. hackers, competitors, and malicious people). These transactions must be protected in their confidentiality and integrity by all means
Reasoning	If any financial transaction gets falsified or financial information gets stolen then the company may get into serious troubles (loss of good image, loss of market shares, legal issues, etc.)
Consequences	The platforms on which the financial transactions take place must support integrity checking mechanisms
	The financial system must regularly be audited
	The confidentiality of financial data transmitted and stored must be preserved
	All actions must have an audit trail

Holistic View

Figure 8.1 shows all the bricks of the Financials (S1) pattern. The Business Architecture consists of three main processes *Analyze and Plan*, *Input Financial Information*, and *Retrieve Financial Information*. Employees modifying and retrieving financial information are represented by the *Business Users*. They may be in the financial department but also in the different business units where financial information is being generated, modified, and interpreted. People who plan und analyze financial information (financial staff, management, etc.) are represented by the role *Financial Staff*.

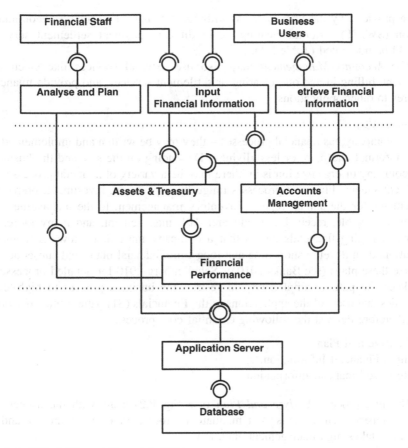

Fig. 8.1 Holistic View of Financials (S1)

This pattern has high interaction with other patterns and external systems. To leverage the effective and efficient implementation of financial processes, the use of electronic billing (in and out) or direct access the financial services like

Table 8.1 Architecture bricks of Financials (S1)

Brick	Description
Asset and treasury	This brick contains all the relevant information about the financial assets of the company
Accounts management	A company manages several accounts (main ledger, payables, receivables, etc.)
Financial performance	This bricks consolidates all financial information from the two other bricks and provides services to measure and forecast the financial performance
Application server	Generic brick for application servers
Database server	Generic brick for database servers

those provided by the Society for Worldwide Interbank Financial Telecommunication (SWIFT), external clearing, or credit card payment settlement services should be integrated (Table 8.1).

The *Accounts Management* may also use external services like electronic payment, billing in and out, clearing or settlement services, and provide financial figures to other applications.

Business View
Every company has financial processes – they may be written and implemented or only informal and more or less «living». Depending on the size and the business the company or organization is in, there may be a variety of financial processes in different shapes. Financial processes range from planning, investment, preparing statements for the annual reports, inventory management to the management of accounts payable, receivable, credit and cash management, and many more. In short, managing financials means that a company must first know its financial situation, then develop short-time and long-time financial plans and subsequently realize these plans (see Banks 2010 or Schellenberg 2010 for detailed processes). To keep the pattern simple, we will restrict the business process to high-level activities that users of the applications in the Financials (S1) pattern must perform. We therefore defined the following essential core processes:

1. Analyze and Plan.
2. Input Financial Information.
3. Retrieve Financial Information.

The first process *Analyze and Plan* (see Fig. 8.2) deals with the aspects of financial performance. This is a mandatory process in every company and it generally takes high management attention.

The basis for every financial model is accounting: Every transaction, movement of financial assets must be recorded according to a defined accounting plan. The financial model is actually a quantitative representation of the company's past, present, and future financial transactions. A comprehensive and consistent financial model is mandatory to be able to measure the performance and to plan for the future.

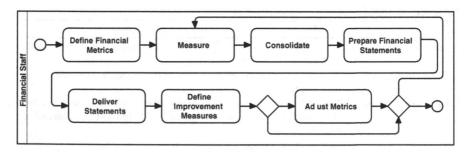

Fig. 8.2 Analyze and plan process

To be able to measure something, the first task is to define a metric (usually using Key Performance Indices and Key Goal Indicators). The metric in financials is normally realized with quarterly financial figures to reach or percentage of financial progression in comparison to past results. Results from the measurement must then be consolidated and prepared for publishing. Depending on the business needs, improvement measures may be defined and the metrics either be adjusted or complemented with new ones. This is a typical Plan-Do-Check-Act process.

A well-known and widely used method to analyze the performance of a company is the use of balanced scorecards (BSC) .

«A Balanced Scorecard is a management tool that provides senior executives with a comprehensive set of measures to assess how the organization is progressing toward meeting its strategic goals.» (Smith 2007, p. 166).

Besides the customer, internal, innovation, and learning perspectives, the financial one is mainly concerned with the shareholders' view of performance. The company will first have to define a financial strategy map and derived strategic initiatives. Then they will have to define metrics concerning market share, return on investment, profitability, growth, cash flow, etc., to be able to measure the financial performance. The BSC method can help to measure the *strategic* progress and must be complemented with other, more *operative* metrics.

The International Financial Reporting Standards (IFRS), released by the International Accounting Standards Board (IASB), defines how financial reports can be defined. The IASB explains the IFRS as:

«The IFRS are designed to apply to the general purpose financial statements and other financial reporting of profit-oriented entities (...). IFRSs apply to all general purpose financial statements. Such financial statements are directed towards the common information needs of a wide range of users, for example, shareholders, creditors, employees and the public at large. The objective of financial statements is to provide information about the financial position, performance and cash flows of an entity that is useful to those users in making economic decisions.» (IFRS 2011)

These standards are a good guideline on how to structure the financial statements. IFRS is mandatory for companies listed in European Union stock exchanges – the equivalent in the United States is the United States Generally Accepted Accounting Principles (US-GAAP).

The eXtensible Business Reporting Language (XBRL) has been developed to classify and analyze financial information. XBRL is a language derived from the eXtensible Markup Language (XML) and is being developed by an international non-profit consortium of major companies, organizations, and governmental agencies (see XBRL 2011). Besides tagging the financial information, it can also help to show how the financial elements are related to each other and thus how they are being calculated. Financial reports can be distributed and loaded into XBRL capable applications for further analysis. The XBRL leverages therefore the interoperability of exchange of financial information within a company, but also across the company's border.

The next process, *Modify Financial Information,* as shown in Fig. 8.3 is quite simple, but must be extremely well implemented and monitored, as incomplete, incorrect, or falsified financial information shall under no circumstances be inputted. Modifying information means in this context inputting new or changing existing information. As stated before, a comprehensive financial model builds the basis for correct input of financial information.

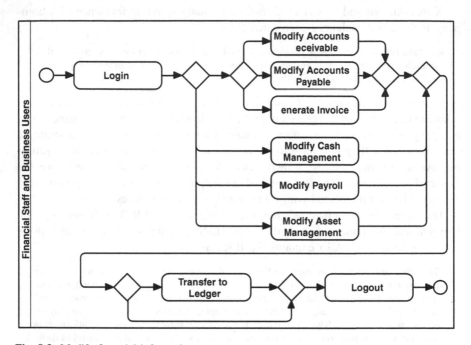

Fig. 8.3 Modify financial information process

The process only shows that financial information is being modified in various accounts and does not show detailed workflows for every activity. In practice, a company will define a subprocess for every activity in the process, with complete workflow information and quality checking activities. The business tells us who should have access to which financial information. This is best done with the definition of a coherent role model with access rights.

The last business process for Financials (S1) is shown in Fig. 8.4. The process is especially interesting, as the correct access rights to financial information are crucial to avoid unwanted information leakage. Even reading financial figures may in certain business situations be a privilege for only a limited group of persons.

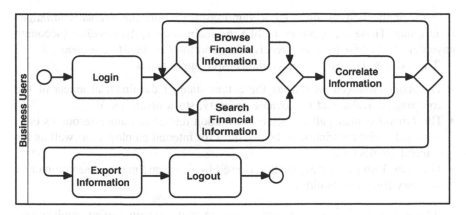

Fig. 8.4 Retrieve financial information

You will find a similar process in different other patterns like InformationChest (S2) or VendingMachine (B2), as working with information always follows a certain path, regardless of the type of information.

Data and Application View
The Data and Application View consists of three application groups. These groups correspond to the application bricks mentioned in the Holistic View.

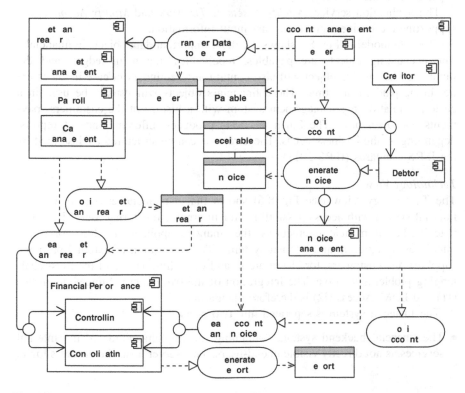

Fig. 8.5 Data and application view of Financials (S1)

Basic applications in financial accountings are within the *Accounts Management* group. These are applications like the main *Ledger*, the *Creditor* (accounts payable), the *Debtor* (accounts receivable), and the *Invoice Management*.

The *Asset & Treasury* group contains three applications:

- The *Asset Management* reflects the actual state of the financial assets of the company (movable and immovable property, stock assets, etc.).
- The *Payroll* contains all financial information related to human resources (salaries and social contributions, bonus, etc.) for internal employees as well as for external contractors.
- The *Cash Management* application is used to assure and manage the company's solvency (financial liquidity).

The *Assets & Treasury* application group may contain further applications depending on the business of the company, e.g., cash forecasting, investment management, treasury risk management, fund raising, etc. (see Bragg 2010).

The *Financial Performance* group centralizes all applications needed to consolidate and report the state of the financial situation. It is therefore connected to the other two groups using the two related application services to read the information (*Read Accounts and Invoices* and *Read Assets and Treasury*). The *Controlling* application is actually a placeholder for different applications, like profit center calculation, product cost controlling, cost center accounting, and others, depending on the business.

The application services *Modify Assets & Treasury* and *Modify Accounts* are supporting the business processes that input information.

The data model in Fig. 8.5 shows the most important data objects in financials: The accounting objects are payables, receivables, the main ledger, and the invoices. The invoice object will also contain any reminders in case invoices are not being paid in due time. These financials objects will usually be used in a customer relationship management system with a history of the customers' payments and open bills. The Financials (S1) produces different kinds of reports, depending on the business needs. These reports can be structured as described by the IFRS standards (IFRS 2011).

Technology View

The Technology View (see Fig. 8.6) shows that a financial environment is an internal system with access possibilities for internal and external users. To eliminate inefficient manual interactions, the financial application offers controlled interfaces for external and internal systems. The integration of external partners, suppliers and customers, for electronic in and out billing is one of the most challenging problems to solve. The integration of the two patterns StoreMyIdentities (I1) and LetMeAccess (I2) is therefore mandatory.

The financial system is separated into two parts:

- The financial backend system, containing the implementation of the internal services, is not directly visible to end-users. This server hosts the business logic.

- The financial application server, which is being accessed by the users and applications. This system provides the presentation services.

The communication between the two systems may occur with well-known standardized protocols or proprietary protocols (e.g., SAP's implementation of remote function call, RFC). Depending on the solution architecture and the chosen products, the financial applications may be spread over more or less systems. For example, the consolidation application may be from another provider than the accounting software.

As the financials system will be accessed by a lot of other applications, we recommend using a decoupling mechanism as provided by an Enterprise Service Bus. Relevant integration patterns can be found in Chappell (2004) and Hohpe and Woolf (2003).

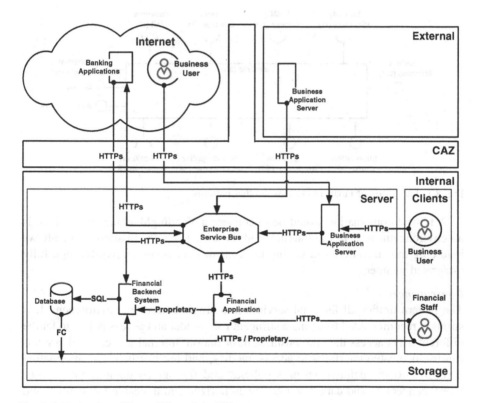

Fig. 8.6 Technology View of Financials (S1)

External applications are, for example, a settlement service for credit card payments, which should also use the enterprise service bus for communication with the internal systems. The use of web services for the communication with external partners is nowadays widely in use, alternatively secure file transfer protocols may be used, an example of which is described in ForYourEyesOnly (S5).

8.1.6 Resulting Context

Interaction

The pattern has a high interaction with other patterns and external systems or services, as it is one of the core elements of every company. The electronic, direct integration may vary depending on the degree of automation implemented and agreed upon with external partners, suppliers, retailers, etc. Direct access to and from external financial services like provided by the SWIFT, electronic banking, billing in and out, purchase and order processing systems, payment services (credit card services, reconciliation services, etc.), or point-of-sales (POS) devices may depend on the business needs. Figure 8.7 shows the possible interactions of the Financials (S1) pattern with the patterns in this book.

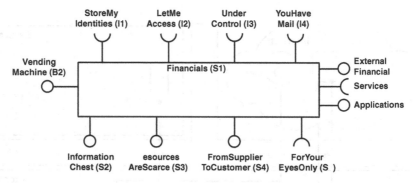

Fig. 8.7 Interaction of Financials (S1) with other patterns

A typical combination would be to connect a VendingMachine (B2), which is an environment near to the Internet, and the Financials (S1) pattern. This allows invoicing the customers and having the control over accounts payable in a fully integrated manner.

Consequences

The pattern unifies all financial services in a single controlled environment. It is strongly recommended to define a stringent role model and access policy to let the different users access the vital business information. Internal and external systems can use dedicated interfaces to access, modify, and retrieve financial information according to the defined business policies and the agreed upon service levels. Every connection and data flow must be authorized and traceable for auditing and compliance purposes.

The pattern can be implemented incrementally, meaning that not all elements must be in place from the beginning. The CFO must be the project sponsor and decide on the priority of the services that must be put in place.

Most of the vendors on the software market for financial solutions sell complete and integrated platforms with connectors for surrounding services. Interoperability between different financial applications can be achieved using standardized transport protocols like SFTP or HTTPS and SOAP as communication protocol. Financial reports can be described using XBRL.

8.2 InformationChest (S2)

«We are drowning in information and starved for knowledge.»

(Naisbitt and Aburdene 1982)

8.2.1 Introduction

Name and Overview

Name	InformationChest
Number	S2
Type of pattern	Infrastructure
Abstract	This pattern deals with the management of structured and semi-structured information. It describes how information can be acquired, transformed, delivered, stored, and archived
Capabilities	Provides control over the lifecycle of business information
	Scanning of information and performing optical character recognition (OCR)
	Classification, versioning, and registering of information according to business needs
	Enabling mobile users to access internal resources
	Delivering information in electronic and hardcopy form
	Long-time preservation of information (archiving)
Referenced patterns	StoreMyIdentities (I1), LetMeAccess (I2), UnderControl (I3), WorkTogether (B1), VendingMachine (B2), KnowYourCustomer (B3), Financials (S1), ResourcesAreScarce (S3), FromSupplierToCustomer (S4), ForYourEyesOnly (S5)
Bricks	Input management, content management, output management, archive management, application server, scanning devices, hardcopy devices, storage components
Impeding forces	A data centric view as stated by this pattern means that the company must define an overall business object model. All divisions or departments must adhere to this model and deliver or get their information from this pattern. This may constrain the particular interests and lead to resistance
Supporting forces	Accurate, consistent, and timely information to support business decisions is essential
	A data centric view of all business objects is being leveraged
	Controlled redundancy (redundancy only where really needed) of information objects, thus less costs for handling information (storage, applications, resources)
Invariance	Medium: the proposed pattern reflects best practices, but depending on the company, it may have more elements than we designed
Complexity	High: the pattern contains many different interacting components

(continued)

(continued)

Connectivity	High: the pattern can be connected to many other patterns that deliver and access information
Keywords	Enterprise content management, information management, input and output management, document management, scanning, archiving, records management, data mining

Definition

The InformationChest (S2) pattern gives a solution for the management of information. Commonly used terms in this context are, for example, *Enterprise Information Management (EIM)*, *Enterprise Content Management (ECM)*, *Information Lifecycle Management (ILM)*, *Records Management (RM)*, or *Information Architecture (IA)*.

Besides the four classical factors of production (the «4 M»: management, machines, materials, and money) information or knowledge has become an important value (see Hillard 2010, p. 22). Knowledge itself is

«the fact or condition of having information or of being learned (…)»

or

«the range of one's information or understanding (…)» (Merriam-Webster 2005).

Information has numerous meanings, depending on the context (Floridi 2010). This means that there is no all-encompassing definition for information. In the world of Information (!) and Communication Technology (ICT) the term is often explained as something between *data* and *knowledge* (Morville and Rosenfeld 2007, pp. 4–5) or (Hillard 2010, p. 13). But a concise, commonly accepted definition would probably never be published. However it can be said that data without contextual knowledge and interpretation would be worthless. The Information-Chest (S2) pattern tries to point out the processes, applications, and infrastructure that are needed to transform data into valuable information.

The InformationChest (S2) pattern provides a solution for the management of electronic content of an enterprise–the Association for Information and Image Management (AIIM) defines Enterprise Content Management as follows:

«Enterprise Content Management (ECM) is the strategies, methods and tools used to capture, manage, store, preserve, and deliver content and documents related to organizational processes. ECM tools and strategies allow the management of an organization's unstructured information, wherever that information exists.»

The ISO 15489-1 Records Management standard defines the term *records management* in Sect. 3.16 as:

«Field of management responsible for the efficient and systematic control of the creation, receipt, maintenance, use and disposition of records, including processes for capturing and maintaining evidence of and information about business activities and transactions in the form of records»

And *records* as

«Information created, received, and maintained as evidence and information by an organization or person, in pursuance of legal obligations or in the transaction of business» (ISO 15489-1:2001a, b).

Tightly coupled with the term enterprise content management is the *Information Lifecycle Management* (*ILM*) concept. The following definition can be found in the official dictionary of the Storage Networking Industry Association (SNIA):

«Information Lifecycle Management comprises the policies, processes, practices, and tools used to align the business value of information with the most appropriate and cost-effective IT infrastructure from the time information conceived through its final disposition. Information is aligned with business processes through management policies and service levels associated with applications, metadata, information, and data.» (SNIA 2011)

To emphasize the business context of the InformationChest (S2) pattern, we will not write about data, but always use the term information. Information is directly related to a business requirement and has a distinct meaning for the business, whereas data have a more technical connotation. When describing electronic documents of any kind (written, video, audio, etc.) we will also use the term information object, or as a synonym, a record. The information objects may be held in a highly structured form (like fields an a database of a business application) or as unstructured objects like free-text documents. The InformationChest (S2) provides a unified view from the business to the infrastructure layer on all aspects of the management of information objects.

8.2.2 Example

The marketing department of TheWineBottle wants to launch a new product called «Wine tasting evening for women». To do so, they first need an aggregated view of all activities concerning this customer group, all the information about similar past events organized by the company, the existing concepts to organize such kinds of events, an analysis of the market, and the corporate identity guidelines.

8.2.3 *Context*

Every company acquires, transforms, aggregates, and produces new information in various electronic forms. The information can be highly structured, like fields in a database, but also in free forms (letters, memos, etc.). For example, the employees and partners of TheWineBottle produce everyday E-mails, office documents, spreadsheets, electronic flyers, web content, etc. Most of the information has an intrinsic value for the business. The InformationChest (S2) pattern can therefore be implemented in every company or organization – the core of every single ICT environment is the input, sorting, searching (find), and output of information.

The InformationChest (S2) pattern helps to manage the immense and always growing amount of information and to define the relationship and responsibilities of the different information objects. In this sense, it provides a data centric view (or better: a business information object centric view), where all other patterns may use the services to store and retrieve information. The implementation of the pattern is not mandatory, but highly recommended.

The InformationChest (S2) pattern unifies different kinds of information management capabilities:

A *Records Management* (*RM*) provides functionalities to store documents according to a registration plan, which reflects the business of the company. The registered documents (records) may then be classified, indexed, and metadata describing the business context can be added (see ISO 15489-1:2001a, b, p. 12 for more details). The lead for storing metadata describing the transaction may be held by a business application or by the records management system itself. A key concept in a records management system is that modifying a document means also creating a new document. This ensures that all changes are always being recorded. Records management systems are made to store business critical information in such a manner that compliance and traceability requirements of the business can be met.

A *Document Management System* (*DMS*) is similar to a records management system, but there is less emphasis on the compliance aspect. A DMS is an interface (application programming or user) that allows storing documents and information objects with metadata or tags and supports versioning and classification functionalities. It is aimed at enriching document with contextual information that facilitates retrieval and processing.

A *Content Management System* (*CMS*), often also used as a synonym for web content management system (WCMS or WMS), provides functionalities to manage and present information like text, video, or images on an Internet platform.

A *file share* is a repository for unstructured information, like documents, videos, or audio files. File shares are organized in a folder structure and the access rights are usually managed on the operating system level. A file share may be used by a document management system to store information.

An *electronic archive* provides functionalities for the long-term preservation of information and represents the last stage of online storage in the ILM. Documents can be searched for and subsequently retrieved for later use. An archive has often also the functionality of making the documents immutable: They cannot be modified and their integrity is warranted. This is an important feature for the compliance with auditing requirements. The access is often slow, due to the storage technologies (e.g., «write once read many» media or magnetic tape).

Business applications often provide highly structured information and must be considered as an important part of an overall information management environment.

8.2.4 Problem

Enterprises have been storing business critical information for hundreds of years. Business transactions, recipes, construction plans, partner contacts, or customer information, etc., have been written down mainly on paper. In the last decade a dramatic switch from paperwork to electronic storage can be observed. Companies are more and more connected electronically, which results in an explosion of information across all industries and in organizations of all sizes. Making business today means also producing a huge amount of electronic information.

> Over the past years, TheWineBottle has gathered a lot of valuable information about their customers: Preferences in wine taste, events attended, payment history, and so on. Unfortunately, all this information is spread over many different systems, the information often being redundant. Employees have made their own copies in spreadsheet applications, small local databases, in E-mails, or have even bought applications for their own needs. This makes it difficult to access up-to-date and accurate business information for employees of TheWineBottle. This has led to exploding costs for information storage, wrong business decisions taken, time-consuming searches for important information, and frustrated employees who tend more and more to keep their own private information store.

Organization's View
Information is a business asset that must be protected, but also shared among the stakeholders, be they internal or external. To manage this information we use applications. Divisions and departments build their specific applications with their own information stores. This ranges from simple spreadsheet applications, local databases up to full-fledged complex applications with data warehouse functionalities. The syndrome «one business need – one project – one application – my data» is widely spread. This lack in information governance leads to uncontrolled data redundancies and inconsistencies, unclear responsibilities for business objects, incomplete assessment of a situation, and subsequently to a high potential

for wrong or suboptimal business decisions. Therefore, a holistic approach to the management of information that allows storing, protecting, searching, and using information according to business needs is an important task for any organization. InformationChest (S2) provides a solution scheme to this problem area.

The problem organizations face does not stop with the massive amount of information. Legal and regulatory requirements like the Sarbanes-Oxley Act (SOX), Basel II or the Health Insurance Portability and Accountability Act (HIPAA) are strong drivers for security, compliance, and integrity in information management environments. If information is actively managed, chances are good to meet regulatory requirements or at least have a good starting point for compliance management. It should be noted that by implementing the InformationChest (S2) pattern, these regulatory requirements are not automatically fulfilled. It is very likely that additional measures are needed outside of the solution scope of this pattern. However, it is strongly recommended to take regulatory requirements into account when designing and implementing the InformationChest (S2) pattern.

Enterprise Architect's View
Improving the management of information is one of the most important tasks any Enterprise Architect has. He must ensure that the enterprise stores its most important asset – information – in a way that is easily searchable and retrievable. As in large enterprises, information is often kept within divisional borders; the Enterprise Architect's first task is to bring together the appropriate stakeholders in order to initiate information management. The InformationChest (S2) pattern may serve him well as a discussion base. When a common understanding has been reached, the Enterprise Architect must ensure that information is actively managed and is available to anyone within the enterprise based on his or her needs and on the security requirements of the actual information. The Enterprise Architect should also have an eye on the lifecycle of information and think in longer terms so that historical information is never lost but archived in a way that allows reading it when needed. Having access to information at any point in time may be a regulatory requirement, especially in the case of financial information. A data centric view as stated by this pattern means that the company must define an overall business object model. All divisions or departments must adhere to this model and deliver or get their information from this pattern. This may constrain the particular interests and lead to opposition. On the other hand controlled redundancy (redundancy only where really needed) of information objects can be leveraged, thus leading to less costs for handling information (storage, applications, resources).

End-User's View
End-users want to have access to any information in an easy and well-structured way. As humans differ in how they memorize the exact location of a piece of information, information should be searchable, accessible via tags, and generally stored in a reproducible way. Ideally, there is a single and user-friendly point of entry to all information requests that allows finding the sought-after information.

Depending on the job profile of the end-user, not only is the single piece of information important but the semantics of information and any correlation with other information as well.

8.2.5 Solution

The solution can be summarized as shown in Fig. 8.8: Information is being produced or acquired (e.g., by scanning documents or applications that let the users fill in a web-form), managed or transformed, and subsequently delivered and preserved in a long-time archive.

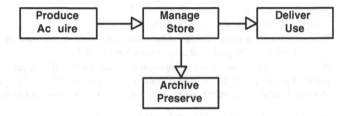

Fig. 8.8 General structure of an information management environment

This structure can be found in all the architecture layers of the Information-Chest (S2) pattern – in fact it is a pattern of its own.

Vision

All electronic information of TheWineBottle is managed in an end-to-end lifecycle and data redundancies are avoided. The information is available according to the requirements defined by the business needs and legislative and compliance requirements can be met.

Principles

1. *Principle*	*A lifecycle management for all information is in place*
Statement	All information items that are produced or acquired by the organization are part of a lifecycle management
Reasoning	Information is a business critical resource. The controlled lifecycle management of every information object is therefore extremely important

(continued)

(continued)

Consequences	Information must be classified according to the business policies and regulations. The pattern must provide the possibilities to classify information on a rule basis
	An information retention policy must be written and approved by the management
	The different stages in the lifecycle of an information object must be defined and the processes to govern the transition from one state to another must be implemented
	Every information object must be in a defined state of its lifecycle
2. Principle	*Instantiate an information-centric view*
Statement	All information produced, transformed, and delivered by the company or organization belongs to a controlled domain. There is no information outside this domain
Reasoning	This principle helps to avoid unwanted information redundancies or information without ownership
Consequences	A business object model must be defined
	Every information object being produced, transformed, or accessed by applications must be part of the business object model
	A governance process for the acquisition or development of new applications must be put in place. These applications must adhere to the stated principle and store and retrieve the information as part of the overall business object model
3. Principle	*Interoperability for accessing applications*
Statement	To leverage the interoperability with internal an external accessing applications, the InformationChest (S2) must provide standardized interfaces and protocols
Reasoning	The information management environment consists of many different systems that must exchange data. This is best done through the use of standardized interfaces and protocols
Consequences	The InformationChest (S2) must support standards like the Content Management Interoperability Services (CMIS 2010)
4. Principle	*Security of information*
Statement	The information must be protected according to the level of security required by the business needs or by regulations
Reasoning	Information is a business asset and must be protected
Consequences	A classification policy must be defined and supported by the underlying infrastructure. The classification should take into account at least the level of confidentiality, integrity, and availability required
	A business continuity plan and derived disaster recovery plans must be written and implemented
	A long-time information preservation plan must be written and implemented according to business needs, legal, and compliance requirements
	For every information object the access rights must be defined and configured
5. Principle	*Accessibility for mobile users*
Statement	The infrastructure must support the online access to information of mobile users
Reasoning	The business of TheWineBottle requires more and more that mobile users (field agents) can access relevant information with handhelds, laptops, or tablet devices
Consequences	A strategy for the use of mobile devices must be defined
	When evaluating components to implement the InformationChest (S2) pattern, the integration of mobile devices is a mandatory requirement

Holistic View

Figure 8.9 shows in the business layer the five typical processes in the context of information management: Users produce, search and retrieve, modify, deliver information, and handle all aspects of the information lifecycle. This sequence of processes can be observed in many different businesses (e.g. gathering statistical data, aggregate, and analyze the data, and deliver them on an Internet platform or internal system). The same four processes may also have an application as an actor. The users can be internal or external and accessing the information with different kinds of electronic devices (workstation, handheld, laptops, tablets, etc.) (Table 8.2).

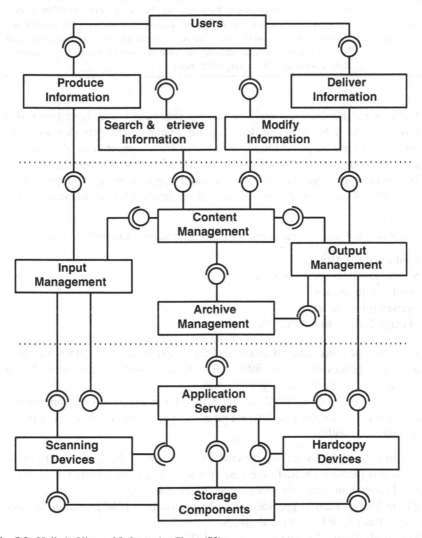

Fig. 8.9 Holistic View of InformationChest (S2)

Table 8.2 Architecture bricks of InformationChest (S2)

Brick	Description
Input management	Allows scanning paper documents and performs OCR on the input data. Other mechanisms for data capture (e.g. forms, document creation, etc.) are also part of this brick. The brick provides an interface for other applications to transfer scanned documents to the store of the requesting applications
Content management	Contains all services and functionalities to search and retrieve information. It also integrates a workflow component to orchestrate the flow of information between the different applications and services to handle metadata, versioning, classification, and access to information. Applications can use an interface to use the functions provided by the brick. The WorkTogether (B1) pattern will typically use this brick to manage content of a collaborative work
Output management	Provides services, also for external applications, to transform the information for publishing on portals or for delivering hardcopy prints or other media
Archive management	Provides capabilities for archiving documents depending on the lifecycle of an information item and the compliance requirements of records management laws and standards. The archive may also be used by external applications to store information on a long-term basis

The *Content Management* and *Archive Management* bricks have two distinct purposes in the ILM: Whereas the *Content Management* provides short-time storage and fast access possibilities, the *Archive Management* brick allows a long-time preservation, revision-proof data archiving with slower access mechanisms.

The technology layer reflects the data and application layer: Input, output, management of information, and the storage are modeled with different bricks.

Business View

We have defined five core processes for the management of information:

1. Produce Information.
2. Search and Retrieve Information.
3. Modify Information.
4. Deliver Information.
5. Manage Information Lifecycle.

There may be more detailed processes (see for example (ISO 15489) for records management processes) in an information management environment, but we believe that these are the most generic ones.

The first process is depicted in Fig. 8.10. The production or acquirement of information may take place in different kinds of applications or media. The process shows three possibilities:

- Scanning of information from paper documents, microfilms, and other physical media and perform OCR. In the case of handwritten documents the use of so-called intelligent character recognition (ICR) can be used.
- «Fill in forms» such as provided by web applications, PDF forms, or any other kind of form-based input possibilities.
- Written electronic document of any kind (E-mail, word processor, etc.).

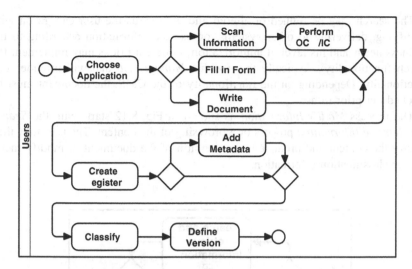

Fig. 8.10 Produce information process

The information may then be stored (registered) in the information management system and then metadata, classification, and versioning information added.

The *Search and Retrieve Information* process as shown in Fig. 8.11 is straightforward: The user must first login in (or, in case of an identity and access management integrated environment, be already logged in) and can then define search criteria based on metadata or free text information.

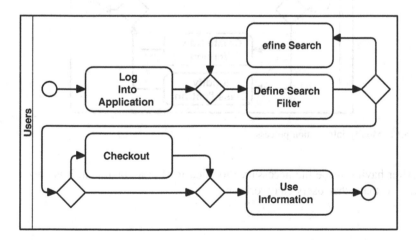

Fig. 8.11 Search and retrieve information process

The search may be refined or altered and afterwards the user can go on with modifying, delivering to other systems, or use the information according to the business needs and his level of authorization. Different bricks may implement the search functionality – typically the *Archive Management* and will provide such functionality. Depending on the functionality of the CMS, the document must be checked out prior to use.

The process *Modify Information* as shown in Fig. 8.12 starts with the *Search and Retrieve Information* process or a browsing of the content. The user may then modify the content and produce a new version of the document or modify meta-data or classification information.

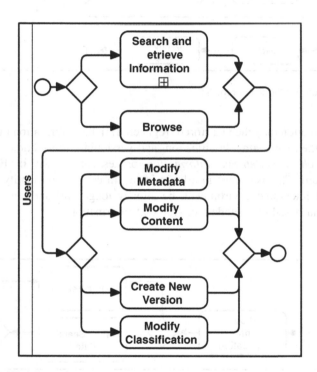

Fig. 8.12 Modify information process

After having made the necessary modifications to a document, it is checked in again, so that other users can work on it.

Figure 8.13 shows the business process to deliver information to different recipients. First the information received or retrieved from the content management brick may be edited with publishing software and checked with a pre-flight software that all fonts, images, crop marks, etc., are correct.

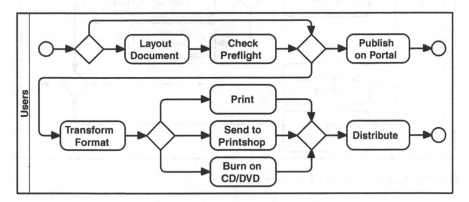

Fig. 8.13 Deliver information process

The file format can afterwards be transformed (e.g., to PDF or Postscript format). Depending on the intended use of the information, the files can then be published on portals as document, video, or audio content. Another possibility is to deliver the information on physical media like paper, DVD, or CD.

An important part in the handling of information is the lifecycle management. The value of information changes for the company over time. An offer may be important today and business critical and must therefore be accessed quickly. Whereas a few months later the same offer will have only informative (or historic) value. The «downgrading» of information objects in relation to their immediate value for the business is typically being handled by storing it on different media or devices during its lifecycle. Important information is stored on fast accessible media like hard disks and in business applications, records management, or CMS. Less important information is being stored on slower but longer living media like tape, write-once-read-many (WORM) disks and handled with an archiving system. Of course the opposite may also happen: An archived document may become important enough, so that it must be brought nearer to a business activity and be «upgraded». The process to handle the lifecycle aspects of information is shown in Fig. 8.14.

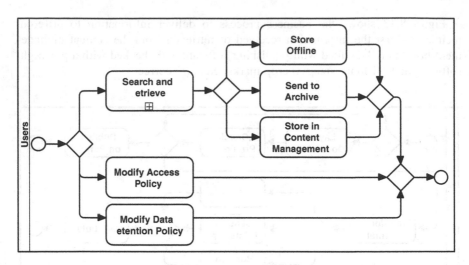

Fig. 8.14 Manage information lifecycle process

In the ILM different tasks must be achieved:

The effective down-or upgrading of an information object in the storage environment can be done after having found the relevant documents. When moving a document from an archive to a CMS, it must be re-registered and made accessible («activated»).

The *Information Retention Policy* (often called data retention policy) determines under which circumstances an information object may live on which type of storage device and can be accessed with the means of which applications. The policy defines the rules that govern the storage of information objects in accordance with compliance requirements from legal and business concerns. Derived from this policy are the effective access rights, which are often stored in Access Control Lists (ACL) and written down in an *Access Policy*. The retention and access policies enable the configuration of a classification scheme, which may even be automated (e.g., all information objects of a certain kind get the classification «Internal» when stored). With the use of a workflow engine (see Fig. 8.15), in conjunction with a role-based access system (see the StoreMyIdentities (I1) and LetMeAccess (I2) patterns for detailed views), the company can then define the appropriate rules to support the business processes.

Data and Application View
The main elements depicted in the application layer of the Holistic View (see Fig. 8.9) correspond in Fig. 8.15 to the application groups named *Input Management, Content Management, Archive Management,* and *Output Management.*

The *Input Management* group is responsible for acquiring or capturing information. This can either be done through applications that provide a form to fill in (e.g., PDF, web-forms) or a scanning system that uses the service of an OCR or ICR application. Of course, the writing of a document or a spreadsheet is also a form of information input. Basically, Input Management deals with the creation of information in a form that later can be managed, retrieved, worked upon, modified, and archived.

The *Content Management* group provides the service *Create and Change Records* to users or applications (e.g. business applications, mail systems, etc.). The main application is the *Records Management* that provides three important services:

- *Versioning Services* for the management of different versions of a document.
- *Meta Data Service* enables indexing and searching for documents based on tags and classification information.
- *Classification Service* is therefore also directly accessible to the *Business Process Management* application. This ensures that no information is being stored without prior classification according to the business requirements.

All the application groups are connected through the service *Apply Rule*, which is realized by the application *Business Process Management*. This application could also be provided by an external application (even in another pattern) – we put it in this application group because it is a core functionality of the information management. Besides the records management, the *Web Content Management* application is an example for another type of content management application. The *Store Management* application provides all necessary functionalities to store information – this is typically a data warehouse system that can be accessed by tools for *Extracting, Transforming, and Loading (ETL)* data. These functionalities are provided by the *Search and Retrieval* application.

The *Output Management* application group contains all functionalities for the publishing of information – as electronic products for different devices or as hardcopies (e.g., CD, DVD, paper). Publishing software provides typographic, layout, and graphics features. Sometimes, the documents must be transformed to a suitable format for publishing. Final documents can then be published or distributed.

As the creation and modification of records may affect a critical business asset, ensuring an audit trail is crucial to comply with business and regulatory needs.

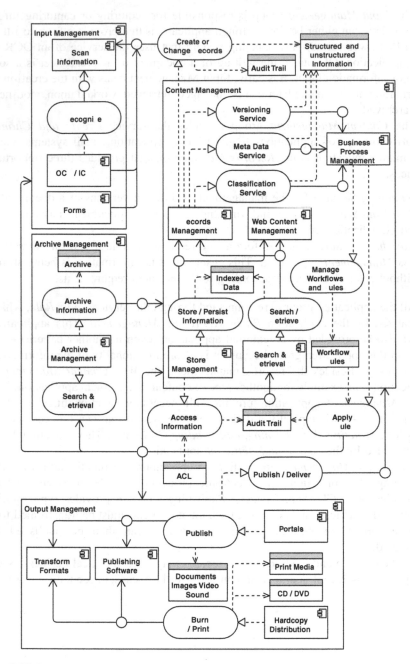

Fig. 8.15 Data and Application View of InformationChest (S2)

The last application group is the *Archive Management*. It contains applications for the long-term preservation of information. Depending on the business needs and the regulations, this group may contain further applications to archive the information on other media (microfilm, slower access media, etc.) and to implement a generation plan for the information objects.

Technology View

Figure 8.16 shows that most of the platforms of this pattern are in the internal networking zone (*DMS, Records Management, CMS,* and *Archiving Server*). Information in these core systems can be accessed with business applications or portal software. As an example we also put a CMS in the external networking zone. This system is being provisioned with information from an internal editorial server. The scanning devices are used to capture information. Depending on the business, this can be a high-speed scanner for large volume capturing. On the other side of the information handling chain there are the printing devices or CD, DVD burning devices.

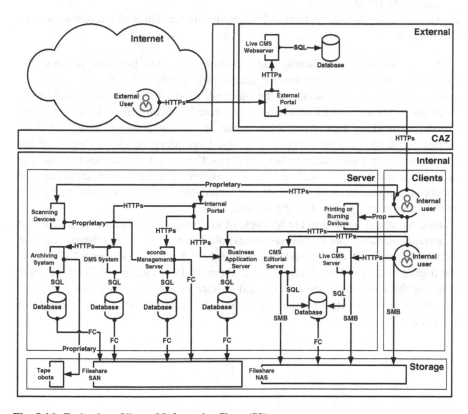

Fig. 8.16 Technology View of InformationChest (S2)

From the user point of view, all information is being accessed through a portal – this serves as an example of how a highly integrated information management environment could be designed. The portal itself helps in increasing the value of the single information objects as the combination of these may create new information. If a portal presents not only the information that the user actually did search for but also related information, it is well possible that he is able to gain new insights.

Concerning the ILM the choice of the storage solution, depending on the business requirements for accessing the information, is crucial. It always represents a trade-off between cost and availability: The faster the storage medium, the more expensive it is. There are typically three types of storage solutions to differentiate:

1. Primary solutions such as Storage Attached Networks (SAN), Network Attached Storage (NAS), and Direct Access Storage Device (DASD) like hard disks.
2. The second class includes online magnetic tapes with tape-robots and online accessible DVD libraries.
3. The last class includes optical and magnetic storage that is stored offline or even off-premise.

As explained in the *Manage Information Lifecycle* business process, the information retention policy and the access policy will define the correct access and storage choice depending on the business needs. In Fig. 8.16 the file share, NAS and SAN are in the internal zone, separated logically from the server in the *Storage* networking zone. A NAS server can be used as an interface to a file share or the file share may be accessed directly. Depending on the strategy and the requirements for information holding systems, the same technologies are going to be used in the external zone as well. The archiving systems with attached tape robots (or similar revision-proof storage capabilities like write-once read many media) are typically placed in the internal zone.

One big challenge during the lifecycle of an information object is to ensure that it remains readable and usable over its whole life span. It is a constant fear that information may become unreadable in the future. If this happens on a large scale, the digital dark age Terry Kuny warned about in 1997 (Kuhn 1997) might come true and the knowledge, the history, and culture of a whole era might disappear. Therefore, it is important to plan the technical infrastructure and the lifecycle of information very carefully.

8.2.6 Resulting Context

Interaction
The pattern has high interaction with other patterns and external systems or services. In Fig. 8.17 the InformationChest (S2) interacts with all EAP described in this book. Depending on the integration in the application landscape of the company or organization other applications may use the services provided.

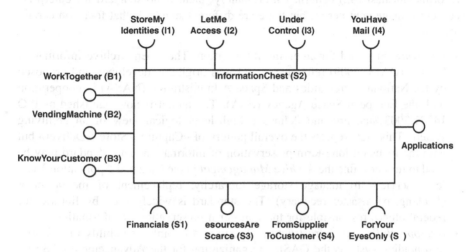

Fig. 8.17 Interaction of InformationChest (S2) with other patterns

The pattern provides a lot of interfaces to other patterns as it implements a central storage for all information of a company. Besides using the interfaces of the three Infrastructure Patterns, it also uses the ForYourEyesOnly (S5) pattern to securely exchange information with other applications.

Consequences
The implementation of the InformationChest (S2) pattern must be thoroughly planned and needs absolute management commitment. Information management is per se a business issue as it is the basis for all decisions. The pattern reflects the complexity of the topic: A high interaction grade with other systems paired with many different implementation possibilities (see the *Invariance* parameter in the overview of the pattern) makes this pattern one of the most complex and challenging ones to implement.

In practice, a lot of the elements shown in the different views will already be instantiated in one way or the other. The InformationChest (S2) enables a comprehensive approach to information management. We recommend first performing an as-is analysis of all information objects and applications used to manage these objects. This analysis may then be used to define the various policies (retention, access, classification, etc.). The identified gaps between the «as-is» analysis and the InformationChest (S2) may then be used to plan the necessary steps.

We strongly recommend adhering to existing standards when implementing the InformationChest (S2) pattern. Unfortunately, there is no standard for enterprise content management per se, but there are different standards that focus on certain aspects:

- *Archiving*. Standard for archiving information: The Open Archive Information System (OAIS 2009) reference model was originally developed and proposed by the National Aeronautics and Space Administration (NASA) in cooperation with the European Space Agency (ESA). The model is now published as ISO 14721:2003 standard and defines a high-level logical view of an archiving system. This view repeats the overall pattern of «Capture – Store – Deliver» but with the focus on long-term preservation of information. This standard may be used to further refine the *Archive Management* in the Data and Application View (e.g., services to manage storage hierarchy, replacement of media, error checking, or disaster recovery). The standard is widely used by libraries or federal offices responsible for the long-term preservation of information.
- *Interoperability and Infrastructure*. To support the interoperability of information holding systems the OASIS (Organization for the Advancement of Structured Information Standards) has published the Content Management Interoperability Standard (CMIS 2010):

  «CMIS provides an interface for an application to access a Repository. To do so, CMIS specifies a core data model that defines the persistent information entities that are managed by the repository, and specifies a set of basic services that an application can use to access and manipulate these entities.»

Another standard in the context of enterprise content management is the *JSR 283 Content Repository for Java Technology* (see JSR 2009). This standard reference is based on different other standards like Java Message Service (JMS), Java Beans Component (JBC), Java Database Connectivity (JDBC) or XML Document Object Model (XML-DOM), and is a specification for the Java platform application programming interface (API) to access enterprise content repositories in a standardized manner.

The CMIS standard defines protocols to access the resource and how a document management model may be defined, whereas the JSR 283 defines an API with a general content repository model. Both standards are evolving and our expectation is that they will become complementary – JSR 283 giving a standard for the *infrastructure* of Java-based applications and CMIS for the *interoperability* between repositories.

The *Resource Description Framework (RDF)* is a standard model for data interchange on the Web (RDF 2004). The framework has been specified by the W3C organization as part of the initiative to create a «Web of data» – a semantic web of linked data:

> «RDF extends the linking structure of the Web to use URIs to name the relationship between things as well as the two ends of the link (this is usually referred to as a "triple"). Using this simple model, it allows structured and semi-structured data to be mixed, exposed, and shared across different applications.» (RDF 2004)

- *Requirements.* The Document Lifecycle Management Forum (short DLM Forum[1]) was created through an initiative of the European Commission in 1997 and holds the MoReq Governance Board (MGB). This board oversees the use and ongoing development of the *Modular Requirements For Records System* standard (MoReq2010 2011), which evolved from the so-called MoReq2 standard:

> «MoReq2 is destined to become the guiding principle used by ERM system suppliers and developers to provide required functionality, and by outsourced records management service providers to define their service offerings. This 'de facto' standard also promises to revolutionize ERM procurement, auditing and training schemes around the globe.»

The standard is best suited for the evaluation of CMS and is a comprehensive guideline on what kind of services an information management environment should provide.

Besides the aforementioned standards, the newest evolution in the fields of federated archives and federated search will help to decouple environments and provide the capabilities to provide, search, and find information across organizational borders. Cloud Computing has a huge impact on enterprise information management: Besides all advantages claimed is the fact that the access to information may not be fully under the control of the owner and new legal aspects and data security issues will arise. These aspects must be thoroughly investigated before agreeing to a service level agreement.

---

[1] Interesting enough, until 2002 the abbreviation stood for «données lisibles par machine» in French, meaning «machine readable data».

8.3 ResourcesAreScarce (S3)

«I love my job, I love my job.»

(from the movie «The Devil Wears Prada»)

8.3.1 Introduction

Name and Overview

Name	ResourcesAreScarce
Number	S3
Type of pattern	Support
Abstract	This pattern provides a solution for an electronic enabled human resource management («e-HRM»)
Capabilities	Management of internal human resources
	Employee can file in requests
	Support for web-based recruiting
	Management of skills including career planning
	Punch in/out and hours reporting spend
Referenced patterns	StoreMyIdentities (I1), LetMeAccess (I2), UnderControl (I3), YouHaveMail (I4), Financials (S1), InformationChest (S2), FromSupplierToCustomer (S4), ForYourEyesOnly (S5), WorkTogether (B1)
Bricks	HR management, ESS portal, electronic dossiers, punch in/out, punch in/out terminal, database, application server
Impeding forces	Lack of necessary resources and management involvement
	Time and effort to re-engineer HR processes
Supporting forces	Compliance with laws
	Enhanced planning capabilities
	Reduced costs for support functions
Invariance	Medium: we believe to have found a pattern that contains most of the needed components, but companies may only use a subset of it
Complexity	Medium: the pattern contains many components, but can be incrementally implemented
Connectivity	Medium: the pattern is a typical Support Pattern that provides services for other applications and patterns using HR information
Keywords	Resources, employee, skills, talent, recruiting, payroll

Definition

The pattern is about the most valuable assets in a company – the employees, although «resource» may be understood as applications, infrastructures, information, or people (COBIT 2012). The topic of human resources has been widely analyzed, written about in literally thousands of publications. Everyone working in a company is part of it.

At the beginning of the twentieth century, Frederick Taylor wrote the book «Principles of Scientific Management» (Taylor 1911) which is considered as the beginning of human resources management. Taylor stated that both the employee and the employer should strive for maximum prosperity and denied that employees and employers had fundamental, antagonistic interests in doing so. According to Taylor, maximum prosperity could only be attained through maximum productivity – both for the employee and the employer. The driver for the scientific management was the statement by Taylor that the human workforce was being wasted and used inefficiently.

Nowadays *human resources* (HR) have become an integral part of every company as a supportive function. HR is responsible for the whole employment lifecycle of an employee – starting from attracting possible candidates and then selecting the right employees through a recruitment process, contracting, training and skills management, career planning, family related issues up to the leaving of the company. Besides these employee-related tasks the HR function is involved in the evolution of organizational leadership and culture and closely works with the legal department to ensure compliance with labor laws and employees rights.

In the context of the *value chain* of a company the planning of the assignment of the employees to projects or tasks is most important. There are always three aspects to it:

- The reporting of the presence of an employee (punch in and out). This has an impact on the payroll and fulfillment of contracts.
- The correct completed hours reporting of the employees for subsequent billing or financial reporting (budgeting, tracking, and reporting costs and profitability).
- To know who will be available or is already assigned to a task. This is a typical enterprise resource-planning topic.

An important term to define in the context of this pattern is the word *employee*. The Business dictionary provides the following definition:

> «An individual who works part-time or full-time under a contract of employment, whether oral or written, express or implied, and has recognized rights and duties. Also called worker.» (BDict 2012)

Closely related is the term *contractor*: Sometimes a company needs to hire external manpower. This may be due to increased demand in production or a lack of knowledge in a certain area. The contractor is usually being hired according to a well-defined specification document, with the definition of what has to be done and the deliverables to produce. An employee normally has a long-term engagement with a company, whereas the (independent) contractor works on a project basis.

8.3.2 Example

The human resources department of TheWineBottle is confronted with an
increasing amount of paperwork due to new employee entering the company,
changes in personal data of the employees (postal address, marital status,
birth of child, etc.), travel activities for training and conferences, etc. The
management of all these tasks has become cumbersome and time-consuming,
leading to mistakes, higher costs, and dissatisfied employees. In order to be
more efficient and effective, the management of TheWineBottle has decided
to reengineer the human resources processes and support them with adequate
applications.

8.3.3 Context

ResourcesAreScarce (S3) is a pattern that can be implemented in every company,
organization, or institution of any kind and size. Every company has to manage
human resources, ranging from simple address changes up to full skills management, time tracking, talent management, contracting, etc. Human resources care
normally about people more than about things like information and communication technologies. But the times when employees began their daily work with a
punch card and filed in handwritten requests for vacations are gone – this has
widely been replaced by the use of electronic systems. The supportive function
human resources is nowadays dependent on the supportive function *information
and communication technologies* in the same degree as the business is.

In the context of ResourcesAreScarce (S3) every employee, internal as well as
external to the company (contractors), is a part of human resources and plays a
more or less active role in the human resources processes. The pattern provides the
most important component to support the management of the employee experience
over the full lifecycle, from attracting possible new employees up to their leave of
the company.

8.3.4 Problem

ResourcesAreScarce (S3) addresses a threefold problem set:

- The fast organizational rate of change that has changed the requirements for any
  HR application dramatically.
- The integration of HR processes and applications into Social Media.
- The expectation of end-users to have all information ready at their fingertips,
  regardless of time, place, and accessing device.

While the last two problem sets are not unique to ResourcesAreScarce (S3) they are a good example of how an application that has been unchanged for a long time now has big changes to go through in order to meet expectations of the organization as well as its end-users.

> The human resource department of TheWineBottle is confronted with different problems: Most of the information about employees cannot be accessed in a timely manner, as it is stored in paper form. The time tracking of sales representatives in the field is inaccurate and cumbersome, as it is still done by weekly paper reports. Moreover, TheWineBottle is in a very competitive market for skilled and qualified sales personnel. In the past, electronic dossiers sent by E-mail by candidates have been lost, leading to interviews that could not take place and possibly not hiring of skilled persons. Employees are disappointed by the long processing time of requests by the HR department.

Organization's View
The shift toward an Internet-enabled society, where all employees, including top-level management, use electronic communication technologies on a daily basis, at home or at work, has become reality. The digital natives (Prensky 2001) are now in the working world and are no longer students. They are part of the deciding processes and help to shape the organization and define the communication culture. Social medias are now emerging within the companies as new communication channels. The human resources are challenged with addressing the needs of a new generation of employees for whom electronic information sharing and online communication is part of their daily life.

Frequent changes in organizations, restructuring, increased compliance requirements, and the fact that human resources is not a profit center demands more and more support from the ICT department.

Enterprise Architect's View
The Enterprise Architect is challenged as different problems are combined. First of all, there exists a strong bond between changes in real-life such as the ever-increasing speed of organizational changes that influences the way resource planning is perceived and what the organization expects from it. Another important problem that is not unique to this pattern but more or less ubiquitous, is the requirement to use an application from everywhere with any device type. In order to have access to valuable talents on the job market, it may be important that the resource planning is integrated into social networks, which is rather a new phenomenon and as such an interesting case study for any Enterprise Architect. The HR function being a cornerstone of every company, the Enterprise Architect must have full commitment by the senior management to get the necessary resources. Reduced costs for HR processes, enhanced planning capabilities, and better proof of compliance with laws and regulations are the supporting forces for the Enterprise Architect's line of argumentation.

End-user's View

End-users are more and more mobile – they have the requirements to access human resources services from anywhere, at any time, using different kinds of communication devices in the same manner as accessing business applications. End-users – especially talents that are potentially new employees – expect a meaningful and up-to-date integration of job opportunities into social media. Social media often form the first impression of an enterprise when it comes to gain interest of «digital natives».

8.3.5 Solution

The proposed solution supports the shift toward *e-HRM* (see Waddill 2011), meaning a consequent support of human resources management with ICT solutions for the following aspects:

- Repetitive tasks must be automated as much as possible and employees and line managers involved in electronic-based workflows to support the human resources management processes. Employee Self-Services (ESS) are an important key success factor to become more efficient.
- Providing management information: Gaining overview of time spent on projects, punch in/out of employees, assignment to tasks and projects. This is especially needed for budgeting, tracking, and reporting costs and profitability.
- Electronic dossiers: All human resources relevant information of an employee is to be maintained in an electronic dossier. This encompasses the curriculum vitae, expenses, memos, time management, training, career planning, performance tracking, and so on.
- Recruiting of new employees: Advertising of open positions, accepting electronic job applications, tracking of application status, and history of communication with candidates up to the contracting must be supported without media breaks.
- Organizational issues: Maintaining organizational chart, job descriptions, and vacancies.

Vision

Applications that allow an efficient and effective performing of HR relevant activities over the full employment cycle of the employees are supporting resource management processes of TheWineBottle. Reoccurring HR activities like approval processes, changes in employee information, or getting management information are being supported by electronic dossiers, employee self-services, and electronic workflow-based applications.

Principles

1. *Principle*	*Electronic-based workflows for human resource processes*
Statement	Reoccurring tasks in human management are being automated as much as possible with ICT means
Reasoning	Human resources processes are characterized by many repetitive tasks, like approval for holidays or training courses, reimbursement of allowances, etc. These tasks should be automated to reduce costs of manual activities
Consequences	Implementation of electronic dossiers to avoid paperwork and media breaks in the processes. The impact is that electronic dossiers become part of the records management
	Implementation of Employee Self Services (ESS) by providing a web-based portal with workflow support for approval processes
2. *Principle*	*Security of employee information*
Statement	Employee information must be protected according to laws and compliance requirements
Reasoning	Human information is highly sensitive and must be protected. Protection of data privacy is regulated through laws
Consequences	Restricted access to employee information through strong authentication
	The core security principles of need-to-know and least-privilege must be adhered to and enforced
3. *Principle*	*Accurate management information*
statement	Management needs accurate information about the human resources planning and availability
Reasoning	For the management it is crucial to have an accurate picture of the capacity of human resources, the skills in the company, the planned use of human resources in projects, and the number of hours spent on projects (chargeable vs. non-chargeable hours)
Consequences	Implementation of a management information system for human resources aspects or integration in an overall system
	Reporting of hours spent on internal services or projects must be supported with the integration of a punch in/out capability

Holistic View

Figure 8.18 shows that the services in the application layer are highly interdependent. We have two main stakeholders, the HR management that uses the HR Management services through the HR processes and the employees who can access the employee self-services portal and the time management application.

We did not detail the business layer – HR processes have been described in many publications, see for example Armstrong (2010) who gives a good overview concerning competency-based HR management processes. The shift towards an e-HR management puts slightly more emphasis on the role of the employee, as he is now empowered to have direct access to personal data via the ESS portal. We took this into account by modeling the employee processes and the candidates' process to file in job applications as two entities (Table 8.3).

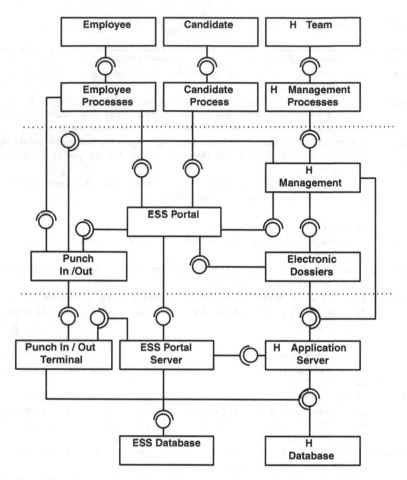

Fig. 8.18 Holistic View of ResourcesAreScarce (S3)

Table 8.3 Architecture bricks of ResourcesAreScarce (S3)

Brick	Description
ESS portal	Access to HR information by employees
HR management	Management applications for HR
Electronic dossiers	Management of the employee dossiers (employee information, skills management, contracting)
Punch In/Out	Application brick for time punch in/out
Punch In/Out terminal	Terminal to punch in with a badge/smartcard
HR application Server	Holds the HR software
ESS portal server	Server for the web-based portal
HR database server	Database with the core HR information

Business View

The business view consists of three processes. As stated before, we will not describe the HR processes in detail, as there is a good deal of excellent literature on this topic.

The first process in Fig. 8.19 shows the high-level activities that the HR department usually performs.

- The *Manage Candidatures* receives its input from the *Candidate Process* (see Fig. 8.21). Managing candidature means publishing job descriptions, selecting dossiers, communicating with candidates, invitations to job interviews, etc.
- The *Manage Employee Requests* is not only performed by the HR department but by line managers, who take part in the defined approval workflow, as well.
- The next group of activities deals with the management of employee topics: Skills, performance and benefits management are activities that have an impact on the electronic dossiers of the employees. The activities in the last group are performed to handle organizational issues, meaning changes in the organizational structure (chart), defining, communicating and keeping track of HR policies, and implementing the appropriate workflow rules across the organization.

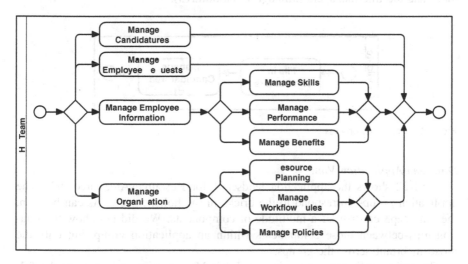

Fig. 8.19 HR management process

The next process as shown in Fig. 8.20 contains all the high-level activities that can be performed by an employee. This encompasses the management of personal information, file in requests (vacation, medical consultation, attending courses, reimbursement of allowances, etc.), finding people in the organization, and reporting work hours. The output of the two activities *File in Requests* and *Report Time* serve as an input for the subprocesses *Manage Employee Requests*, respectively, *Manage Organization* led by the HR department.

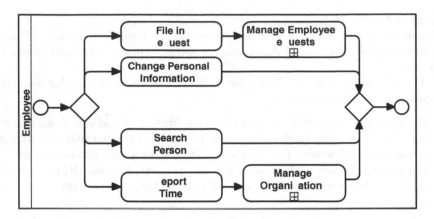

Fig. 8.20 Employee process

The last process in Fig. 8.21 enables candidates to apply for open job positions. The process is part of the overall recruiting process managed by the HR department and the line managers (*Manage Candidatures*).

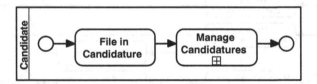

Fig. 8.21 Candidate process

Data and Application View

Figure 8.22 shows the application landscape for ResourcesAreScarce (S3). The application groups correspond to the bricks in the holistic view. As can be seen, the landscape consists of a multitude of components. We did not show the relationships between those components within an application group, but only the most important across the groups.

The main application group is called *HR Management* and contains the following applications:

- *Workflow Management.* HR management processes, which involve different roles and are supported by applications, can use the workflow capabilities. This component allows implementing approval processes in an automated way. Workflow rules represent actually a part of the implemented HR policies.
- *Policy Management.* HR management means also regulating and communication of rules. This application can be used to manage the policies in a consistent and traceable manner.

- *Organization.* Management of the organizational chart, including job descriptions, vacant job positions.
- *Payroll.* The payroll application uses an interface of the main ledger, see the *Assets and Treasury* application group of the pattern Financials (S1).
- *Performance Management.* This component supports the measurement of the performance of the organization. The individual performance goals of the employees, organizational units, and different management levels can be managed, tracked, and reported.
- *Benefits Management.* provides the necessary services for organizations to administer employee participation in benefits programs. These typically encompass compensation, insurance, profit sharing, and retirement.
- *Leave Management* is a mandatory component in HR as it provides the necessary services for the planning of holidays and other absences of employees. According to the organizations leave policy, employees can file in requests for vacation allowances, sick days, or trainings off-premise. The leave management application communicates with workflow management and the policy management.
- *Talent Management* refers to the capability of attracting highly skilled candidates, of integrating new employees, and developing and retaining current employees to meet current and future business objectives.
- *Skills Management* is closely related to the aforementioned Talent Management: The application enables the organization to keep track of employee expertise and skills. The application helps in recording certifications, attended trainings, and for the identification of potentials within the organization.
- *Resource Planning* builds the basis to assign job tasks to employees taking into consideration all the necessary parameters from other HR applications (*Leave Management, Talent Management, Organization,* etc.). This application also serves as an important source of information for the FromSupplierToCustomer (S4) pattern.

The application group provides two services: The *Manage Human Resources* service which is a generic way of accessing all the functions and services within the application group and the *Management Information* provides the relevant information from the different applications to enable the organization to take decisions.

The *Electronic Dossiers* application group provides applications that are directly related to the management of the information of the employee. The inventory application manages the records of items placed at the disposal of employees (keys, cars, etc.) whereas the *Employee Management* provides the necessary services and interfaces to change and store the employee information in one location. It receives inputs from the *PIM* application in the ESS portal and from various applications in the *HR Management* application group. The *Contracts Management* application provides the capabilities to handle contract information – be it from internal personnel or from contractors. This information may also be provided by the pattern FromSupplierToCustomer (S4), depending on the business

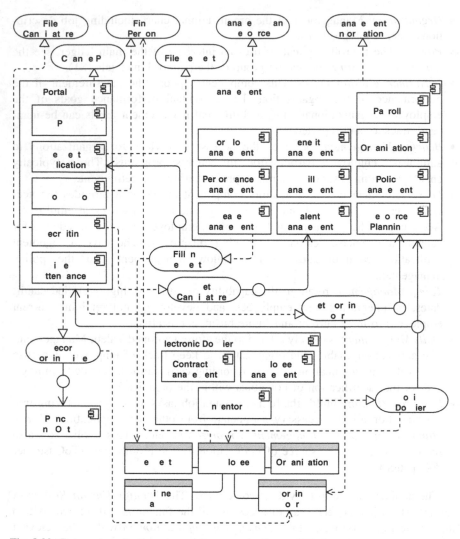

Fig. 8.22 Data and application view of ResourcesAreScarce (S3)

the company is in. We designed only one service that provides the interface to change and access the information in the *Electronic Dossiers* application group.

The *ESS Portal* group contains applications that allow employees or applicants for open job positions to file requests, candidatures, find persons, or change personal information:

- *PIM* is short for *Personal Information Manager* and allows the employee to change their address and other personal information like marital status or interests.

- The *Request Application* provides web-forms to file in requests for taking vacations, reimbursement of allowances, etc. The application communicates with the corresponding components in the *HR Management* application group.
- The *Who is Who* application can be queried to find persons in the organization.
- The *Recruiting* application is the frontend for candidates to file in their applications for open job positions.
- The *Time & Attendance* application provides the functions to keep track of accomplished hours and presence at work. This information is the basis for resource planning.

It is interesting to note that the *ESS Portal* has the potential to be used as a social media tool: With a few more functionalities, employees can use the portal to present themselves and form group of interests, find other people, or exchange information on virtual pin boards as known from online social media portals.

The last application is the software needed to record the working hours with a batch (proximity sensor card or smartcard) – usually called «punch in». The application communicates with the *Time & Attendance* application to enable the employees to track and report their achieved hours of work.

We designed a fairly simply data model that reflects the most important objects that are managed by the application landscape of ResourcesAreScarce (S3). The data object *Employee* holds all information pertaining to the employee, meaning contact information, curriculum vitae, correspondence with HR, skills, attended trainings, contract information, and so on. The data objects *Working Hours* and *Assigned Tasks* store the information needed for resource planning.

Technology View
The technology view in Fig. 8.23 shows that the infrastructure is usually split into three parts: The *ESS Portal Server,* the *Punch In/Out Terminal,* and the *HR Management Server.* We put the *ESS Portal* with all applications as depicted in Fig. 8.22 in the *Extranet.* Depending on the networking policies, you could also consider splitting the portal in an internal and external part. You may want to implement a self-registration for the *Recruiting* application, so that candidates can upload their dossiers and query the status of their application for a job. Probably you are going to want to let external people query your directory (*Who is Who*) to get into contact with the right persons in the organization. The *Recruiting* and *Who is Who* applications would then reside on a server in the *Extranet* and the other applications in the *Intranet.* Such a decision must of course be taken considering the usual factors like costs, requirements, security, complexity of the architecture, and so on. It certainly makes sense to investigate thoroughly where to place those applications. Moreover, mobility is also an important topic for HR processes: Line managers want to be able to approve employees' request on the road, traveling from one meeting to another. Mechanisms like those depicted in LetMeAccess (I2) and UnderControl (I3) may help to implement a secure access to HR information.

The *HR Management* and the *Electronic Dossiers* application groups reside on the *HR Application Server.* As this server and the associated database server hold the most sensitive information, special care must be taken to protect these assets.

The last physical component is the *Punch In/Out Terminal*. Depending on the geographical situation, you may have more than one terminal, even in different locations (towns, countries). The employees will have a personalized card with a proximity sensor or chip to enable registering their attendances. The rollout of such a (smart)-card usually triggers the discussion concerning the «all-in-one card»: The same physical card can be used for certificate-based authentication, digital signature and encryption (see the LetMeAccess (I2) pattern), access to premises, payment for beverages and meals and time registration.

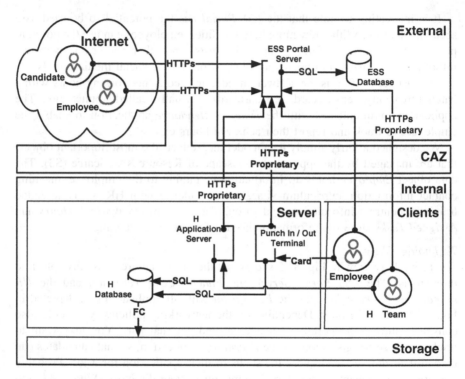

Fig. 8.23 Technology View of ResourcesAreScarce (S3)

8.3.6 Resulting Context

Interaction
Figure 8.24 shows the resulting context for ResourcesAreScarce (S3). The pattern is mainly surrounded by infrastructure and Support Pattern. Business Pattern may use some information provided by ResourcesAreScarce (S3), e.g., organizational hierarchy, planning information, or hours spend on projects.

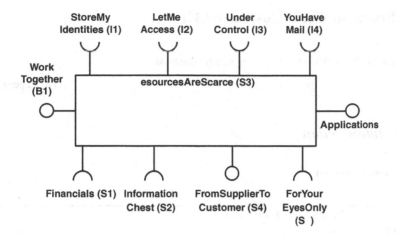

Fig. 8.24 Interaction of ResourcesAreScarce (S3) with other patterns

Consequences

Not all the components presented in this pattern may be in use in every context, but we think that we have found a pretty stable and reusable pattern. The pattern is not extremely complex, but shows in itself a high connectivity, as most of the application components are interacting. It acts as a typical Support Pattern, providing information to other patterns, but using only services from other support or Infrastructure Patterns. When implementing the ResourcesAreScarces (S3) pattern, you will probably not realize all the components shown in Fig. 8.22 from the start. As the pattern shows a very modular view on the HR application landscape, we think that it will help in prioritizing which components should be implemented first.

ResourcesAreScarce (S3) manages employee information that is per se sensitive – the electronic dossiers contain highly personal information that must be protected according to laws in order to ensure privacy. When implementing the pattern special care must be taken to ensure that security measures on all levels, at the business (defining roles, access rights to information, liabilities, etc.), the data and application (encryption, user rights, etc.) and technology level (multi-tier architecture, operating system hardening, etc.).

The pattern contains all the important components to support and help to streamline typical HR tasks, independent of whether the function is being outsourced or not. The implementation of an ESS portal is actually an important part of a service delivery model in conjunction with an *HR Shared Service Centre* (*SCC*): Questions and requests of employees are being answered by means of the ESS portal, thus disburdening the HR specialists from answering frequent questions. This may be achieved by incorporating a knowledge base (e.g. FAQ) into the ESS portal. Moving toward an e-HRM means also adapting and re-engineering the HR processes. Existing process must be analyzed and possibly changed. This change could also mean a complete outsourcing of the HR functionality.

Although this pattern depicts an ICT approach to human resources, one must not forget that in HR the human (person) plays the most important part!

8.4 FromSupplierToCustomer (S4)

«I am like any other man. All I do is supply a demand.»

(Al Capone)

8.4.1 Introduction

Name and Overview

Name	FromSupplierToCustomer
Number	S4
Type of pattern	Support
Abstract	Supply chain management encompasses the planning and management of all activities involved in sourcing and procurement, conversion, and all logistics management activities
Capabilities	Seamless integration of all partners, from the suppliers to the customers, in the context of buying, adding value to products, and selling the products
	Supporting the delivery chain and planning the internal resources
	Unification of core processes involved in supply chain management activities
	Optimizing costs, and improvement in efficiency and effectiveness from demand to procurement
Referenced patterns	KnowYourCustomer (B3), StoreMyIdentities (I1), LetMeAccess (I2), UnderControl (I3), Financials (S1), InfoChest (S2), ResourcesAreScarce (S3)
Bricks	Planning, Production, Supply Management, Delivery Management, Inventory Management, Application Servers, Database Servers
Impeding forces	Organizational silos, heterogeneous or inconsistent process landscape, missing or inadequate business or ICT strategy
Supporting forces	Constant pressure to optimize costs, market competition
Invariance	Low
Complexity	High
Connectivity	High
Keywords	Supply, delivery, procurement, purchase, inventory, warehouse, production control

Definition

The name of the pattern relates it quite clearly to a term that has been defined and redefined many times in the last three decades: Supply Chain Management (SCM). The term was first introduced in 1982 in an article in the Financial Times and is regularly credited to Keith Oliver, a senior consultant of Booz Allen Hamilton (Mol 2009). Oliver defined SCM as

«Supply chain management (SCM) is the process of planning, implementing, and controlling the operations of the supply chain with the purpose to satisfy customer requirements as efficiently as possible. Supply chain management spans all movement and storage of raw materials, work-in-process inventory, and finished goods from point-of-origin to point-of-consumption.»

Since then different organizations and industry associations committed to SCM have been founded. One of them is the Council for Supply Chain Management Professionals (CSCMP) that defines SCM on their webpage as follows:

«Supply chain management encompasses the planning and management of all activities involved in sourcing and procurement, conversion, and all logistics management activities. Importantly, it also includes coordination and collaboration with channel partners, which can be suppliers, intermediaries, third party service providers, and customers. In essence, supply chain management integrates supply and demand management within and across companies.» (CSCMP 2011)

The supply chain management is a business model – not a bunch of tools. It is an integrative function that coordinates processes within the enterprise and across the enterprise border. The supply chain management extends the enterprise and its processes across the traditional organizational borders to integrate external functions and services (Davis 2003).

It is not our intention to write another book on SCM – the literature dealing with this topic is already quite extensive – and still growing. When digging into the topic you will be confronted with a lot of terms and concepts like distribution planning, logistics, fulfillment, forecast, material planning, product design, value chain, warehouse management, information flow, customer service, and so on. We will therefore highlight a few of these concepts to get a better understanding of what we are going to describe in the FromSupplierToCustomer (S4) pattern.

Supply chain management must not be confused with *logistics management* – this is a part of the overall supply chain management that deals with all aspects of the movement of goods (see CSCMP 2011 for a definition).

Another term, which is closely related to supply chain, is the *value chain*. The value chain has been first introduced by (Porter 1998) as

«Every firm is a collection of activities that are performed to design, produce, market, deliver and support its products. All these activities can be represented using a value chain (…).»

The value chain represents the capabilities of an enterprise to valorize a product in such a way that a profit results – you should get more money for the product than the costs involved in creating it. The APICS dictionary defines it as

«The functions within a company that add value to the products or services that the organization sells to customers and for which it receives payment.» (APICS 2011)

In this sense, the value chain is an integral part of the supply chain management. The business strategy of a company and the business processes to create and deliver a product define the value chain. The supply chain couples these processes with the supplier and the customer to get an end-to-end process. This chain can also be depicted as a seamless integration of the processes involving supplier relationship management, enterprise resource management, and customer relationship management. In fact, it is a management approach that integrates a set of interrelated processes for planning and controlling the flow of materials, information and financials from purchase to delivery. This means that in the context of the pattern presented in this book, the ResourceAreScarce (S3) and KnowYourCustomer (B3) patterns must be integrated.

The last term which needs explanation is *procurement*. The term procurement is often used interchangeably with *acquisition* or *purchasing*. When digging into the topics a more differentiated point of view must be taken. There have been lots of debates on the Internet about the correct definition of procurement versus purchasing (see Procurement Insights 2008 for posts on this topic). For the purpose of this pattern we will make the following distinction:

Procurement is a planning process to ensure that the company has done everything to buy the necessary goods or services in such a manner that the value chain of the company benefits. The process encompasses all aspects of contract management with suppliers, price discussions, risk mitigation, formulating quality requirements, and scheduling aspects. *Purchasing* is the action of buying the goods or services according to the defined procurement rules. In this sense, purchasing is a part of the overall procurement process.

8.4.2 Example

TheWineBottle sells different combined products in a basket consisting of a fine bottle of wine, a corkscrew, a recipe, and depending on the season, assorted Italian food specialties. Many different partners in various countries are supplying the items in the basket. Moreover, a customer can customize such a product (e.g., choice of wine, gift card, etc.) and have it delivered as a gift at a defined date. TheWineBottle has different stores and warehouses in the country to deliver from. To manage the whole chain from the choice of the supplying partners, to the confection of the combined product and the delivery to the customers, the management of TheWineBottle has decided to adopt a supply chain management approach to reach their business goals.

8.4.3 Context

The FromSupplierToCustomer (S4) pattern may be applied to every company that buys products from suppliers and uses those products to generate new products and to sell them to customers (retailers, distributors, end-users). Figure 8.25 shows an overview, derived from Taylor (2004) and complemented by us. The elements are the following:

In the horizontal the three phases *Supply*, *Make*, and *Deliver* can be considered as a high-level view of a business model. Whereas the *Make* is the core of the production of goods (manufacturing) within a company, the other two are oriented to the outside. The sequence of supply, make, and deliver reflects the flow of information and goods through the different stages from the suppliers to the customers. For each of these phases there exists an ICT counterpart: *Supplier Relationship Management* (*SRM*), *Enterprise Resource Planning* (*ERP*) and *Customer Relationship Management* (*CRM*).

The vertical is subdivided into four streams:

Strategy. The supply chain management strategy is derived from the business strategy and encompasses all the strategic decisions concerning the choice of the suppliers, the goals to achieve with the supply chain management, and how to support the value chain and the alignment with the business. The strategy is of course dependent on the desired positioning of the company's products or services in the market (e.g. low-cost product leader, best service leader, innovative products, etc.). Ideally, the strategy is being written in tight cooperation with the sales, operations, and marketing divisions of an enterprise (Handfield 2002, Chap. 4).

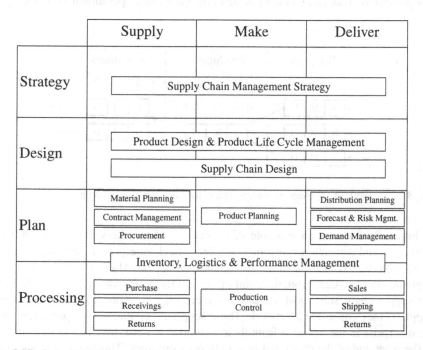

Fig. 8.25 Overview of the components in a supply chain

Design. The design of the supply chain describes how the different components will work seamlessly together. This encompasses the metrics (see SCOR 2011) to measure the performance, how the integration within a virtual network of partners will be achieved, which information must flow from one end to the other of the chain, how procurement and order management will fit in, and the organizational aspects with responsibilities and accountability. The supply chain design is sometimes also described as the supply chain planning. The design of the supply chain depends on the enterprise's business, as the same is obviously true for the product design and lifecycle management.

Plan. This stream encompasses all aspects of planning in the three phases (supply, make, deliver). The planning begins with the material and contracts, to the effective production and product planning and ends with the distribution, the demand, and forecast planning. An expression often used in this context is *advanced planning*, meaning that all the different planning aspects can be unified in an integrated way (Stadtler 2005).

Processing. This is often also called the execution of the supply chain and contains the operational activities that must be performed (handling purchase, returns of goods on both ends of the chain, the production itself, the sales, and shipping of goods).

When looking from the top to the bottom of Fig. 8.25 the four rows can be categorized as strategic, tactical (*Design and Plan*), and operational (*Processing*).

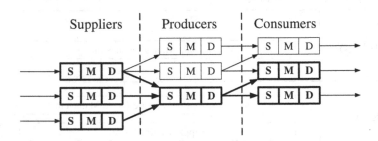

Fig. 8.26 Network of suppliers, producers, and consumers in a supply chain

Figure 8.26 shows an example of a network of suppliers, producers (manu-facturers), and consumers (customer, retailers). Each enterprise is represented with a rectangle that is divided in the three phases *S(upply)*, *M(ake)*, and *D(eliver)* as explained in Fig. 8.25. From the point of view of the enterprise in the center (bold), the supply chain starts with suppliers – there may be more than one and these suppliers may constitute a network. These suppliers are themselves producers and the enterprise in the center is from their viewpoint a consumer. The same happens at the other end of the chain, but now with inversed roles. This leads to a complex network of enterprises, with three different roles, depending on the context.

The chain continues on both sides of the picture: On the left side, suppliers are consumers of products from other producers and on the right side the chain is extended with consumers being suppliers for other producers. This leads to the following conclusion: In every company there is an internal supply chain (illustrated with the *S, M* and *D* in Fig. 8.26), which is a part of a broader chain. The overall chain extends the internal chain at both ends – at one end with connections to the suppliers and the other with connections to the customers. Figure 8.26 is a representation of what (Davis 2003) calls «the extended enterprise». To round this picture up, it is also possible that the manufacturing phase (*M*) may even be sourced outside of the company.

8.4.4 Problem

As the FromSupplierToCustomer (S4) pattern addresses the whole chain of production and selling of goods, the challenges are numerous, but well described in the SCM literature:

- *Globalization* of markets leads to increased competition: The upcoming of Internet technologies has shortened the geographical distances, information travels much faster and the competitor is also well informed. With globalization, the enterprises are able to seek for the lowest prices for the supply of materials and so heating up the competition. The drawback of a global network of suppliers is that the enterprise buying and selling goods can only exert a limited control over the different stakeholders in the full supply chain (Muller 2011).
- *Organizational issues* within an enterprise: A lack of governance and historically grown organizational structures lead often to a mix of inconsistent policies, business processes, bad information flow, contradictory performance measures, or unclear accountability. The results are often functional silos, little kingdoms, and no clear understanding about the enterprise's actual performance (Davis 2003).
- *Rising costs and sinking revenue.* Due to the increased competition it becomes more and more difficult to balance the production costs and the revenue. Shorter time-to-market and more competitors put a constant pressure on the cost-structure of an enterprise.
- *Manual processing and error-prone data interchange.* Due to fragmented business processes with manual data entries (and copying), incompatible system interfaces and heterogeneous application and system landscapes of the different parties in a supply chain, a consistent and up-to-date information flow that reflects the actual business situation, is not possible. This leads to false decisions and management errors.
- *Divergent interests.* As shown in Fig. 8.26 a company as a producer in a supply chain is one of many: A supplier may have different business sectors and customers to provide with products or materials. These may even be direct

competitors of the company. The supplier may therefore pursue different interests than the company it provides with goods.

- *The bullwhip effect.* This is a well-known phenomenon in the supply chain literature: A slight variability on the demand side (from the customer, the market) is being magnified when the information travels upstream in the chain towards the suppliers. This can lead to an oversized inventory, bad customer service, higher product costs, inefficient planning, and so on (Russel and Taylor 2010).

The variety of goods of TheWineBottle has been constantly extended with products from different suppliers worldwide. Whereas in the beginning the company only sold bottles of wine, the catalog includes now also non-food products that are manufactured in different countries. The company is confronted with an increasing complexity in managing their suppliers and the expectations of customers to order and receive bundles of products in due time and at a competitive price. Suppliers still send their offers by mail and their price lists are being manually entered into TheWineBottle's system. This has led to wrong entries (prices, articles) and subsequent financial problems for TheWineBottle.

Organization's View

The following problem areas that an organization needs to solve summarize the aforementioned challenges:

- Managing a distributed, often global network of suppliers. This makes accurate and up-to-date information in the supply chain management system crucial.
- Delivering goods in a timely manner to customers worldwide.
- Constant pressure to reorganize organizational structures in order to remain competitive demands a flexible and easily adaptable supply chain management.
- Providing a highly responsive and accurate supply chain management in order to balance supplies and demands.

The organization must search for a solution to the supply chain management that is efficient and enables it to balance supply and demand. It must be able to react in a timely way and to provide information about supply chain status, demand in real-time and enable management to make sound forecasts based upon this information.

Enterprise Architect's View

The Enterprise Architect has the challenging task to plan and integrate applications that are absolutely crucial to the organization. As they have so many dependencies and are strategically significant, changes at the supply chain management need to be carefully planned. Organizational silos, heterogeneous or inconsistent process landscape, missing or inadequate business or ICT strategy, are impeding forces that must be taken into account. The Enterprise Architect must find a solution that guarantees to have a very long lifecycle but that is adaptable to quickly changing conditions. He must closely watch the definition of the interfaces to the outside, starting with the information flow between the enterprise and its suppliers, continuing with the interfaces to production, and ending with the interfaces from the demand side. All information gathered and produced must be kept available and must be provided to the employees in an easily readable and timely way. As always – mobility and device independency is an important requirement.

End-user's View
We must distinguish between employees that are involved in the supply chain management process and customers who expect the delivery of their orders. Both have expectations – often unspoken – to the supply chain management. An important area of concern is to have access to the information from any device at any time from anywhere – this is a requirement that is not unique to FromSupplierToCustomer (S4) but that is formulated very often. Due to the complexity of a supply chain management the fulfillment of this requirement can be challenging.

In order to successfully implement the FromSupplierToCustomer (S4) solution scheme, especially the problem of organizational silos and an ICT strategy that does not cover supply chain management should be kept in mind. The market pressure and the everlasting quest for competitive advantage are important forces that support the implementation of this pattern.

8.4.5 Solution

Vision

The management of the supply chain of the TheWineBottle is a strategic element to support the business activities. It results from the conjoint efforts of all divisions of the company and must support the following goals: It must enable an efficient delivery of products to customers. By integrating external and internal services, a seamless flow of information, financial transactions, and goods through the supply chain is possible. All services and actions are monitored by performance measures and accurate reporting that is based on the business needs. All these things together enable TheWineBottle to achieve a better cost-efficiency from the purchase to the delivery of products

Principles
One of the most requested articles in the «Supply Chain Management Review»
appeared 1997 with the title «The 7 Principles of Supply Chain Management» and
was reissued in 2007 (Andersen et al. 2007). The principles give guidance for all
main elements of a supply chain: for the customer segmentation and the management of suppliers, for the demand management, product differentiation and
market signals, for the strategy and technology of the supply chain, as well as for
performance measurements. The following principles relate partly to these still
valid statements, but also directly to the formulated vision in this pattern.

1. Principle	*Achieve better cost-efficiency*
Statement	The instantiation of the supply chain has a main goal: the overall operational, production and inventory costs from the purchase of goods to the delivery of the products to the customer must decrease
Reasoning	TheWineBottle gains a competitive advantage on the market and can increase market shares
	Better use of internal and external resources
Consequences	Manage sources of supply strategically to reduce the total cost of owning materials and services. (Andersen et al. 2007)
	Alignment with the business strategy of TheWineBottle must be achieved
	The financial flow along the supply chain must be documented, controlled, and monitored
	Segment customers based on the service needs of distinct groups and adapt the supply chain to serve these segments profitably (Andersen et al. 2007)
2. Principle	*Add value*
Statement	Supply chain management is about economic value added. It is not just about cost. It is about the total content of a final product or service, including quality, technology, delivery, and after-sales service. If we cannot manage the total content, we will be unable to meet the needs of our customers (Handfield 2002)
Reasoning	A simple business rule is to earn more money than spending. The supply chain must support the value chain of TheWineBottle in contributing to make profit. The supply chain management is a core function to add value to the products of TheWineBottle
Consequences	Segment customers based on the service needs of distinct groups and adapt the supply chain to serve these segments profitably (Andersen et al. 2007)
3. Principle	*From interfacing to integration*
Statement	Partner at both end of the supply chain (suppliers, distributors, retailers) must be integrated in the overall supply chain management of TheWineBottle. The goal is to instantiate a collaborative supply chain management
Reasoning	Integration means a tighter coupling of the business activities between the partners in a supply chain than only interfacing with them. Suppliers get accurate, immediate information about the material needs and defective parts of delivered goods to the TheWineBottle. Retailers have a synchronous view with TheWineBottle on all the orders and status of these, including financial aspects. This tighter integration leads to the same level of information among all participants, better management of material inventories, procurement, and demand management

(continued)

(continued)

Consequences	The integration begins at the process level: TheWineBottle and its partners must cooperate and align their processes involved in the common parts of the supply chain management
	The system and application landscape must support a tighter integration of partner systems
	A too tight coupling on all the layers, from the business down to the technology, may lead to inflexibilities and unwanted dependencies among the participants in the supply chain. This may hinder timely reactions to new business opportunities
4. Principle	*Controlled flow of goods, information, knowledge, and financial values*
Statement	In order to gain full control over the supply chain of TheWineBottle, it is mandatory that the flow of goods, information, knowledge, and financial values along the supply chain must be known and managed
Reasoning	At every stage within the supply chain, the participants are modifying information and financial values. To be able to take the right decisions and manage the supply chain, it is crucial that a correct information basis is available. The participants in a supply chain gain also knowledge on a daily basis. This knowledge is extremely valuable to improve the processes
Consequences	Develop a supply chain-wide technology strategy that supports multiple levels of decision-making and gives a clear view of the flow of products, services, and information (Andersen et al. 2007)
5. Principle	*Measure, learn, and improve*
Statement	To be able to improve the performance of the supply chain, measurement metrics must be defined and monitored. The participants should take an active part in helping to enhance the supply chain by means of continuous learning and collaboration
Reasoning	The performance of the supply chain must closely be monitored to know how the state is. Without clear objectives and derived performance metrics it is not possible to get better. A good supply chain is also a collaborative work, where participants learn from each other and collaborate in the improvement of the common business activities
Consequences	Adopt channel-spanning performance measures to gauge collective success in reaching the end-user effectively and efficiently (Andersen et al. 2007)
	Listen to market signals and align demand planning accordingly across the supply chain, ensuring consistent forecasts and optimal resource allocation (Andersen et al. 2007)
	Cooperate with partners at both ends of the supply chain with joint projects, workshops, and meetings to gain a common understanding of supply chain activities and improvement possibilities
	Benchmark your supply chain management with other companies

Holistic View

The Holistic View of this pattern as shown in Fig. 8.27 reflects the structure defined in Fig. 8.25 as well in the business layer as in the data and application layer. The four main components for planning, procuring (supply), make, and delivering can be found on both layers.

The pattern contains many different business roles. The reason for this is that a supply chain encompasses many different departments within a company and beyond. We will therefore describe the following stakeholders, who take an active part in the planning and execution of the supply chain:

- *Supplier*. This role has an important part in a collaborative supply chain, in the sense of integrating rather that only interfacing with suppliers.
- *CPO*. The Chief Procurement Officer (CPO) as an executive role is responsible for the procurement, sourcing decisions, and supply chain management in general.
- *Maker*. This is a general term for all the persons involved in the production and production control within the company.
- *Product Manager*. The product manager is responsible for the lifecycle management, the pricing, and the selection of the products. The definition of the product manager varies widely among the enterprises.
- *Customer Department*. These are all persons who communicate with the customers (distributors, retailers, end-users).
- *Customers*. This represents an external group of persons or enterprises (distributors, retailers) that are tightly involved in the supply chain. Their involvement is similar to the *Supplier* role.

The list of business roles involved in the supply chain management may differ from company to company and is certainly not exhaustive. Other roles from marketing, financials, business units, customer services, sales, or export departments may also be mentioned.

The data and application layer contains the four aforementioned main components and an application group for the inventory management. The technology layer contains only a placeholder for the application and database servers. Supply chain management is an integrative function, which has also an impact on the technological layer: Different systems must be integrated and exchange information through well-defined interfaces. As we will see in the Technology View, the interoperability issues and the use of integration technologies can be a challenge when adopting the supply chain approach (Table 8.4).

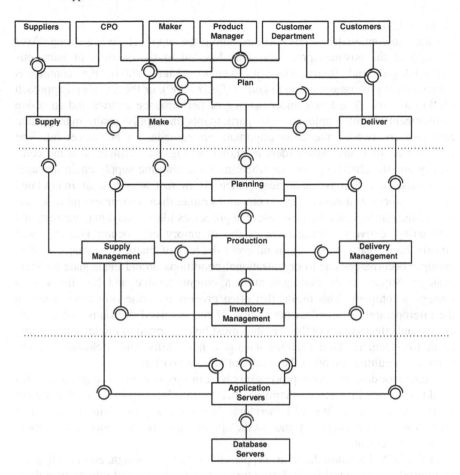

Fig. 8.27 Holistic View of FromSupplierToCustomer (S4)

Table 8.4 Architecture bricks of FromSupplierToCustomer (S4)

Brick	Description
Planning	Planning of material, demand, product, procurement, etc.
Supply management	Services for supply management, e.g., purchase, handling of returns to suppliers
Delivery management	Delivery of goods and management of returns from customers
Inventory management	Handling of inventories and warehouse stocks
Application servers	Placeholder for different application platforms
Database servers	Placeholder for different database systems

Business View

The need to continually reduce cost throughout the supply chain is a strong driver to improve the business processes. This has led to the creation of numerous methodologies and frameworks, like *kanban* (Liker 2004), the continuous improvement process according to *kaizen* (Ortiz 2009), or the *Six Sigma* approach (Zinkgraf 2006). The better understanding of performance metrics and an active involvement of all employees and participants in supply chain management activities are two of the most important prerequisites to be successful. The involvement of many stakeholders as shown in Fig. 8.27 defines also the complexity and the challenges to face when implementing the supply chain management processes. Supply chain management is in fact a system of interrelated complex processes across different companies rather than companies and functions doing business together. In most cases the processes like demand management and forecasting, delivery, management of the inventory or procurement, etc., will already be in place. Certainly in different degrees of maturity, perhaps even in multiple occurrences due to organizational conditions or/and inadequate business strategy. Supply chain management is a comprehensive and holistic way to manage a company. This means that often process reengineering tasks to assure the interoperability, seamless integration of the involved divisions and the efficiency and effectiveness of the activities must be performed to implement a supply chain management. Organizational changes, new skills, and a change in communication culture are often the results of such activities.

We cannot describe every process involved in supply chain management – this would be a book in itself. Furthermore, there are industry specificities that are not generic in character. We will therefore depict the supply chain management process in a very generic way and not the operational business processes in supply chain management.

In the SCM literature the terms supply chain strategy, design, and planning are often used interchangeably. In the context of this book, we will differentiate these terms as shown in the horizontal streams in Fig. 8.25. In our understanding, the two streams, strategy and design, are directly related to the business model and goals of the company and will give directions for the underlying streams of planning and processing. Furthermore, you do not need specialized software to write a supply chain strategy or design it, whereas planning and processing will be supported by adequate applications and technologies. In a real-life scenario the streams will not be executed sequentially but every stream will have a cycle of its own and take outputs from other streams in the form of monitoring information into account. In place of a business process, we propose a cycle as depicted in Fig. 8.28.

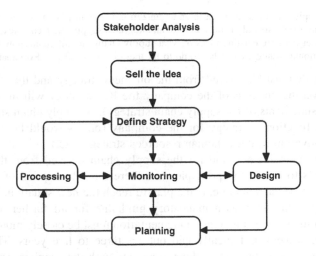

Fig. 8.28 Supply chain management cycle

To successfully realize a supply chain initiative, you need first to *identify the stakeholders* who will support the idea and actively participate in the initiative. According to the SCOR model (SCOR 2011) you need at least the following four roles:

- The *evangelist*: This role is most crucial, as he must be able to sell the project to the upper management. The evangelist is an experienced person in supply chain management projects and people will follow the directions given by him.
- An *active executive sponsor*: You need money, resources, and management support.
- The *core members of an executive steering team*: As in every strategic project, you will need a strong and competent steering team. These persons are responsible to assess the project's results at the different milestones, take decisions on the executive level, perform corrections, and overview the financial aspects.
- The *analytical design team*: These people are the specialists and will have to design the supply chain according to the business needs.

Before being able to start to formulate the supply chain strategy, the company will already have been on the road: It is most probable that a green field approach is not possible, as many components, like processes, applications, etc., will already be in place. The shift toward a comprehensive supply change initiative starts with *selling the idea* to the organization. Bolstorff and Rosenbaum formulated this phase as:

«Selling supply chain management to an organization is tough. It's an educational sell to
everyone involved. Not only is the reality of an integrated supply chain complex; everyone
has his or her own pre-existing ideas of what supply chains are all about, how they fit in
with operational strategy, and what to do to fix them.» (Bolstorff and Rosenbaum 2007)

The *strategy* must be derived from the business strategy and the ICT strategy
(depending on the business of the company the ICT strategy will in fact contain
most of the statements of the supply chain strategy). A supply chain strategy is in
this sense a functional strategy for the company (others would be a marketing
strategy, innovation strategy, human resources strategy, etc.)

A strategy contains a vision for the supply chain derived from the business
strategy, goals to reach, and principles to adhere to, a description of the «as-is»
situation, a «to-be» architecture, and a plan to reach the new situation. The supply
chain strategy will serve as a mandatory guideline for all further activities in
supply chain management and the implementation must be closely monitored. The
supply chain strategy is typically laid out for three to five years. The strategy
contains directions on the partnerships to engage with the suppliers and retailers,
the locations of productions and delivery, sourcing decisions, the products to be
manufactured, and which resources are to be allocated to the supply chain. As the
strategy has a timeline up to five years, the company must ensure constant
monitoring, as there will always be a certain amount of uncertainty about the
market conditions (see for example Chopra and Meindl 2010). According to
(Sanders 2011) the five following competitive priorities must be clearly addressed
when writing a supply chain strategy:

- Cost.
- Time.
- Innovation.
- Quality.
- Service.

The company must clearly formulate on which of these priorities it is going to
have a competitive advantage when defining the supply chain.

The *design* phase is often being mentioned as a synonym for the strategy,
although in our opinion other stakeholders will be engaged and more in-depth
know-how on how a supply chain management operates is asked for. The design
defines how the network of partners and the involved business processes will
work together. Factors like overall capacity of the chain, optimization of existing
processes versus new design of processes, vertical integration versus transversal
coordination in the company, or flexibility versus stability of the supply chain
structure, etc., must be addressed and a suitable design found for.

Starting from this high-level design, the ICT department will be challenged to
derive the application, data, and technology architectures that support the overall
design of the supply chain (ideally the ICT department will be involved at the
beginning of the design phase).

The *planning* phase takes place in all the different stages of the supply chain, from the material planning, procurement and product planning, to the delivery planning. Specialized tools are nowadays supporting all of these planning aspects. The plans should take the key performance indexes and the constraints (resources, dependencies, etc.) into account. Besides these operative aspects of planning, an overall plan for the evolution of the entire supply chain, with statements about the integration of functionalities, process (re-) engineering, resource allocation, and organizational changes must be defined.

Finally, the *processing* (or execution) stream deals with the effective providing of the supply chain management services. These are the purchasing of goods and handling of defective parts, the manufacturing of the products, the sales, and delivery to the customer or retailers.

We put the *monitoring at* the center of Fig. 8.28: The monitoring must occur for every stream, from the strategy down to the planning. From the point of view of the strategy this means to report on an annual basis on the state of the supply chain in relation to the goals, whereas for the processing this means the ongoing measurement of the agreed upon key performance indicators (KPI). The monitoring values may then be used as a feedback to all streams to improve the overall performance of the supply chain. For every described phase in Fig. 8.28 there will be a *Plan-Do-Check-Act* (also known as *Deming cycle*) sequence of activities, with the longest cycles starting at the strategy (e.g. check improvement every year) and getting shorter to the processing activities (intervals of minutes or even seconds for real-time transactions).

In the above paragraphs we depicted the overall supply chain management process in a top-down fashion, we can also distinguish between three groups of processes that reflect the generic parts of supply, make, and deliver. These process groups combine the components from the design, planning, and processing rows of Fig. 8.25 in a vertical view.

- *Supply processes*. This encompasses typically the procurement, purchasing as a subprocess, material planning, and handling of returning defective parts to suppliers.
- *Make processes*. This is the actual production process, which may differ greatly from company to company. In supply chain management an important part of this process is the production control.
- *Delivery processes*. Distribution planning, handling of returned goods from customers, sales, and forecasting must be performed.

Data and Application View
The Data and Application View shows the different integration challenges that must be faced when implementing a supply chain management application landscape. As integration must occur not only with internal but also with external functions to the organization (i.e. procurement, handling returns, logistics, etc.) a

supply chain management application landscape will use different services from various systems. Connaughton (2008) has identified 19 key applications for SCM, categorized in four core areas (manufacturing, distribution, retail, service). As already shown in the Holistic View, we have defined similar categories (supply management, production, planning, and delivery), which can easily be mapped to Connaughton's proposal.

The shift from an interfacing to an integrating supply chain management strategy has a huge impact on the application landscape: Partners like suppliers or retailers will have a direct integration of their systems (i.e., procurement systems, customer relationship management systems, inventory/warehouse management systems) with the company's environment. Retailers will be able to track in their system the status of a product delivery from the manufacturer in real-time, the information being provided by a direct integration of the manufacturers system. Figure 8.29 shows the Data and Application View. The different application groups correspond to the bricks of Fig. 8.28.

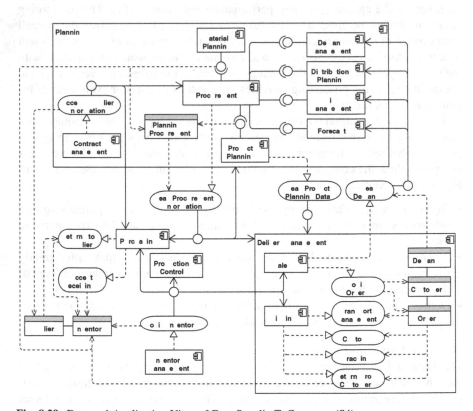

Fig. 8.29 Data and Application View of FromSupplierToCustomer (S4)

The application group *Planning* contains all the services and application components involved in the different planning activities from the supplier side to the customer side of the supply chain. The terms *Advanced Planning* or *Advanced Planning and Optimizer* or *ERP II* are often used to describe systems that address the overall planning activities.

- The contract management provides information about the partners (suppliers) and is a part of the overall *Supplier Relationship Management* (*SRM*) function.
- The central component is the *Procurement* application that hooks into the different surrounding applications that are necessary to plan the whole procurement. According to the definition given in this pattern, the procurement process involves many stakeholders, internal and external to the organization and aggregates different planning information to provide the ability to buy the necessary amount of goods or services, at the right time and place from the right suppliers. The aggregation of this planning information is vital to mitigate the bullwhip effect and to contribute to the value chain in a positive way.
- On the right side of Fig. 8.29 we put different applications that provide services to help to plan, like *Demand Management, Demand Forecast,* or *Risk Assessment* applications. All these applications access the information provided by the *Delivery* application group and help planning the procurement, production, and delivery of the products, depending on the different constraints given (capacity, resources, availability, etc.).
- The *Product Planning* application provides all necessary functions and services to perform the Product Lifecycle Management (PLM), from the first idea up to the retirement of a product.
- The application group uses extensively the services provided by Financials (S1) as the main goal of the planning activities is to contribute positively to the value chain, reduce the overall costs, keep an eye on the enterprise's asset management, and mitigate any financial risks.

The next application group deals with all aspects of delivery. This group contains all services to sell and deliver the products to the customers:

- The *Sales* application is a placeholder for all channels used to sell the products. This can be the VendingMachine (B2) for the online web-shop, but also a customer relationship management system as described in KnowYourCustomer (B3).
- The *Shipping* application is used to ship the goods to the right addresses, change the amount in the inventory, and provide services for tracking (e.g., radio frequency identification RFID, print package slips, etc.). An important service is the transport management. In cases where the company manages its own fleet of transport vehicles, this application provides a whole bunch of functionalities for efficient routing of the transported goods, global positioning system

(GPS)-based location information, capacity utilization, and scheduling services for the drivers. If the company sells products abroad, a service for handling customs issues (electronic declaration of goods, customs clearance, handling of export permits, etc.) will be implemented.

- Returns of defective parts of products must be considered at both ends of the supply chain. The correct handling of returned products involves the change in the inventory, financials, customer relationship, changes in procurements, and should also lead to increased knowledge to improve the products and reliability of the offered services.

The *Purchasing* application handles all aspects of the effective buying of materials according to the defined procurement rules and strategy.

The *Production Control* application depends highly on the business of the company. We consider it as a generic application that should provide information about the correct functioning of the production process to the whole supply chain management. The application may be a full management system for production processes or a simple application that tracks the output of the number of assembled products. Terms used for these kinds of applications are often *Manufacturing Execution Systems* (*MES*) or *Operations Execution Systems* (*OES*).

Closely related to the production control is the *Supply Chain Events* application. This application monitors all components of the supply chain and fires alerts when events occur that are outside of the defined normal operating values (key performance index).

An important component of the FromSupplierToCustomer (S4) application architecture is the *Inventory Management*, as its services will be used by many other applications throughout the whole supply chain. The *Inventory Management* application provides, depending on the degree of integration with the supply chain partners, also services for the access of external parties. Closely related with *Inventory Management* is the *Warehouse Management*: This application handles all aspects of the physical location and movements of goods in the warehouse(s). The *Warehouse Management System* (*WMS*) operates in conjunction with all the applications in the delivery application group (e.g. transportation, picking up of goods).

When talking about supply chain management applications, two other applications are always mentioned: Enterprise Resource Planning (ERP) and Customer Relationship Management (CRM). Today, the dominant software used in manufacturing companies is certainly the ERP. The emphasis of an ERP system is the planning of internal resources, whereas SCM provides explicit services to interface (or better: integrate) with external partners. Nowadays ERP packages tend to integrate more and more services and functionalities that are part of an SCM package. The FromSupplierToCustomer (S4) pattern is therefore closely related to

ResourcesAreScarce (S3) and share some common capabilities (e.g., resource planning). The same can be said for CRM functionalities on the other end of the supply chain: The pattern KnowYourCustomer (B3) is directly related to From-SupplierToCustomer (S4) and ResourcesAreScarce (S3).

The data architecture shows only the most important data objects (in fact it is more a business object view). Depending on the integration with other patterns, like ResourcesAreScarce (S3) or KnowYourCustomers (B3), the master for these objects will be in one of the applications of these patterns.

Technology View
Depending on the business and the ICT strategy of the company, the technology architecture may be spread over different geographic regions, countries, or even continents. There may be therefore different computing centers that can work as autonomous entities, but will certainly have to share common information, like financial statements, procurement information, user identities, or customer relationship data. Figure 8.30 shows the technology architecture in the different network zones:

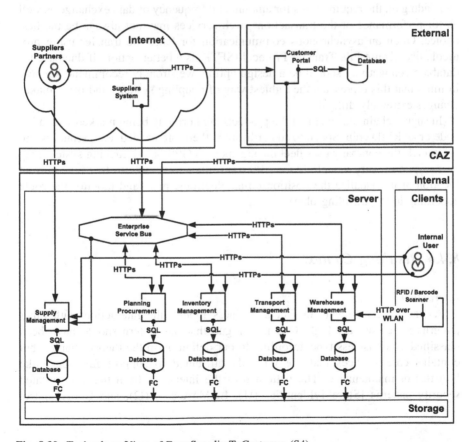

Fig. 8.30 Technology View of FromSupplierToCustomer (S4)

The systems in the external zone provide the necessary services for the sales channel (e.g. web platform like VendingMachine (B2) or a portal software). Nowadays it is common that the customer also gets the possibility to track the status of ordered goods via a web interface.

To allow a timely communication with partners (suppliers, retailers), the system at the two ends of the supply chain must be accessible through direct integration. A common way to do this is by using web services. To protect the internal systems, the use of a web service gateway with filtering capabilities for XML documents can be used. Depending on the product chosen by the company, the integration may also be made with proprietary technologies (e.g. a SAP protocol like RFC).

The integration in the internal networking zone is best done with the use of *Enterprise Service Bus* (*ESB*) functionalities. The ESB may also be used to integrate legacy systems or systems with proprietary protocols and thus decouple the systems. In a global acting company, the internal systems may even be geographically dispersed and will communicate over the network boundaries. As the need for information exchange is per se very high in a supply chain management environment, a thorough design of the network architecture is mandatory. Depending on the requirements for amount and frequency of data exchange as well as for performance of the transactions, web services may not always be the best choice. Often an asynchronous communication for large file transfer using protocols like Secure File Transfer Protocol (SFTP) is a better option. If database-to-database connectivity should be a design option, we strongly recommend keeping in mind that this represents the tightest way of coupling systems and often makes changes extremely difficult.

In supply chain management the products are normally being marked with a bar code or an RFID chip. Specialized hardware is therefore needed, e.g., scanners and printers. If the company uses fleet management, a GPS-based tracking system may be an option (every vehicle has a GPS transmitter to be able to track the current location of it, visualize the position on an electronic map, and monitor the route according to the traveling plan).

8.4.6 Resulting Context

Interaction

As the pattern reflects in fact a business model, the interaction with other patterns is per se very high. One may argue that the pattern should have been classified as a business type according to our definition in the theory chapter, but contains core services that are typically attributed to support functions, like logistics or maintenance. The pattern uses the interfaces from the three related security patterns [StoreMyIdentities (I1), LetMeAccess (I2), and UnderControl

(I3)], as well as the interfaces of the three other Support Patterns. As we have seen in the previous paragraphs, KnowYourCustomers (B3) and RessourcesAreScarce (S3) are closely related to this pattern and can be fully integrated to provide the necessary services. Depending on the degree of integration, other applications

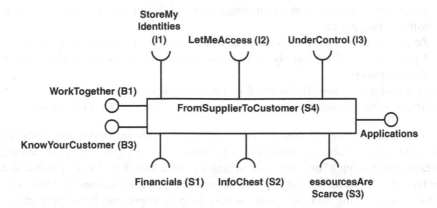

Fig. 8.31 Interaction of FromSupplierToCustomer (S4) with other patterns

(internal and external to the company) will have to access the information provided by the different services.

The pattern is not mandatory for every company, but we assume that a lot of the provided services will be used in most companies. FromSupplierToCustomer (S4) is only a guideline: There will be many different implementations, with a great variance in the services provided (Fig. 8.31).

The pattern provides the necessary interfaces to other applications accessing information like inventory, planning, or demand management (see Fig. 8.29 for the explicit services). You will hopefully have only one instantiation of a supply chain management in your company.

Consequences

The successful implementation of a supply chain management is a big challenge and requires many resources, often a change of mind and culture. A clear leadership is asked for. All employees are participants, even the partners at the border of the company (suppliers, retailers). ICT can act as an enabler for better supply chain management activities, but a bad supply chain design can lead to higher costs. Connaughton (2008) advises to first try to gather the low hanging fruits, meaning realizing a fast *Return On Investment (ROI)*. This can be realized by local optimization of processes or infrastructure, but always keeping the big picture in mind.

The *Supply Chain Operations Reference* (*SCOR*®) model strongly advises to define monitoring values in order to be able to measure the performance of the supply chain and comparing against internal and external industry goals. SCOR (2011) states that

Supply chain performance is focused on:

- Reliability – achievement of customer demand fulfillment on-time, complete, without damage, etc.
- Responsiveness – the time it takes to react to and fulfil customer demand.
- Agility – the ability of supply chain to increase/decrease demand within a given planned period.
- Cost – objective assessment of all components of supply chain cost.
- Assets – the assessment of all resources used to fulfill customer demand.

When introducing the measurement metrics, not only the performance should be addressed, but also the constant improvement of the supply chain. A mature measurement setup allows not only managing the chain, but also to predict to a certain degree the future and perform the necessary risk management. Moreover, information sharing with the partners may help in improving the supply chain, Handfield (2002) states that

«Finally, collaborative sharing of forecasting and demand information can better help plan long-term capacity, inventory, and human resource requirements.»

With the upcoming of cloud technologies and related concepts, supply chain strategies will have to be adapted. Companies will be able to choose to which degree a certain service will be sourced from a cloud provider. A company may choose to source a service from the business process down to the technology, or to only source a technology solution. Examples are call-center services, transportation management, computing power, storage, etc. The word sourcing in supply chain management activities becomes therefore twofolded: The sourcing from the point of view of the business process («Which are our suppliers?») and the sourcing from the point of view of the supporting ICT landscape («Which ICT services should we source from whom?»).

8.5 ForYourEyesOnly (S5)

«Melina: For your eyes only, darling.»

(From the movie «For Your Eyes Only»)

8.5.1 Introduction

Name and Overview

Name	ForYourEyesOnly
Number	S5
Type of pattern	Support
Abstract	The pattern supports the manual and automatic exchange of files between internal and external persons or systems in an asynchronous way. The pattern provides the necessary mechanisms to protect the files during transport and storage
Capabilities	Secure data exchange between internal and external partners using different transport and communication protocols
	Automatic system-to-system data exchange using put and fetch mechanisms
	Guaranteed delivery of files with integrity and antivirus checks
	Notification of systems and users when new documents/files have been placed on or fetched from the secure data exchange environment
Referenced patterns	StoreMyIdentities (I1), LetMeAccess (I2), UnderControl (I3), YouHaveMail (I4), Financials (S1), InformationChest (S2), ResourcesAreScarce (S4), WorkTogether (B1)
Bricks	Secure Transfer Service, Application Server, Database Server
Impeding forces	Lost of control over all services in an existing environment: Often, file or documents exchange capabilities are already implemented and the application owner is not keen to make changes
	Use of SMTP to exchange files: This is a common way to implement file exchange, although there is no guaranteed delivery and weak security mechanisms to protect the content during transport and storage
Supporting forces	Need to securely exchange information. Governance, risk, and compliance requirements
	Need to consolidate similar environments and reduce overall costs
	Reduce overall complexity by providing a generic service for secure data exchange
	The pattern can easily be implemented and will rapidly be effective
Invariance	High: we believe to have defined a very stable and generic pattern
Complexity	Low: the pattern consists of only a few components and can easily be implemented
Connectivity	Medium: not all patterns will need the services provided by this pattern
Keywords	Secure file exchange, WebDAV, SSH, SFTP, FTPS

Definition

The pattern provides means to securely exchange files and documents between different communication partners. The requirement to be able to transfer documents is as old as trading. In electronic communication the first systems used punched cards, later on magnetic tapes, which were sent by conventional mail. In the 1980s the first online protocols emerged. All these methods describe some kind of data exchange. Therefore, we need to clarify the following terms to understand the pattern:

Asynchronous file exchange.

In the pure sense of the word, asynchronous means «not in time». Applied in our context, an asynchronous file transfer means that files or electronic documents can be exchanged without having the sender and the receiving party to be simultaneously online. The sender can send the file to a system from which the intended receiver can fetch the file.

The following paragraphs explain a few protocols that are used in this pattern:

FTP (File Transfer Protocol) has been specified 1985 in Postel and Reynolds (1985) and is one of the oldest protocols used on the Internet. FTP allows transferring files, browsing, and creating remotely directories on a server. The protocol uses a control port for sending and receiving commands and a data port for the transfer of the files. The design of the protocol does not include mechanisms to protect the integrity or confidentiality of the transferred files – the whole communication takes place in clear text.

WebDAV (Web-based Distributed Authoring and Versioning) is an open standard for the access to files on the Internet. Technically speaking, it is a set of extensions to the HTTP 1.1 protocol, which allows users to collaboratively edit and manage files on remote web servers (Whitehead 2010). WebDAV functionalities can easily be integrated into web applications and can therefore use all security mechanisms provided by the *Secure Socket Layer (SSL)* protocol, including certificate-based authentication. When accessing a WebDAV server with a web browser you don't even need to install a specific WebDAV client.

SSH (Secure Shell) is a network protocol for secure communication based on a client–server model. The protocol provides different functionalities, like remote administration, secure file transfer (*Secure Copy Protocol, SCP* or *Secure File Transfer Protocol, SFTP*), port-forwarding or tunneling of other protocols into an SSH session. SSH in its open source variant OpenSSH uses public-key cryptography to authenticate subjects (remote servers, users) and only verifies that the presented public key matches the private key. It is therefore extremely important that only authorized and valid public keys are deployed to the server. There exist commercial variants as well as patches that allow a certificate-based authentication.

FTPS (File Transfer Protocol over SSL) is a protocol to securely transfer files in an encrypted channel using FTP-like commands. The data channel as well as the control channel is being encrypted using the Secure Socket Library (SSL). The protocol supports two modes of operation: The explicit mode allows using FTP and FTPS clients to access the same server, whereas the implicit mode requires FTPS clients only. The FTPS protocol is today widely implemented in FTP client software.

8.5.2 Example

> External partners and employees of TheWineBottle need to exchange documents to keep the business running. The documents often contain sensitive information that needs to be protected during transport and storage.

8.5.3 Context

The pattern can be used in almost any company, irrespective of its size and business. The pattern itself provides no business logic – it works like a postbox with a notification mechanism if needed. The pattern can therefore be used, when no synchronous communication is required. Besides the support for file transfer, the pattern provides also the following capabilities:

- Strong authentication of senders and receivers: Both the sending and the receiving party can be authenticated using mechanisms based on asymmetric cryptography provided by certificates. The pattern allows also simpler means of authentication with less security features (e.g. username/password).
- Integrity and authenticity check: All transferred files can be checked upon receiving that they have not been tampered or did not arrive corrupted. This is done using digital signatures.
- Support for large file transfers.
- Supports both batch transfers as well as interactive transfers (e.g. a user uploads or downloads a file).

To be able to fulfill the security requirements, the pattern relies heavily on StoreMyIdentities (I1), LetMeAccess (I2), and UnderControl (I3) – all Infrastructure Patterns by themselves.

8.5.4 Problem

The transfer of files is a common use case in an application landscape. Users and systems must be able to exchange securely data in the form of files. As these files often contain sensitive information, only authorized persons or systems should be allowed to access the documents.

The transfer can be characterized by the following parameters:

- Amount of data.
- Security requirements (e.g., confidentiality, integrity, availability, authenticity, traceability).
- Asynchronous versus synchronous.
- Frequency of transfers (e.g., hourly, daily, etc.).
- Type of data to be transferred.
- Type of users or systems involved in the file transfer.

TheWineBottle exchanges information with partners on a regular basis. This is done mainly by E-mail. The exchanged information often contains sensitive information (drafts of contracts, planned details for new products, human resource information, etc.) and vastly differs in frequency and amount. E-mails with important attachments have been lost in the past, wrong persons got sensitive information not intended for them and large amounts of data must always be sent on CD or on a USB stick. Secure file exchange functionalities have been implemented in different applications, leading to redundancies, increased maintenance, and high licensing costs.

Organization's View

Any organization regardless of its size and business must exchange data in the form of files. Most often, this is done in many different ways and not always with the protocol best suited but with the one that is available, e.g., SMTP or a publically available cloud service. This can lead to data that are not delivered in the expected timeframe, to data leakage or exposure of sensitive information. In order to harmonize the use of file exchange platforms, the organization must decide about the aforementioned parameters as well as about security requirements such as:

- *Confidentiality*. Protection of the files during the transport from the uploading party to the downloading user or system and storage on the file transfer service through encryption.
- *Integrity and Authenticity*. Proof of origin and that the files have not been tampered with. Integrity means also that the files can be delivered free of malware.
- *Availability*. The files and the service must be available according to the business needs. Another aspect of availability is that the service must guarantee the secure delivery of the files according to the service level agreement.
- *Traceability*. All actions must be traceable in order to fulfill regulatory and compliance requirements. This means that the service must log all actions relevant to audits.

According to these settings, it is going to be relatively easy to introduce a central platform that suits most needs of file exchange. The more important and difficult part follows afterwards by convincing projects, divisions, and users to solely use the platform that has been defined and to abandon the other ways of exchanging files. This process can be long as we are talking about a change in behavior.

Enterprise Architect's View
In practice chances are high that multiple solutions for the transfer of files will already be in place. As the need for file exchange is a typical reoccurring problem, the ForYourEyesOnly (S5) pattern helps the Enterprise Architect to address new needs and consolidate existing solutions. The Enterprise Architect must first get an oversight of the various solutions as this gives him valuable insight into the requirements the new platform has to fulfill. When arguing for the new platform, the cost factor is very important, as all these particulate solutions require know-how, maintenance, and further development and investments. Another important point is security and reliability arguments. As file exchange is something that is just done and that is not perceived as an isolated task but very often is integrated in a workflow, it may well take some time and marketing efforts to convince projects and end-users to abandon their old solutions in favor of the new and centralized one.

End-User's View
End-users tend to use the solution that comes in handy and/or that they are used to work with. They are likely to be willing to use the new solution if it meets their needs, especially in terms of usability and speed. Another important requirement is going to be the availability of the service for any device and from any location. As many end-users have also the need to share file-based information with users outside the enterprise such as customers or employees of partner organizations, it is crucial that the new solution supports this requirement in an easy and comfortable yet secure way.

8.5.5 Solution

Vision

> Providing a generic service for secure file transfer for internal and external users and systems of the application landscape of TheWineBottle. The service supports strong security mechanisms for the protection of the files during transport and storing according to the business requirements. The service uses standard protocols and can easily be integrated in existing and new applications.

Principles

1. *Principle*	*Ease of integration*
Statement	The file transfer service must be easy to integrate
Reasoning	A service that requires little effort to be integrated will help to shorten the projects throughput times and thus decreasing costs
Consequences	Use of standard interfaces and protocols
	Accurate and comprehensible documentation for solution architects and developers must be provided
	Adequate, efficient tools must support the administration of the service (new users, postboxes, reporting, etc.)
2. *Principle*	*Attractive pricing*
Statement	The service must be financially attractive to use in comparison to a particulate solution
Reasoning	The service will be shared by different applications and the costs will be shared among those. As the service is not very complex, a financial advantage by using it must be possible
Consequences	A price model on a per use basis should be defined
	Accounting and reporting functionalities must be built in
3. *Principle*	*Separation of data (confidentiality)*
Statement	The documents on the file exchange server are only to be seen by authorized users or systems according to the document owner's specifications
Reasoning	Many different applications (systems) and users will use the service. The protection of the confidentiality (who is allowed to see the documents) of the documents is a core requirement of the service
Consequences	The service must provide mechanisms to build secure compartments for the users/applications that store documents on the system as well as the possibility to encrypt the documents on the fly
4. *Principle*	*Protection of the integrity and authenticity of data*
Statement	The service must provide mechanisms ensuring the integrity and authenticity of the data transmitted
Reasoning	The acceptor of the files transmitted should have the possibility to verify the integrity and the authenticity of the files transferred
Consequences	Cryptographic hashes and signatures must be easily implemented in order to fulfil these security requirements
5. *Principle*	*Traceability*
Statement	All security relevant actions performed on the system must be logged
Reasoning	As security of data is a core feature of this service, the traceability of actions must be logged in accordance with the business requirements
Consequences	Logging (for subsequent analysis) and security monitoring (for immediate analysis) must be implemented

(continued)

(continued)

6. *Principle*	*Support for large files*
Statement	The service must support the transport and storage of large files (gigabytes)
Reasoning	Secure bulk transfer between systems must still be addressed
Consequences	Transfer of large files must be designed into the service and tested

Holistic View

As shown in Fig. 8.32 the pattern is quite simple. There are three actors who use the pattern: A person who uploads files, his counterpart who fetches the files, and the administrator who is responsible for customizing the service. Either user may be internal or external to the organization – accessing the service is handled by the StoreMyIdentities (I1) and LetMeAccess (I2) patterns. The roles *Uploader* and *Downloader* may also be systems (in a service-oriented architecture we would speak of «service consumers») that interact with the file exchange service. A single brick that provides all the necessary interfaces to the users represents the file transfer service. For the three main transfer protocols we put a single interface (SFTP, FTPS, HTTPS) that is going to be explained in greater detail in the application and data view. The second interface is for the administrator to access the privileged administration functions of the service (e.g., setting up new users and access rights, analyzing log files, etc.).

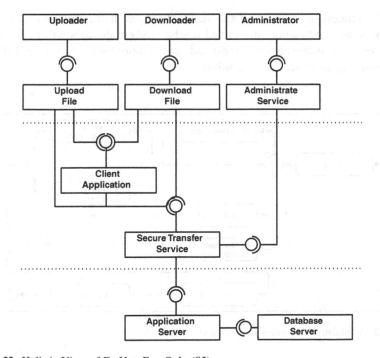

Fig. 8.32 Holistic View of ForYourEyesOnly (S5)

Depending on the security needs, the users, or systems using the service may also have a local application installed (*Client Application*) to perform the secure signing and encryption of the data.

The technology layer consists of the application and database servers. Depending on the availability requirements, there may be more than one server each; even a cluster may be necessary (Table 8.5).

Table 8.5 Architecture bricks of ForYourEyesOnly (S5)

Brick	Description
Client application	Locally installed client application for security relevant operations (digital signing of files, verification of signatures, de- and encryption of files)
Secure transfer service	Core service for transferring files. Provides all necessary interfaces for the different transfer protocols and the administration of the service
Application servers	System that hosts the secure transfer application
Database servers	Database for the storing of metadata and service-related attributes

Business View

The business view consists of three processes:

- Administration of the service.
- Use of the service from the point of view of the *Uploader*.
- Use of the service from the point of view of the *Downloader*.

In the processes we will use the «term client» with the following meaning: A client is the combination of a virtual postbox (where the files will be uploaded on the system and downloaded from) and one or more users or systems with the appropriate rights to access the postbox.

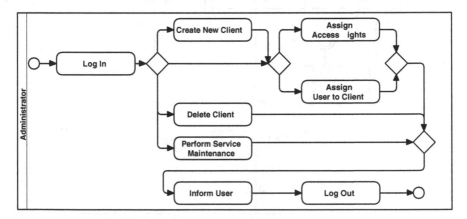

Fig. 8.33 Administration process for ForYourEyesOnly (S5)

As shown in Fig. 8.33 the administration of the service starts with the login of the administrator. Afterwards the administrator has different options: Creating a new client, modifying an existing client (protocols to allow, assign access rights or assign a user to a client), deleting a client according to the policies (this could also mean archiving the client for compliance reasons) and performing maintenance of the service (log file analysis, statistics for accounting, etc.). The process ends with the logout of the administrator. The administrator does not only create clients for users but also for system-to-system communication without user interaction.

The security level of the service depends not only on technical capabilities, but also on how strong or restrictive the administrative processes are being designed. For example, the company may decide that a postbox may only be created for internal users and external users may be invited to use the service. Or, on the other side of the spectrum, even a self-registration and self-creation of a postbox and associated clients by a user (internal or external to the company) may be allowed. As many Internet Services such as Teamdrive or Dropbox prove, the provisioning of a data exchange service can be a business opportunity itself. The pattern may also be applied in order to provide such a service.

The next process in Fig. 8.34 shows the interaction of the user who wants to upload one or more files onto the system. The user must first login and then has different possibilities to protect the files: He can encrypt the files using the public key of the receiver of the files and/or sign the files with his own certificate using the private key. Later the file(s) can be uploaded using the protocol assigned by the administrator and subsequently the user will have to inform the receiver (e.g., sending a link to the files) and log out of the service.

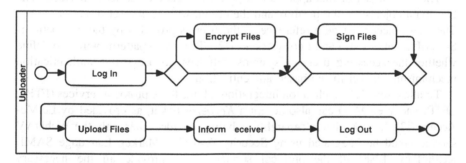

Fig. 8.34 Uploader process for ForYourEyesOnly (S5)

The last process is being shown in Fig. 8.35. The user who wants to download the files must also first login using the information received by the uploading party. If the files have been previously digitally signed and/or encrypted, the user will first have to verify the signature and then decrypt the files using public key mechanisms. Note the reverse order of verifying and decrypting the files in comparison to Fig. 8.34.

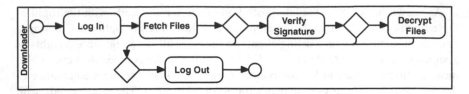

Fig. 8.35 Downloader process for ForYourEyesOnly (S5)

Data and Application View

The data and application view, as shown in Fig. 8.36, consists of the core group of applications for the secure transfer service. The group contains six applications:

- The three applications for handling the direct communication with the users or systems by implementing the necessary protocols (SFTP, FTPS and WebDAV).
- The *Postboxes* application in which the files for the clients will be held. This application is responsible for the secure compartmentalization of the postboxes on the system. The application must enforce that only authorized clients may have access to their specific postboxes.
- The *Clients Management* application, which allows creating and modifying the clients and assigning users to the clients.
- An *Administration* application that uses services from all other applications in this group to customize the different parts. The administration application also provides service for getting usage data (accounting). The administration application can be accessed through means of the administration service.

The data model of this applications group reflects the services provided: The two main objects are the postbox and the client, with each a set of access rights. The user object must be a reference to the user as provided by the two patterns StoreMyIdentities (I1) and LetMeAccess (I2). These two patterns will also define whether the accessing users or systems will have to use strong authentication mechanisms like certificate-based authentication.

To allow seamless application integration, all the three protocol services (FTPS, SFTP, and WebDAV) can also accept a *Kerberos* ticket, as provided by LetMe-Access (I2). If no Kerberos capability is being provided, then only the WebDAV service could be integrated using Security Assertion Markup Language SAML technology. Else, all the protocol services must provide all the necessary authentication and authorization services by themselves (username and password, certificate-based authentication, one-time password, etc.).

We propose to use a client application to allow for more security: The client application must be installed on the accessing hardware (server, pc, laptop, tablet, and smartphone) and provides services to encrypt and decrypt files (protection of confidentiality) and sign the files (proof of integrity and originator). This is best done using *Public Key Infrastructure* (PKI) services. Using certificates from a PKI serves three different purposes: Digitally sign files, encrypt files, and authenticate the user or systems to use the secure transfer service.

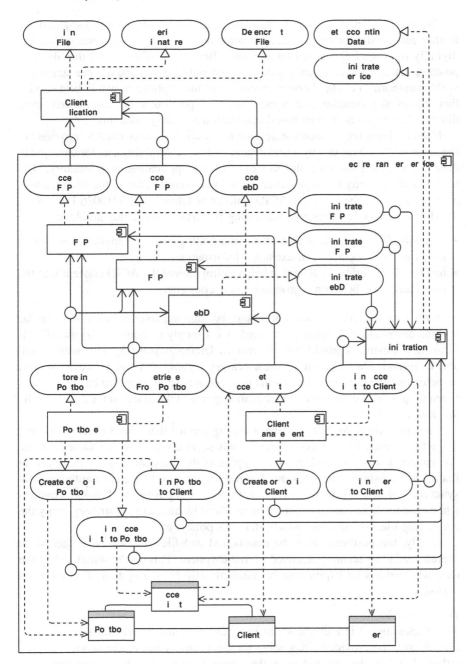

Fig. 8.36 Application and Data View of ForYourEyesOnly (S5)

The proposed data and application view of ForYourEyesOnly (S5) may be further enhanced with other security mechanisms, like automatic encryption and digitally signing of files based on assigned clients to postboxes: All the files in a postbox get automatically encrypted and can only be decrypted when accessing with an authorized client. Another extension of the application would be a service that allows the creation and management of postboxes and associated users directly by end-users. A web-based application normally does this.

If the business requirements states that transaction security must be provided in the sense of ACID (atomicity, consistency, isolation, durability), as for example in database transactions, then the use of a client application is mandatory. The transactional security mechanisms are then to be incorporated in the client as well as in the server application. The ACID concept is defined in (ISO10026 1998, Sect. 4). Hohpe (2004) describes two interesting patterns to solve this problem:

- The *File Transfer* pattern that helps «integrating multiple applications so that they can work together and exchange information»
- and the *Transactional Client* that helps to implement the ACID concept into the communication between a producer and a consumer.

A file transfer service always bears the risk that malware-infected files may be up- and downloaded. To mitigate this risk, we strongly recommend the use of anti-virus mechanisms as provided in the pattern UnderControl (I3). This pattern will also be responsible for providing the necessary logging services. However, it must be noted that there may exist a conflict of objective when an end-to-end encryption is required. In that case, the malware scanning must take place on the device of the up- and downloader.

Another optional feature is a time stamping service that allows proving the time that a file is ready for delivery. Generally this service would be maintained outside this pattern. Closely related to time stamping is the integration of a synchronizing feature when using client software: The modification of files can be automatically synchronized across different clients that access the postboxes. Possible conflicts when changes have been made must be resolved by an adequate strategy (copy the conflicting file, let the users decide, define a policy, etc.).

Finally, the postboxes must be maintained and files that are no longer to be shared need to be securely removed from the system. This can be initialized by the user who defines an expiry date or automatically by the system after a certain period.

Technology View
The Technology View as shown in Fig. 8.37 is quite simple, as only one core service must be provided. Depending on the business needs, the service may be either placed in the external or in the internal zone. The choice depends on to which degree external partners are to use the service. We chose to put the secure

transfer service in the external zone. The access to the service is being protected by the technology provided by LetMeAccess (I2): The users accessing the service must first authenticate in the *Central Access Zone* before being routed to the

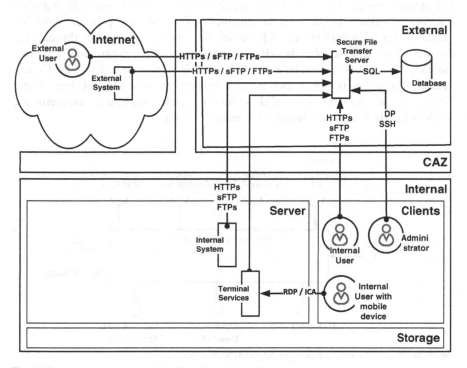

Fig. 8.37 Technology View of ForYourEyesOnly (S5)

service. The administration of the service is done via a separate physical Ethernet interface, whereas the business users can access the service through yet another interface. The metadata for the postboxes (access rights, assignment of clients and their parameters to a postbox) are being held in a database. Depending on the chosen product, the files to be exchanged may themselves be stored in a database, on a file system or on other storage technologies (SAN, NAS).

Users accessing the service are in the internal or external zone and must adhere to the defined network policies. As mobility is a big challenge that must be addressed, we put a terminal service in front of the secure file transfer service: This is a common way to let users access business content with their mobile devices, when data leakage caused by the theft of mobile devices should be avoided. The user needs to have a terminal service client installed on his device. Another method is to use virtual private network (VPN) technology and install the corresponding client software.

8.5.6 Resulting Context

Interaction

The pattern provides interfaces for all applications as shown in Fig. 8.38 that need a secure asynchronous file transfer capability. Typically the patterns WorkTogether (B1) or InformationChest (S2) can use the services provided by this pattern. On the other hand, it relies heavily on the three other Infrastructure Patterns, StoreMyIdentities (I1), LetMeAccess (I2), and UnderControl (I3). The UnderControl (I3) pattern is most important as it provides all necessary services for the logging of actions and thus fulfill regulatory and compliance requirements, whereas LetMeAccess (I2) handles the authentication.

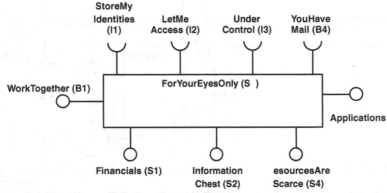

Fig. 8.38 Interaction of ForYourEyesOnly (S5) with other patterns

The pattern YouHaveMail (B4) is being used for the notification of the users (new postbox created, initial password, invitation to fetch files, etc.).

Consequences

The pattern provides complementary capabilities in an application landscape for secure data exchange. The complexity is rather simple and the pattern can easily be implemented. The pattern ensures the necessary technical security measures (encryption, secure storage on the file transfer server, etc.), but the administrative tasks are equally important to provide a secure service. We therefore strongly recommend to define a policy that defines the liability issues, which can use the service under which circumstances, how a user can enroll in a registration process, which security level will be supported, and so on.

Patterns for data exchange exist in numerous variations and have been documented in many books and publications: Hohpe (2004) proposes patterns for message-based communication, OSA (2011) has documented a secure file exchange pattern based on HTTPS, and SFTP or (Chappell 2004) describes the use of an enterprise service bus as integration component.

As the need to exchange documents in an application landscape will always emerge when new applications must be integrated or existing applications changed, the pattern and the possible implementation should be well documented and well known by the stakeholders (project managers, solution architects), so that they can incorporate it into their design and planning. Depending on the problem to solve, it may be sometimes better (e.g. cheaper) to integrate the document exchanging functionalities directly in the application than using an external service as stated in this pattern. In an application landscape that has evolved over many years, the use of insecure transport protocols like FTP will be widely in use. It can be challenging for an enterprise to replace FTP by secure protocols, but can be done sequentially, at every migration point of an application landscape.

The secure exchange of documents (files) is a core use case when interacting with governmental offices: Citizens must exchange information with governmental institutions (G2C, government-to-citizen) as well as enterprises (G2B, government to business) or governmental agencies must securely transfer files to another agency (G2G, government-to-government). The shift from a paper-based to a paper-less communication involves therefore the providing of a secure file transfer service. The German government has specified the Online Services Computer Interface (OSCI) protocol standards to help the exchange of XML-based document in an e-government environment. Typical use cases are the secure transfer of files with strong authentication mechanisms, full traceability, integrity, authenticity and non-repudiation using digital signatures, and the notification of senders and receivers. The OSCI (2011) protocol suite is based on web-services and uses well-known standards and protocols like SOAP, XML-signature, and XML-encryption. Often in e-government environments not only is the secure transport of the documents being specified, but also how these documents are to be structured: The semantic of the entries are being described by standards (e.g., how the address of a citizen is to be structured). Specifications for e-government based on XML and web-services exist in other countries around the world.

The market delivers many solutions to solve the problem stated in this pattern. The solutions are often part of an information management system management suite and are often being advertised as «secure document exchange» solutions.

References

Anderson D, Britt FF, Favre D (2007) The 7 principles of supply chain management. Supply Chain Manage Rev 11(3):41–46

APICS (2011) APICS dictionary. http://www.apics.org/gsa-main-search?q=#!dictionary. Accessed 23 June 2013

Armstrong M (2010) Armstrong's essential human resource management practice: a guide to people management. Kogan Page, London, Philadelphia

Banks E (2010) Finance: the basics. Routledge, New York

Basware (2010) Lost in transaction 2010. http://www.basware.com/news-and-events/blog/2010-07-08/lost-in-transaction-2010-%E2%80%93-weak-finance-processes-hitting-global-bus. Accessed 8 Aug 2011

BDict (2012) Business dictionary http://www.businessdictionary.com/definition/employee.html. Accessed 3 Feb 2012

Bolstorff P, Rosenbaum R (2007) Supply chain excellence: a handbook for dramatic improvement using the SCOR model. AMACOM-American Management Association, New York

Bragg S (2010) Treasury management: the practitioner's guide. Wiley Corporate F&A, Hoboken

Chappell D (2004) Enterprise service bus. O'Reilly, USA

Chopra S, Meindl P (2010) Supply chain management. Pearson Education (US), Boston

CMIS (2010) Content management interoperability services (CMIS) version 1.0. http://docs.oasis-open.org/cmis/CMIS/v1.0/os/cmis-spec-v1.0.html. Accessed 1 July 2011

Connaughton P (2008) Forrester TechRadarTM: the extended supply chain application ecosystem, Q2 2008. Forrester Research Inc

CSCMP (2011) Council of Supply Chain Management Professionals. http://cscmp.org/aboutcscmp/definitions.asp. Accessed 10 Aug 2011

Davis E (2003) The extended enterprise: gaining competitive advantage through collaborative supply chains. Financial Times/Prentice Hall, Upper Saddle River

Floridi L (2010) Information: a very short introduction. Oxford University Press, USA

Handfield R (2002) Supply chain redesign: transforming supply chains into integrated value system. Financial Times Prentice Hall, Upper Saddle River

Hillard R (2010) Information-driven business. Wiley, New York

Hohpe G (2004) Enterprise integration patterns: designing, building, and deploying messaging solutions. Addison-Wesley, Boston

Hohpe G, Woolf B (2003) Enterprise integrations patterns. Addison-Wesley, USA

IFRS (2011) Preface to international financial reporting standards. IFRS Foundation, London

ISO10026 (1998) Information technology–open systems interconnection–distributed transaction processing–part 1: OSI TP Model. ISO Copyright Office, Geneva

ISO 15489-1 (2001) ISO/TR 15489-1 Technical report information and documentation – records management – part 1 general. International Organization for Standardization, Geneva

ISO 15489-2 (2001) Information and documentation – records management – part 2 guidelines. International Organization for Standardization, Geneva

JSR (2009) JSR-000283 content repository for Java technology 2.0. Final release http://download.oracle.com/otndocs/jcp/content_repository-2.0-fr-oth-JSpec/. Accessed 4 Feb 2011

Kuny T (1997) A digital dark ages? Challenges in the preservation of electronic information. http://archive.ifla.org/IV/ifla63/63kuny1.pdf. Accessed 6 Aug 2011

Liker J (2004) The Toyota way. McGraw-Hill, New York

Merriam-Webster (2005) The Merriam-Webster dictionary. Merriam-Webster, Springfield, Massachusetts

Mol M (2009) Giant steps in management creating innovations that change the way we work. Prentice Hall/Financial Times, Harlow

MoReq2010 (2011) Modular requirements for records system version 1.0. http://moreq2010.eu/. Accessed 28 Aug 2011

Morville P, Rosenfeld L (2007) Information architecture for the World Wide Web. O'Reilly, Sebastopol

Müller M (2011) Essentials of inventory management. Amacom, New York

Naisbitt J, Aburdene P (1982) Megatrend. Avon, New York

OAIS (2009) Reference model for an open archival information system (OAIS) draft recommended standard CCSDS 650.0-P-1.1. http://public.ccsds.org/sites/cwe/rids/Lists/CCSDS%206500P11/Attachments/650x0p11.pdf. Accessed 4 Feb 2011

Ortiz C (2009) Kaizen and Kaizen event implementation. Prentice Hall PTR, Upper Saddle River

OSA (2011) SP-019: secure ad-hoc file exchange pattern. http://www.opensecurityarchitecture.org/cms/library/patternlandscape/276-pattern-secure-ad-hoc-file-exchange. Accessed 30 Dec 2011

OSCI (2011) XÖV Standardisierung: Anwendung von XML in der öffentlichen Verwaltung. http://www.xoev.de/sixcms/detail.php?gsid=bremen83.c.2405.de. Accessed 6 Jan 2012

Porter M (1998) Competitive advantage: creating and sustaining superior performance, 1st edn. Free Press

Postel J, Reynolds J (1985) RFC 959: file transfer protocol. IETF Networking Group. http://tools.ietf.org/html/rfc959. Accessed 10 Dec 2011

Prensky M (2001) Digital natives, digital immigrants in on the horizon, vol 9(5). MCB University Press

Procurement Insights (2008) Is there a difference between purchasing and procurement? (A PI Q&A). http://procureinsights.wordpress.com/2008/07/21/is-there-a-difference-between-purchasing-and-procurement-a-pi-qa/. Accesses 14 Aug 2011

RDF (2004) Resource description framework (RDF). http://www.w3.org/RDF/. Accessed 6 Aug 2011

Russel SR, Taylor B (2010) Operations management: creating value along the supply chain, 7th edn. Wiley, New York

Sanders N (2011) Supply chain management: a global perspective. Wiley, Hoboken

Schellenberg A (2010) Rechnungswesen Grundlagen, Zusammenhänge. Interpretationen, Versus, Zürich

SCOR (2011) Supply chain operations reference-model (SCOR). http://supply-chain.org/scor. Accessed 10 Aug 2011

Smith R (2007) Business process management and the balanced scorecard: using processes as strategic drivers. Wiley, Hoboken

SNIA (2011) The 2011 SNIA dictionary. http://www.snia.org/education/dictionary. Accessed 4 Aug 2011

Stadtler H (2005) Supply chain management and advanced planning: concepts, models, software and case studies; with 56 tables, 3rd edn. Springer, New York

Taylor F (1911) Principles of scientific management. Project Gutenberg EBook #6435

Taylor D (2004) Supply chains: a manager's guide. Addison-Wesley, Boston

Waddill D (2011) The e-HR advantage: the complete handbook for technology-enabled human resources. Nicholas Brealey Pub, Boston

Whitehead J (2010) WebDAV resources. http://webdav.org/. Accessed 10 Dec 2011

XBRL (2011) An introduction to XBRL. http://www.xbrl.org/WhatIsXBRL/. Accessed 4 Aug 2011

Zinkgraf S (2006) Six sigma. Prentice Hall, Englewood Cliffs

Chapter 9
Infrastructure Patterns

Abstract In this chapter, we present five patterns that provide services for all the other patterns in this book. The services are often not directly visible to end-users, but are essentials for the effective and efficient functioning of an ICT environment.

9.1 StoreMyIdentities (I1)

«Who Am I and If So How Many?»

(Precht 2011)

9.1.1 Introduction

Name and Overview

Name	StoreMyIdentities
Number	I1
Type of pattern	Infrastructure
Abstract	This pattern describes how electronic identities are created, stored, managed, and used. Identities may refer to internal or external collaborators, customers, suppliers, or other persons or entities that have a relationship to the enterprise. Tightly connected to the management of identities are credentials and authorization rights, which shall also be covered by this pattern
Capabilities	Create and manage identities
	Provision identities
	Use identities

(continued)

T. Perroud and R. Inversini, *Enterprise Architecture Patterns*,
DOI: 10.1007/978-3-642-37561-3_9, © Springer-Verlag Berlin Heidelberg 2013

(continued)

Referenced patterns	LetMeAccess (I2), UnderControl (I3), Vending machine (B2), and KnowYourCustomer (B3)
Bricks	Identity management, Credential management, Identity management system, Directory, and Database
Impeding forces	An impeding force may arise by privacy considerations as the aggregation of various attributes may lead to new and privacy relevant information Financial constraints can be an impeding force, as realizing this pattern causes the approval of long running projects with high costs Inertia is often an impeding force. As the implementation for the identity management pattern can cause many changes in processes that have been long running, a careful planning and communication strategy is crucial
Supporting forces	In the long term, any centralized and well-defined identity management is most likely to have a positive financial impact By implementing this pattern, any business application is developed much quicker as there is no need for the project to deal itself with the tedious task of developing an identity management component An enterprise implementing this pattern has the chance to realize new business opportunities as it may access the existing customer base in a quick and simple way The end-user satisfaction is greatly enhanced because a user has not to deal with multiple identities but with just one Even if we defined security also as an impeding force, the security of the enterprise can benefit and may be considered as a supporting force. A centralized identity management helps streamlining the provisioning and revocation of identities in a traceable way
Invariance	Medium
Complexity	High
Connectivity	High
Keywords	Identity, Access, Authorization, Federation, and Synchronization

Definition

The StoreMyIdentities (I1) pattern solves the problem of managing multiple electronic identities of employees, customers, partners, and suppliers. It is used as a supporting pattern for internal processes as well as for business-to-consumer (B2C) or business-to-business (B2B) processes.

In order to avoid confusion, a few central concepts are defined and explained:

A digital identity is typically defined by a combination of

- Generic attributes, such as name, address, and contact details.
- One or more specific attributes that are meaningful to the organization maintaining the identity details (Williamson et al. 2009).

Digital identity management is about creating, managing, using, and eventually destroying records [...] (Windley 2005).

The definition in this book is nearly the same, but differs in a few expressions used:

Identity management is about the processes and infrastructure needed to provision, use, maintain, and de-provision digital identities.

An identity management system has the following mandatory capabilities:

- Provisioning of identities: Meaning the creation, modification, and synchronization of identities in order to enable the user to work with his identities.
- Management of identities: As identities must be kept current, processes and services must be in place to ensure this.
- Usage of identities: Identities need to be queried and used for different purposes such as authentication, authorization, but also as the base for other patterns such as KnowYourCustomer (B3).

The following capabilities are not considered as mandatory, but are recommended and often at least partly implemented:

- Federation: This capability describes what is necessary in order to use one single identity over the borders of different organizations or domains.
- Synchronization: The capability of synchronizing identities or parts of them across different directories is important if multiple sources for identities exist or if an identity is composed with attributes from different sources.
- Authorization: Authorization describes the process of granting, managing, and revoking access rights to resources. Assigning rights to roles or claims do this. Whether to use role-based or claim-based access depends upon the environment an enterprise is operating in.

9.1.2 Example

The company TheWineBottle has different directories, each one storing identity data. An internal collaborator has at least four different identities, depending on whether he uses his internal computer, his telephone, his salary is paid, or whether he acts as a customer himself. Some people with special tasks, such as the Webmaster, even have more identities to deal with. After having had a security incident during which an ex-employee abused his identity that had not been revoked after his job termination, TheWineBottle's management decides to centralize and streamline identity management in a way that there exists only one visible identity per person.

9.1.3 Context

This pattern is suitable for every kind of organization in any size. However, the more identities are used in the company, the more important the successful implementation of this pattern gets. At least a basic identity management must be in place in order to successfully implement the other patterns described in this book, because StoreMyIdentities (I1) is part of the core of every Information Technology infrastructure.

The main actors are the end-users, internal or external. The administrators provisioning and maintaining the identities are very important for a successful implementation of this pattern. But there are more people concerned by this pattern: The chief security officer is disburdened of the always menacing risk of forgotten identities that should have been disabled. On the other hand, he must take a careful look at privacy issues. Another important actor is the group of project leaders and software architects implementing new applications (hopefully using some of the other patterns described in this book). They benefit greatly as they need not take care of the laborious task of implementing the management of the needed identities by themselves but can access well-defined interfaces. The StoreMyIdentities (I1) pattern is coupled to the LetMeAccess (I2) pattern. In fact, these two are often considered as one piece of infrastructure concept called IAM. Figure 9.1 shows the context in which the patterns are to be considered.

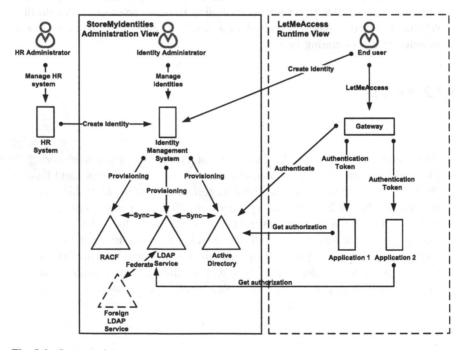

Fig. 9.1 Context of the pattern

LetMeAccess (I2) is mainly responsible for the runtime part of the IAM, whereas StoreMyIdentities (I1) has a much stronger focus on the management of the digital identities. This means that in the StoreMyIdentities (I1) pattern processes, applications, and infrastructure must be defined in order to create, provision, maintain, synchronize, and federate digital identities as well as make them accessible for other patterns such as LetMeAccess (I2). By providing the necessary interfaces, StoreMyIdentities (I1) eases the burden of managing digital identities from the other patterns. By providing access during normal use of the ICT infrastructure, LetMeAccess (I2) does the same for authentication and authorization.

It is important to note that there is no exact borderline between the StoreMyIdentities (I1) and the LetMeAccess (I2) pattern, but the distinction nonetheless makes sense at it lowers complexity and supports the step-by-step implementation of patterns in an enterprise.

9.1.4 Problem

The management of digital identities is one of the most challenging tasks within any organization. Commonly encountered problems are:

- Incomplete processes that lead to lost identities that are, for example, not deprovisioned after an employee leaves the enterprise.
- High costs for maintaining an up-to-date user base due to identity management processes. The management is often done by different units and is neither centralized nor automated.
- Time-consuming development processes for new applications, as these have to deal with the complex process and infrastructure of managing digital identities and developing an identity management component.
- Low user experience as many different identities and credentials must be remembered and used by customers, suppliers, and employees.
- Compliance requirements cannot be met, as the traceability of the creation, modification, and archiving of identities and attributes are not supported.

The problem of the management of identities and its consequences are widespread. Therefore, the following story is certainly going to sound familiar:

At TheWineBottle, Bob, the new sales representative has his first day on the job. Mary from human resource (HR) gives him an envelope with three usernames and the corresponding passwords in it, one for accessing his laptop, one for the CRM system, and one PIN with a swipe card for accessing the office building beyond office hours. She concludes that he should go to the webmaster's office for the Intranet account and if anything fails, he could open a support ticket at the service line.

Organization's View
The enterprise is forced to support different systems and applications in order to keep the decentralized identity management working. This leads to a huge overhead in terms of investments and operating costs. As every user has different digital identities, all these must be kept in a lifecycle, the identities must be provisioned and de-provisioned as collaborators enter the enterprise, get new assignments or leave the enterprise. This results in highly complex provisioning, change, and de-provisioning processes. Even if these processes are designed and maintained with the highest effort, the risk that identity information is inaccurate remains too high. As nearly every use of an ICT technology requires access to digital identities, all problems must be solved again and again, mostly on a project basis, which leads to higher costs and longer project durations. All these problems result in lost business opportunities, money, and therefore, a lower competitive ability.

Enterprise Architect's View
In most organizations, strategic initiatives and projects have been started in order to centralize and streamline the management of digital identities. Enterprise Architects are (and must be) deeply involved in these initiatives and projects. With their broad view of the problems they can gather all the necessary people and can facilitate discussion and solution finding. The use of StoreMyIdentities (I1) as a solution scheme in order to build a centralized and efficient identity management supports reusability of architectural elements. The Enterprise Architect must have a close look at the definition of protocols and standards and should insist that their use is defined in advance as well as the data model for storing the identities. By governing the Enterprise Architecture he must work toward the goal of having finally one application where all identity information is stored centrally. As identity information is security sensitive, care should be taken to implement all necessary controls in order to protect the information. This helps to avoid security breaches as well as privacy concerns. One time-consuming task is talking and convincing: Talking to the management for the necessary funding, convincing project leaders and solution architects that they do not implement an identity management system of their own, and talking to many different persons who are involved in the existing identity management processes about the changes needed. In fact, we are once again speaking about a cultural change that must happen in the organization.

End-user's View
It is not only the enterprise which suffers from an inefficient identity management but the owner of the digital identities as well. He must keep information about his different identities and must often change identity information attributes by himself. Having no centralized identity management lowers the end-user experience and therefore customer/employee satisfaction.

9.1.5 Solution

Vision

To facilitate the management of digital identities, to increase end-user experience, and to stay competitive, the TheWineBottle implements well-defined processes, applications, and infrastructure. This leads to a minimal redundancy when storing digital identities and enables other patterns to have clear and well-structured interfaces for accessing these identities.

Principles

1. *Principle*	*Well-formed and standardized interfaces*
Statement	The StoreMyIdentities (I1) pattern provides well-formed and standardized interfaces for the other patterns
Reasoning	As this is a core pattern, it must be easily accessible and usable for the other patterns. Defining and implementing well-formed and standardized interfaces at every architectural level can reach this
Consequences	The definition of the interfaces is one of the most important tasks in order to successfully implement this pattern. After that the interfaces and their correct use must be communicated to all stakeholders. It is strongly recommended to use broadly accepted standards for these interfaces such as lightweight directory access protocol (LDAP) for the directory access
2. *Principle*	*Identity information is edited at exactly one place*
Statement	For each piece of information, it is defined where it is edited and this place must be the only one
Reasoning	Adhering to this principle avoids having inconsistencies
Consequences	The whole system must be designed in a way that ensures, that for every identity and every attribute, it is clear where it is written and how it is synchronized to other directories
3. *Principle*	*There can only be one—the number of instances of this pattern is exactly one (1)*
Statement	There must exist exactly one implementation of the StoreMyIdentities (I1) pattern in an organization
Reasoning	If various independent processes, applications, or infrastructures exist within an enterprise, the main advantage of implementing this pattern is lost and the problems that were to be solved continue to exist
Consequences	Strong governance is needed, which ensures that there exists only one instance of this pattern. Every activity concerning identity management must be guided by the Enterprise Architects

(continued)

(continued)

4. *Principle*	*Security by design*
Statement	The StoreMyIdentities (I1) pattern must be implemented with security in mind
Reasoning	The storage of identities affects privacy. Any breach may not only result in financial or reputational damage but in legal problems as well
Consequences	Security is a mandatory requirement for any solution dealing with identities. The security requirements must be examined and fulfilled in every project phase
5. *Principle*	*Ensuring the principle of least privilege*
Statement	Access to the identities is granted based on the principle of least privilege. This means that the requester has exactly these identities and attributes provided, which he needs in order to fulfill his tasks
Reasoning	Ensuring the principle of least privilege helps in guarding the privacy and security of the identities stored in an organization
Consequences	Least privilege is a central design requirement when implementing this pattern. Any solution chosen must support a well-structured system of authorization. A thorough risk analysis should be made before and after the implementation
6. *Principle*	*Well-defined and implemented identity management processes*
Statement	The StoreMyIdentities (I1) pattern is only useful when the identity management processes for creating, changing, and archiving identities and access rights have been defined and implemented
Reasoning	Identity management processes are the basis for StoreMyIdentities (I1). The definition and implementation of these processes ensures the traceability, accountability, and compliance with regulative and legal requirements. Highly repetitive tasks like creating identities, granting rights, changing attributes, etc., must be done according to well-defined rules and specifications
Consequences	The as-is processes must be documented and analyzed
	The to-be processes must be defined and a gap analysis must be performed
	Depending on the maturity of the enterprise, an organizational change must be performed and new skills acquired and people trained

Holistic View

Figure 9.2 shows how the StoreMyIdentities (I1) pattern is organized. At the application layer, the two main bricks are clearly visible, named identity management and credential management. These two applications provide all the functionality needed by the business processes.

- The core elements are connected by the directory catalog, which makes the connection between an identity and its credentials. Both core elements share the same interfaces to other patterns.
- The most important interfaces to another pattern are the ones offered to Let-MeAccess (I2) as StoreMyIdentities (I1) and LetMeAccess (I2) are tightly coupled.

- Even if StoreMyIdentities (I1) could – theoretically – work without LetMe-Access (I2), it is advisable to provide access to the services of this pattern using a gateway as defined by LetMeAccess (I2).
- Nearly every other pattern needs to access the interfaces to the credential management and to the identity management, as there seldom exists an application without identities and credentials.

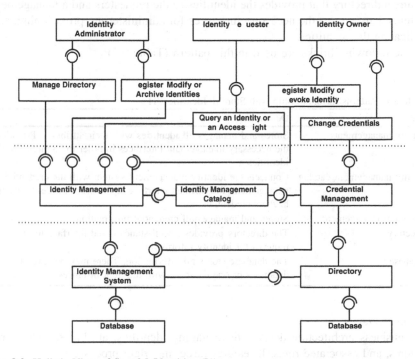

Fig. 9.2 Holistic View of StoreMyIdentities (I1)

The fact that the StoreMyIdentities (I1) pattern mainly deals with the management of identities (IdM) and their assigned credentials are reflected in its business processes. The main actors on the business level are the identity owner, the identity requester, and the identity administrator. The identity owner is the person who owns the digital identity. The identity requester is a person or a service that requests information about a certain identity. As identities need to be managed and must have a lifecycle, the identity administrator has an important role. In some scenarios, he is also responsible for the initial identification of a person before generating a digital identity on behalf of this user. The processes on the business level either deal with the generation and administration of an identity or the credentials linked to a certain identity. Access rights form an important relationship between the identity they are granted to and the resource they take effect on.

The application level consists of two elements, the identity management and the credential management interconnected by the identity catalog. Identity management provides interfaces to all identity-related business processes, whereas credential management provides an interface to manage its own credential, most often just to be able to change a password.

The technical layer is fairly simple. The actual implementation strongly depends upon the actual implementation or vendor. However, all implementations feature a directory that provides the identities to the requesters and a management systems that features the necessary interfaces for administering, provisioning, and replicating the identities.

The following bricks are used in this pattern (Table 9.1):

Table 9.1 Patterns in relationship with StoreMyIdentities (I1)

Brick	Description
Identity management	Stores and manages all identities with their attributes. Provides the necessary management interfaces in order to administrate the identities
Identity management catalog	Connects the identity management system with the credential management. Provides an interface to the user in order to change his/hers credentials
Credential management	Stores and manages all credential information
Directory	The directory provides a well-standardized interface to all requests for identity information
Database	The database stores all information. There may be several databases or one database with different instances

Business View

The business architecture deals with managing identities, attributes, rights, credentials, and associated rules. It features three important processes:

- Managing identities
- Query identities
- Change credentials

Managing identities includes the role of the identity administrator as well as the role of the identity owner. The first is able to manage identities that do not belong to him and of which he is the «custodian», the latter can manage his own identity within the limits given by the organization. This normally means that the Identity Owner is allowed to alter certain attributes such as address, mobile phone, and so on. Figure 9.3 shows the process of Managing Identities and its subprocesses or tasks. These cover all activities with the goal to administer identities, attributes, roles, and rules. Normally, these activities require an authentication, as identities need to be protected from unauthorized access. The next step is to query the identity that is going to be administered or to work with synchronization or federation rules.

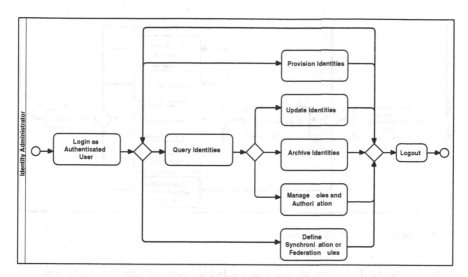

Fig. 9.3 Managing identities process

The second business process treats the process of querying an identity. Figure 9.4 shows the process of how an identity may be queried. It is important to note that this can be done in an anonymous way, without doing any authentication or as an authenticated user. Depending on whether someone is authenticated or not and depending on the associated rights, he is going to see different subsets of identity information. Querying identities is an important part of the process shown in Fig. 9.3. In fact it is needed for nearly every operation with identities.

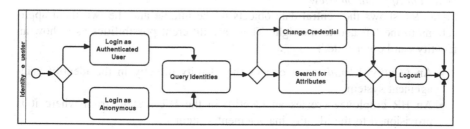

Fig. 9.4 Query identities process

The third business process handles the management of credentials. How credentials are handled is treated in the StoreMyIdentities (I1) pattern, because it is primarily a question of management and only to a lesser extent a question of runtime actions. The use of the credentials, however, belongs to the pattern LetMeAccess (I2). Figure 9.5 shows how the process is organized. It resembles the business process *Managing Identities* (Fig. 9.3) just with other tasks and subprocesses.

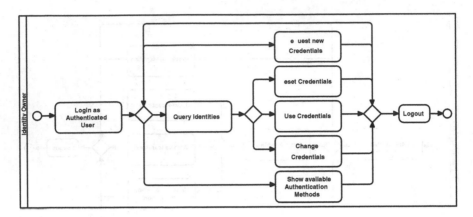

Fig. 9.5 Manage credentials process

It must be said that not all tasks and subprocesses are open to every actor:

- An end-user may change and reset its password but he is certainly not allowed to do this for other users.
- If the user has forgotten his credentials he is unable to login as an authenticated user. In this case he needs to prove his identity by other means.
- Resetting passwords is a task for the identity administrator, together with many other tasks such as implementing password rules.
- Credential management is not just about passwords. There may be other means of authentication in place, e.g., smartcards or one-time-password (OTP) tokens.

Data and Application View

Figure 9.6 shows the central data objects in the middle and the two main applications to the left and to the right. There are different possibilities as to how an identity can be generated:

- An *Identity Administrator* creates the identity directly in the identity management system.
- An HR employee creates an identity in the HR system from where it is provisioned to the identity management system.
- The *Identity Owner* himself creates an identity. This is also called a self-registration.

The core bricks identity management and credential management are explained in more detail showing all services necessary for their correct functioning.

Identity management consists of the following services:

- Adding, querying, modifying, and archiving identities are the most commonly used services. We assume that identities are never deleted. In the case that they are no longer in use, they are archived.

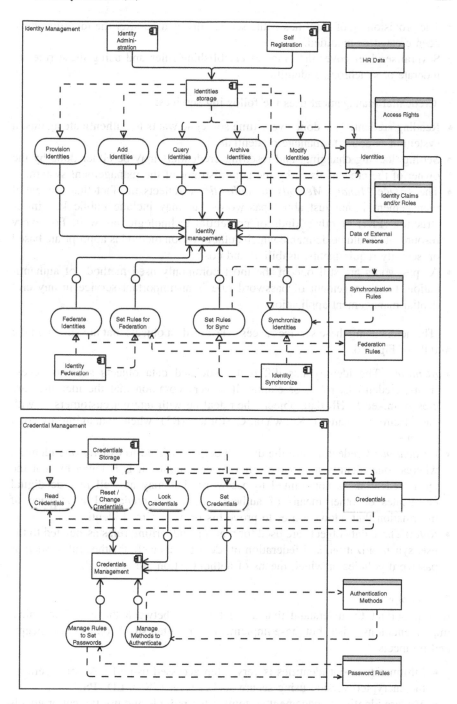

Fig. 9.6 Application and data architecture of StoreMyIdentities (I1)

- The provisioning of identities is the service that is used after the identities have been created or modified.
- Several services cover the areas of establishing rules and using these rules to federate or synchronize identities.

Credential management uses the following services:

- Reading credentials is done every time someone wants to authenticate against a system or is about to manage credentials.
- Setting, locking changing, and resetting credentials may be either done by the owner of the credentials or by the administrator of the management system.
- The service *Manage Methods to Authenticate* reflects the fact that credential management is not just about passwords but may include public key infrastructure (PKI) or other kinds of credential technologies as well. For every resource it should be definable which authentication method is appropriate based on security requirements, usability, and costs.
- As passwords are still one of the most commonly used methods of authentication, the management of password rule is an important service in any credential management application.

The actors using these services access various data objects that are shown in the middle of Fig. 9.6.

- *Identities*: The identity has different associated data objects such as access rights, credentials, roles, or claims. It is very common that the identities are closely linked to HR data object when dealing with internal customers or with data from the pattern KnowYourCustomer (B3) when managing external persons.
- *Credentials*: Credentials are the data objects associated to exactly one identity, whereas one identity may have different credentials. It is noteworthy that the term credentials is not limited to passwords but may as well include digital certificates or other means of authentication. The credential is a piece of information that allows a user to prove his or her claimed identity.
- *Rules*: These data objects are used for reading and writing rules associated to the use, synchronization, and federation of identities as well as other rules, such as password policies or which means of authentication are accepted.

Technology View
It is important to understand that a great variety between the actual technical implementations exists, but these implementations often share some core concepts and protocols:

- Information about identities is very often accessed using LDAP or – better – the encrypted version using secure socket layer (SSL), LDAPS.
- Modern identity management systems often provide and use typical protocols for web services such as SOAP over HTTPS.

- The core of the identity management system with its administration interfaces, its synchronization rules, its definition of how and when an identity is provisioned and de-provisioned lies in the center, often located in a well-protected internal networking zone.
- The directories where the identities can be accessed are dispersed over the different networking zones trying to be as near as possible to the resource requesting this information.

Figure 9.7 shows how this pattern is organized from a technical point of view:

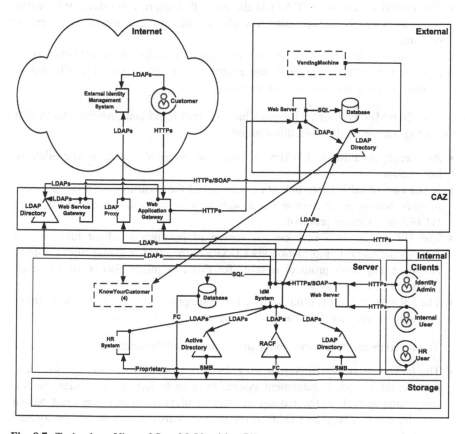

Fig. 9.7 Technology View of StoreMyIdentities (I1)

The technology view is spread over four different networking zones with the main part, the actual identity management system, being positioned in the internal server zone.

- The main storage and several directories are located in the internal networking zone for servers.
- The HR system, one of the most important sources for identity information, is also located in the internal zone.
- In the internal zone for clients, three different types of users can be identified: the identity administrator, the internal user, and the HR responsible for managing the HR system.
- Identity information needed by external users is located in a directory in the external zone.
- The central access zone (CAZ) is the zone that queries the directories when someone wants to authenticate himself in order to get access to a certain resource.
- External users located in the Internet may create identities by a self-registration process that is taking place in the external zone where they are allowed to manage and use this information as well.

The StoreMyIdentities (I1) pattern has different important protocol stacks that are being widely used within this context:

- As already mentioned LDAPS is the base protocol for accessing identity information.
- In the case of self-registration via a web portal the identities are brought to the *Identity Management System* via a web service normally using SOAP over HTTPS or a similar protocol.
- The HR service is a very central source of information about identities. It delivers the identity information via LDAPS to the identity management system. However, any other protocol suitable for this task might also be in use, even proprietary interfaces.
- The HR system itself is often accessed by a proprietary protocol. In recent times providing a web interface has become more and more common.

A few noteworthy remarks about the technical implementation:

- The *Identity Management System* may also be connected to the outside world, to an external identity management system in order to federate identities. Such a connection as well as the request of internal identity information must pass a security gateway (e.g. an LDAP proxy server). This gateway should be located in the CAZ.
- Internal and external users, who need to identify themselves, access identities. Normally, the query is done by the resource they are requesting. This resource is often another pattern such as the VendingMachine (B2) or the KnowYour-Customer (B3) or any other pattern needing identities.

- The *Identity Management System* provides an interface to manage and provision the identities. Depending upon the solution implemented, the actual identity data are not stored within this system but in various other directories. In this case, the *Identity Management System* functions as an information hub with rules for synchronization, provision, and federation of identity information. However, also the opposite exists where the *Identity Management System* has a rather monolithic and more integrated approach where the directories – be they source or destination for provisioning identities – are included as well. Figure 9.7 shows the first approach where the *Identity Management Systems* relies on directories that are often already in place for a long time such as resource access control facility (RACF) and active directory (AD). It is important to note that the *Identity Management System* as shown here is a concept and not an off-the-shelf solution. Most suppliers offer all in one solutions with interfaces to popular directory services.

9.1.6 Resulting Context

Interaction
Figure 9.8 shows the interaction of the pattern with the surrounding EAPs.

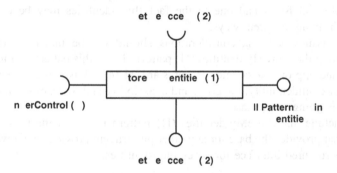

Fig. 9.8 Resulting context for the StoreMyIdentities (I1) pattern

Being a typical Infrastructure Pattern, StoreMyIdentities (I1) offers an interface to all other patterns that require identity information. The only interfaces that are required by StoreMyIdentities (I1) are provided by LetMeAccess (I2) as the use of identities must be controlled and by UnderControl (I3) as the information must be protected. Therefore the connectivity is high in the context of all patterns in the catalog.

Consequences

As identities tend to be dispersed among many different systems, databases, and directories, strong governance is needed to implement this pattern. The way may be long and painful but the reward is great. Having a centralized identity management with well-defined and communicated processes supports the enterprise in saving costs, shortening time-to-market for new applications (as they need not deal with this complex topic), and lowering risks of identity theft.

All stakeholders should be aware of the fact that this pattern cannot be implemented fully in short terms and that there may be great obstacles to overcome in the process of doing so. First of all, a clear understanding of the identities and their purposes must be established and their creation, management, and provisioning must be understood. The technical implementation normally is much smaller than the definition, adoption, and enforcement of the accompanying processes, the definition of responsibilities, and the communication within the enterprise. From a technical point of view, many proven protocols and even fully fledged software suites exist that support the implementation of this pattern. But even after having successfully implemented this pattern, the work does not stop as the centralized provisioning of identities must be guarded and defended in order to avoid having another *Identity Management System* growing secretly. Therefore, the question of how identities are managed should be asked in every information technology project and the solution adopted must be actively communicated. It is likely that this pattern has different forms depending on the type of enterprise and its technological focus and due to the fact that identities may be created and managed in many different ways.

Privacy issues and risk considerations should not be underestimated when implementing the StoreMyIdentities (I1) pattern. But if this pattern is implemented correctly and appropriate countermeasures are taken, risk is going to decrease and the level of confidentiality, integrity, and availability and traceability of the stored identities is going to increase.

To conclude, the StoreMyIdentities (I1) pattern is one of the most important patterns that provides the base for any other pattern and provides them with a clear and well-structured interface for accessing identities.

9.2 LetMeAccess (I2)

«The doors of Durin, Lord of Moria. Speak friend and enter.»

(J.R.R. Tolkien, Lord of the Rings)

9.2.1 Introduction

Name and Overview

Name	LetMeAcccess
Number	I2
Type of pattern	Infrastructure
Abstract	This pattern describes how access to resources is granted, how the requester is authenticated, and how the traffic is transported between different security zones
Capabilities	Manage access to resources Authenticate Filter
Referenced patterns	StoreMyIdentities (I1), KnowYourCustomer (B3), VendingMachine (B2), and UnderControl (I3)
Bricks	Manage Access, Authenticate, Filter, Authorize, Authentication Server, remote access service (RAS) Gateway, Filtering Gateway, Web Services Gateway, and Web Application Gateway
Impeding forces	Financial constraints are one of the forces that may ward you off from successfully implementing this pattern Security considerations may slow down the project but as security is one of the most interested stakeholders, there is nevertheless a strong interest in the successful implementation of this pattern The technical complexity may be considered as a hindering point as it may be difficult to implement some parts of this pattern
Supporting Forces	By implementing this pattern many activities regarding authentication and authorization are greatly simplified and the end-user satisfaction is most likely to increase, especially if Single-Sign-On (SSO) is implemented as well Development is going to support this pattern as the implementation of this pattern builds a well-defined interface to the authentication service The end-user satisfaction is greatly enhanced because a user has not to deal with multiple identities but with just one Even if security is also defined as an impeding force, security is going to be on a higher level as the access management is centralized and can therefore be designed in a coherent, secure, and traceable way
Invariance	Medium
Complexity	High
Connectivity	High
Keywords	Access, Authorization, Credential, Token, and SSO

Definition

The LetMeAccess (I2) pattern solves the problem of granting access to users requesting a resource. This requires that a user authenticate himself using appropriate credentials. It is an Infrastructure Pattern for all processes – whether internal, B2C, or B2B processes.

To avoid confusion, a few central concepts are defined and explained:

Authentication is the process of validating the identity of someone or something.
(Joseph Migga Kizza 2008)

The meaning of *access* is:

Fundamentally, access refers to the ability of a subject and an object to interact.
(Ballad et al. 2010)

Access control is defined as follows:

Access control is the formalization of those rules for allowing or denying access. Access control defines exactly who can interact with what, and what the subject may do during that interaction. It is based on the granting of rights or privileges, to a subject with respect to an object.
(Ballad et al. 2010)

Authorization is defined as follows:

Authorization is often defined as the process of enforcing policies; that is, it determines what types or qualities of activities, resources, or services a user is permitted.
(Ciampa Mark 2009)

We summarize these definitions in a way to include all the aforementioned aspects:

LetMeAccess (I2) encompasses all aspects on how a subject (user, process, and service) accesses a resource, defining the necessary processes, and infrastructures to authenticate and authorize him/her, to generate an audit trail and to ensure the security of the resource that is being access according to the business need.

9.2.2 Example

The company TheWineBottle wants to enable its collaborators to access any resource, regardless of whether a co-worker is on-site and connected to the local network or whether he is on the road using his tablet. Furthermore, access from customers to suppliers (users as well as systems) must be authenticated at the network border in order to not expose the systems and applications. Until now, for every new access requirement or for every new application, the TheWineBottle had to start a new ICT project in order to find a solution. The implementation of this pattern must support TheWineBottle in reaching its goals.

9.2.3 Context

An access management system has the following mandatory capabilities:

- *Central Access Zone* (CAZ): A central networking zone, in which all access systems are concentrated is an important capability of this pattern.
- *Authentication* methods: The authentication system must accept commonly used authentication mechanisms such as passwords, smartcards, and challenge/response technologies.
- *Authenticated Tokens*: The authentication system must be capable to provide authentication tokens in the form of commonly used protocols such as *security assertion markup language* (*SAML*) or *Kerberos*.
- *Authorization*: Authorization describes the process of granting, managing, and revoking access rights to resources. Assigning rights to roles or claims does this. Whether to use role-based or claim-based access depends upon the environment an enterprise is operating in.

The following capabilities are not considered as mandatory, but are recommended and often at least partly implemented:

- Filtering against malicious access attempts: There is a strong need for filtering devices that are capable of detecting and eliminating malicious access attempts.
- Centralized audit trail: Every access to a resource leaves an audit trail that is resilient against alteration. It is strongly recommended that this audit trail is stored and analyzed at a central location.

The more complex an environment is, the more helpful this pattern gets. However, only the smallest companies with few or no external access requirements will not benefit from implementing such a pattern. As the purpose of any authentication is proving the identity of a person or a process, an identity management must be in place. We strongly recommend implementing the StoreMyIdentities (I1) pattern first.

As there is virtually no action that does not need any form of authentication, LetMeAccess (I2) is going to affect most users in an enterprise, regardless of whether they are collaborators working on-site or on the road, administrators, customers, or suppliers. Developers, project leaders, and architects may benefit as well from the implementation of this pattern as they do not need to solve the authentication problem every time they develop or integrate a new application. They can rely on a well-defined interface and only need to implement the correct processing of the authentication token. As the LetMeAccess (I2) pattern has a strong impact on security, the security officer is one of the most concerned stakeholders and he will accompany its implementation and operation closely.

The LetMeAccess (I2) pattern is coupled to the StoreMyIdentities (I1) pattern. In fact, these two are often considered as one piece of infrastructure concept called IAM. Figure 9.9 shows the context of these two patterns.

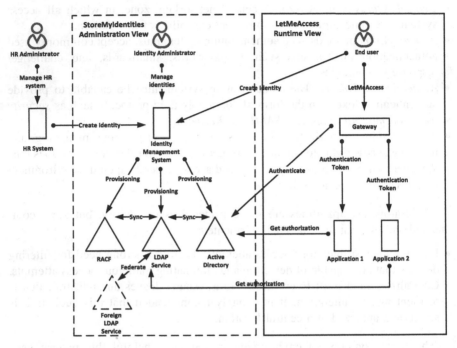

Fig. 9.9 Context of the pattern

LetMeAccess (I2) is mainly responsible for the runtime part of the identity and access management (IAM), whereas StoreMyIdentities (I1) has a much stronger focus on the management of the digital identities. LetMeAccess (I2) facilitates the secure authentication by using the identity information provided by StoreMyIdentities (I1) in order to authenticate persons or processes querying access to a resource. This is done by implementing different means of authentication and by providing different authentication tokens to other patterns. In order to decide which actions are allowed to perform on a certain resource, the StoreMyIdentities (I1) pattern is used again to authorize the requesting entity. If the identity is not stored within the organization but in a trustworthy external entity with its own identity management system, identity federation allows using the foreign identity information for the purpose of authentication and authorization.

It is possible to divide the whole IAM discussion into four levels as proposed by (Mezler-Andelberg 2008) in Fig 9.10:

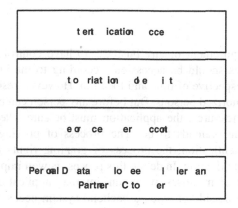

Fig. 9.10 Layers as described by Mezler-Andelberg

For the use in this pattern this model is slightly modified (Table 9.2):

Table 9.2 Modified Mezler-Andelberg model

Level	Description	Example
Identity	The identity of a person or a process using the IAM systems. This level is described in the StoreMyIdentities (I1) pattern	Peter of TheWineBottle
Resources/ Accounts	This layer describes the information and systems that are made accessible for the identity	Gets user accounts for windows, SAP, and Messaging
Authorization/ Roles	The authorization layer answers the question of which identity has which rights on the requested resources. As assigning rights directly to an identity is neither feasible nor economic. These rights are normally assigned to roles or groups	Has the role of accountant in SAP and domain user in windows
Authentication/ Access	The proof of the claimed identity is done by authenticating with an appropriate authentication method. This can be a password or something more secure such as a smartcard. Often, it depends on the information accessed or on the location from where the authentication is done	Uses a smartcard for authentication against Windows which provides a Single-Sign-On to SAP as well. When working from remote Peter uses an OTP key

The model is well suited to show the interdependence between who requests a resource from where and how this authentication is done.

9.2.4 Problem

It is a common requirement of any business to have control over access to its resources. Resources should be accessible according to the business needs, this may even mean irrespective of time and location. However, resources should only be accessible to authorized persons. But before any person can be granted the right to access a certain resource, the application must be sure whether this person is really the person he pretends to be. The process of proving one's identity is considered the authentication; the process of granting rights to perform certain actions is called authorization. In detail, this process is well implemented and fully functional. The problem arises when an internal application must be made accessible from the outside or when a backend system needs to be connected to systems facing the Internet. Such an endeavor may make it necessary to traverse security perimeter zones needing an additional authentication or demanding a second authentication factor.

Anne from TheWineBottle is going to tell a short story about a problem she experienced with access management when she was visiting customers.

Anne, TheWineBottle's best sales agent is on the road and tries to access the internal network using her VPN Client. Unfortunately, she mistakes her Intranet password for the one she should have used for the Remote Access and locks herself out. She calls her Helpdesk to regain access, but the Helpdesk employee is unsure whether it is really Anne or someone trying to attack TheWineBottle using social engineering techniques. Finally, Anne calls her boss who goes directly to the IAM administrator who resets the locked account of Anne. Now she is able to connect into the internal network and has 15 minutes left to prepare for her next meeting with a customer.

Organization's View
Without an access management strategy, each single application and system must handle access management on its own. Security perimeter transgressing access is done by different gateway systems. This often leads to high costs and complicated access matrixes that are only partially understood. The monitoring and auditing is difficult as well and is mostly done on an ad hoc basis. The intricateness, therefore, leads to a reduction of the overall security. Another repetitively encountered problem is that each and every application needs to reinvent the wheel when it comes to authentication. As granting access is needed in nearly any use of ICT technology, the problem of access management must be solved by every project individually. This leads to higher project costs and durations. Generally spoken, an organization has higher risks and higher overall costs and is less competitive if it fails to manage access to its resources in a foresighted and coherent way.

Enterprise Architect's View

Streamlining access management is on the top of the priority list of most Enterprise Architects. In order to have a well-structured access zone with all gateway systems and to have well-defined and mature processes, the Enterprise Architect must have a master plan for access management as well as a continuous monitoring of projects that influence the access management landscape. By implementing a better structured and centralized access management, the Enterprise Architect helps in preventing the reinvention of the wheel in every project. He must ensure that clear interfaces and widely used protocols are implemented, which can be used by any project without big hassles. Although it is normally unquestionable that access management strategies are a reasonable idea, the Enterprise Architect must take security concerns seriously. By centralizing access management, a successful attack against this system would be devastating. This requires the organization to implement appropriate security controls to detect any attack, to provide an audit trail, and to reduce the overall risks. The overall complexity of redesigning access management should not be underestimated and good planning and thoughtful engineering are indispensable. The Enterprise Architect must summon experienced people from various areas such as process management, system- and network engineering, as well as from support and enable a tight collaboration between them.

End-user's View

The end-user faces problems of access management everyday. He must memorize many different credentials for all his accounts as, if he forgets one of these, he must have security questions ready in order to reset his password. An end-user utilizing a well-designed access management that proves his identity in an unobtrusive yet secure way is most likely to result in a greater level of satisfaction. In the case of an employee productivity raises as well.

9.2.5 Solution

Vision

> Any resource of TheWineBottle is accessible from everywhere by passing a centralized authentication infrastructure. This infrastructure consists of all services that are needed to provide a secure and efficient way of accessing resources in the different networking zones. Whenever possible, the accessing user has to provide his proof of identity only once therefore using a true SSO.

Principles

1. Principle	*Well-formed and standardized interfaces*
Statement	The LetMeAccess (I2) pattern provides well-formed and standardized interfaces for the other patterns
Reasoning	As this is a core patterns, it must be easily accessible and usable for the other patterns. Defining and implementing well-formed and standardized interfaces at every architectural level can reach this
Consequences	The definition of the interfaces is one of the most important tasks to successfully implement this pattern. The choice of accepted authentication means and of the tokens used is crucial and must be well thought out
2. Principle	*One infrastructure—multiple gateways*
Statement	There exists only one infrastructure for authentication. However, the infrastructure may well consist of different gateways from different suppliers. These gateways are concentrated in one central network zone (CAZ)
Reasoning	Authentication should be implemented, managed, and monitored centrally to keep track of every access to a resource
Consequences	A migration project must be started to summon all the different authentication solutions in one networking zone with one clear and strongly governed concept of how authentication takes place
3. Principle	*One implementation*
Statement	There must exist exactly one implementation of the LetMeAccess (I2) pattern in an organization. Even if this is not that crucial as in the StoreMyIdentities (I1) pattern it is important enough to state it as a principle
Reasoning	It is neither cost-effective nor secure to deploy several instances of this pattern
Consequences	Strong governance is needed to ensure that there exists only one instance of this pattern and that every activity concerning identity management is guided by the Enterprise Architects
4. Principle	*Security by design*
Statement	The LetMeAccess (I2) pattern must be implemented with security in mind
Reasoning	If authentication fails, the attacker has all the means to realize his evil plot
Consequences	Security is a mandatory and crucial requirement for this pattern. A thorough and regularly repeated risk assessment must be done; the whole infrastructure and the corresponding processes must be monitored and regularly audited
5. Principle	*Ensuring the principle of least privilege*
Statement	Every access to a resource must adhere to the principle of least privilege
Reasoning	By following this principle the attack surface for any kind of attacks—be it a malevolent insider or an external hacker—is reduced
Consequences	There need to be processes in place that govern the implementation and up-keeping of this principle. The design and configuration of the gateway systems must be done in a way that support its adherence
6. Principle	*Support for different means of authentication*
Statement	The authentication systems must support different means of authentication such as username/password, smartcards with certificates, and challenge/response technologies
Reasoning	The way of authentication may differ depending on the location from which a resource is accessed and on the security requirements of the resource
Consequences	There must exist a matrix, which is individual for every organization that states which authentication technique is used under which circumstance. The implementation of the pattern must incorporate this matrix

(continued)

(continued)

7. *Principle*	*Standardized authentication token*
Statement	The access management infrastructure must be able to provide a token that shows the requested resource whether a user has been successfully authenticated. The authors suggest using Kerberos and/or SAML
Reasoning	Relying on a standardized authentication token leverages the implementation of an SSO system. It fastens the development of new applications as well
Consequences	The product for the issuing party of the authentication token must be carefully chosen. When developing new applications, precautions must be made that these are able to use the authentication token

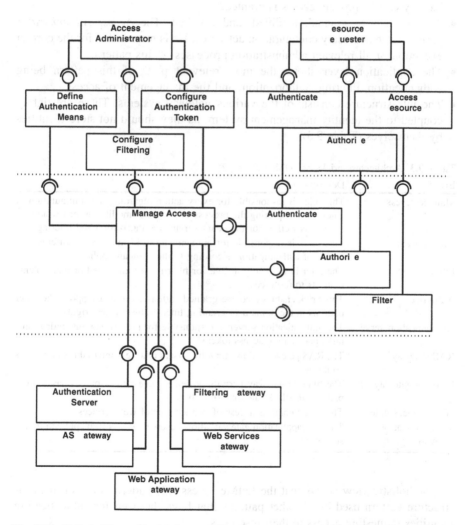

Fig. 9.11 Holistic View of LetMeAccess (I2)

Holistic View

Figure 9.11 shows how the LetMeAccess (I2) pattern is organized. At the application layer, the main bricks of this pattern are clearly visible. These are named *Managing Access, Authenticate, Filter*, and *Authorize.*

The most important interface to another pattern is the one offered to StoreMyIdentities (I1) as these two patterns are tightly coupled. It is impossible to provide an authentication without having stored the identities that are to be verified (authenticated). A few important attributes of these bricks should be enumerated at this place:

- The end-user of this pattern is called *Resource Requester* and may be a human being as well as a process, a service or another application. If the claimed identity can be proven, access is granted.
- Access must be granted, modified, and revoked. The *Access Administrator* performs the necessary configuration activities. He is responsible for the correct execution of all relevant administration processes of this pattern.
- The application layer shows the most relevant parts of this pattern being authentication, filtering, authorization, and the management of access.
- The infrastructure consists of the various gateway systems. These are tightly coupled to the identity management system, as they should not store identities by themselves (Table 9.3).

Table 9.3 Architecture bricks of LetMeAccess (I2)

Brick	Description
Manage access	This brick is responsible for every action regarding the configuration of gateways, supporting the process of granting, modifying, or revoking access, as well as for the coarse-grained authorization and filtering
Authenticate	This brick is responsible for authentication. It must accept different means of authentication according to the company policy
Filter	The filter brick is responsible for filtering out unwanted or malevolent requests to resources
Authorize	This brick enables a coarse-grained authorization and supports the other patterns in the domain of granting finer grained access rights
Authentication server	The authentication server is responsible for performing authentication tasks and writing access tokens
RAS gateway	The RAS gateway allows traveling users to access internal resources in a secure way
Filtering gateway	The filtering gateway permits or denies access to resources based on patterns in Black- and/or White lists
Web services gateway	This brick controls access of connections of web services
Web application gateway	The web application gateway allows users to access web application in a secure way

The holistic view shows that the LetMeAccess (I2) pattern is a typical Infrastructure Pattern used by all other patterns that have the need for authenticating identities requesting access to their resources.

Business View

The business architecture deals with requesting access to a certain resource. This can be shown as a concatenation of subprocesses as shown in Fig. 9.12:

As Fig. 9.12 shows, there are the following four core processes that – put together – form the access to a resource:

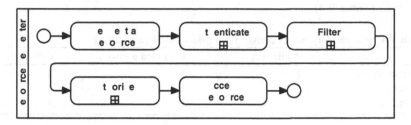

Fig. 9.12 Overview of the processes in LetMeAccess (I2)

- Authentication
- Authorization
- Filtering
- Managing access

Authentication, as shown in Fig. 9.13, proves the requester's identity. The requester asks to access a resource and tells the system who he is. The system decides

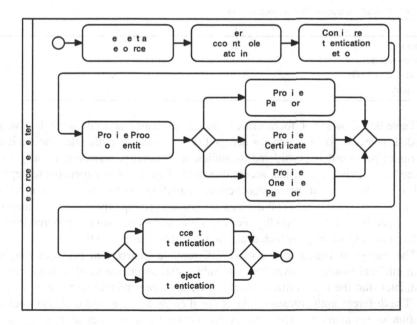

Fig. 9.13 Authenticate process

based on the resource requested, the role of the requester and the location of the requester, proof of which is necessary to be sure that no one is wrongfully admitted.

The decision of how the requester must prove his identity depends on the resource he requests, the location from where he requests the resource, and the role he wants to incorporate. According to his decision it can be based upon a risk category matrix (Mezler-Andelberg 2008, p. 55) for accessing data, as shown in Fig. 9.13 (Table 9.4).

Table 9.4 Risk category matrix derived from (Mezler-Andelberg 2008)

	Public access	Restricted access	Critical access
External access	2	3	3
Partner access	2	2	3
Internal access	1	2	3

Whereas Mezler-Andelberg writes of public data/normal rights we define the horizontal line in public, restricted, and critical access assuming that this may correspond to the type of data as well as to the rights the requester claims. As an example: Reading public data is certainly something considered to be low risk, whereas writing this publicly available information may be something that is considered at least a restricted or even critical access.

Depending on the risk matrix it may be defined how a requester must authenticate in order to get access. The following matrix is just an example and depends on the organization and its strategy:

Table 9.5 Authentication factors and access

	1	2	3
Password	X		
Soft certificate	X	X	
Smartcard or OTP	X	X	X
Biometry			X

Table 9.5 shows that for a critical access a «hard» second factor is always needed, whereas for a «normal» access (1) a one-factor authentication such as username/password is considered as sufficient. Biometry, however, is only considered appropriate for critical access due to the fact that it is expensive to deploy and often there exist privacy concerns regarding biometrical authentication methods. Smartcards and OTP devices are considered equally secure and may be used depending on the feasibility. For example, when accessing a resource from a tablet, a smartcard may be technically not feasible, but an OTP is.

The European Union uses a more differentiate matrix that provides ranging from minimal assurance, over low, and substantial assurance to high assurance. It postulates that the more critical an access is, the more reliable an assurance must be. The different authentication tokens are then matched to the different authentication tokens available. The hard crypto token is the only token allowed to cover all four assurance levels (iDABC 2007).

It is noteworthy that the assurance level is not only dependent on the security token but at least as much on the reliability of the process that performs the initial identification of the requester before handing out the token. This matter is a topic that is dealt with in the StoreMyIdentities (I1) pattern.

After getting access filtering takes place (Fig. 9.14). We recommend to implement a filtering whenever feasible and to agree upon a filtering strategy. It is important to note that filtering may take place in all directions: Someone from the outside requesting an internal resource passes a filtering device as well as someone surfing the Internet from the local area network (LAN).

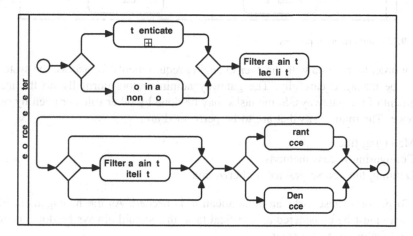

Fig. 9.14 Filtering process

Figure 9.14 shows that filtering can be done in two different ways, filtering against a blacklist (filtering out, what is explicitly forbidden) and filtering against a whitelist (filtering everything out, which is not explicitly allowed). While filtering against a blacklist is much easier to implement and needs less resources, the risk of overlooking something is also bigger. Therefore, the recommendation is to implement blacklisting first and always and to enhance its protection by using whitelists for access to very critical resources.

After having passed the filtering successfully, it must be decided which operations are allowed for this user/process. This process is called authorization (see Fig. 9.15). It may take place in a coarse-grained way at the gateway, deciding whether the requester has access to a certain application (or more specifically a certain uniform resource locator, URL) or in a much finer grained way at the application level when it is decided whether access should be granted to a certain data set or function.

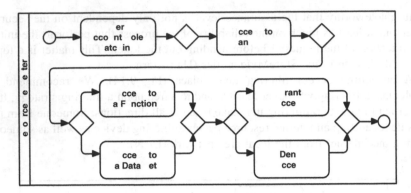

Fig. 9.15 Authorization process

In order to keep up with the ever-changing requirements for access, the systems must be managed carefully. The gateway administrators normally do the management of the gateways. Some tasks may be done by other roles or even by self-service. The main tasks that are to be performed are:

- Managing filters
- Configuring access methods
- Defining the coarse-grained authorization

To perform these tasks an authentication is needed. As the management of a gateway must be considered as a critical task, this should always be done using a second factor such as a smartcard.

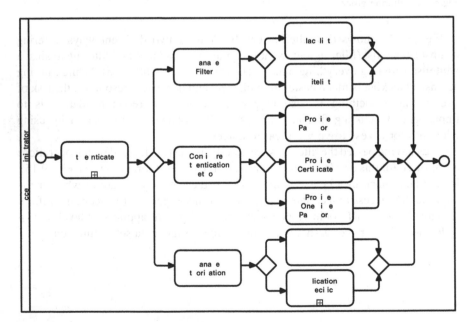

Fig. 9.16 Administration process

Figure 9.16 shows the different administration tasks that need to be done in order to have a secure and reliable access management infrastructure.

Data and Application View

Figure 9.17 shows the central data objects in the middle and the main applications grouped around them. There are three main components, the administration (*Administrate Access*), the actual authentication (*Authenticate*), the filtering (*Filter*), and the authorization (*Authorize*).

Normally the process begins by authentication, followed by filtering and authorization. The administration of access is a component of its own that is normally only used by few people or roles. Authentication provides the following services:

- Authenticate: this is the actual implementation of the authentication. It consists of verifying the claimed identity with the help of the authentication token provided, ensuring that the token used is sufficient for the resources accessed and – if everything is completed successfully – issuing an authentication ticket that is transmitted to the resource requested.
- Provide authentication ticket: The authentication application provides the ticket that later allows the requester to access the desired resource. The ticket should be standardized such as Kerberos or SAML.

Administration uses services from all the other core applications, always in order to administrate these. Generally spoken, administration consists of defining, modifying, and querying elements. These elements that are worked upon by the administration application are the data objects of the other services.

The actors using these services access various data objects that are shown on the right side of Fig. 9.17.

- *Filters* consist of blacklists and whitelists. While blacklists are much easier to implement they are only successful against known attacks. Whitelists only allow traffic or requests to pass that are explicitly allowed by an administrator. This makes them much more complex to implement. Filtering can also be seen as a compensating control when an authentication is not feasible or is only done based on self-registration.
- *Identities*: The StoreMyIdentities (I1) pattern manages identities: As these are crucial for any authentication and authorization process, they are visible in the LetMeAccess (I2) pattern as well.
- *Credentials* represent the method of how an identity is proven. Normally these are passwords, certificates, or OTP tokens. Other means of authentication may also be in place such as biometric authentication systems. One part of the management of this data object – what identity has which authentication method associated – is treated by the StoreMyIdentities (I1) pattern. The LetMeAccess (I2) pattern is responsible for the other part, for the configuration of the gateway system with the various authentication methods and authentication tickets.

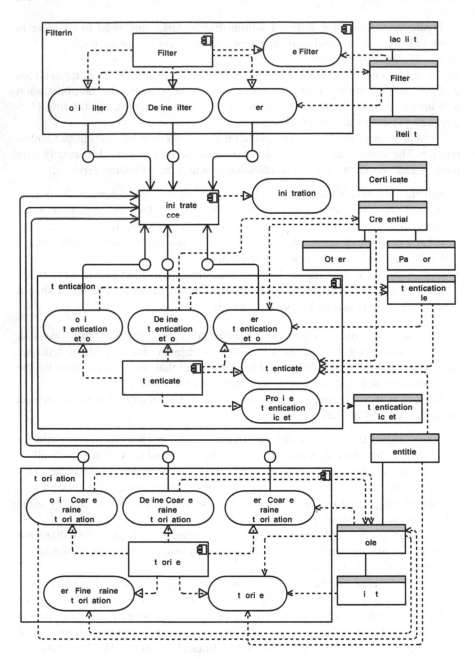

Fig. 9.17 Data and application view of LetMeAccess (I2)

- After being successfully authenticated the authentication system may provide an *Authentication Ticket* that is passed to the requested resource. Often this is a Kerberos or a SAML ticket.
- A *Role* is often used as the base for any authorization. Instead of giving access rights to every identity, it is much more efficient to define roles with corresponding rights and to add these roles to the actual identities.
- Other data objects exist, which may be seen as supplementary such as rules for authentication that are used to build the authentication system according to the risk/location matrix.

These data objects are used by different services provided by the four main applications of the LetMeAccess (I2) pattern:

- *Authenticate*: The main purpose of this application is to provide the services needed to authenticate people and processes. The user faces the authenticate service, whereas the application requested faces the authentication ticket service. The latter is creating a ticket that makes proof of the successful authentication against the authenticate service. Apart from these two crucial services other services exist that configure the gateway systems with the various authentication methods.
- *Authorize*: This application provides authorization for the resource requested. First, it is a coarse-grained authorization during which the gateway checks whether a resource or a certain URL should be accessible for a certain role or identity. The finer grained authorization is mostly done by the application itself but it must query the identity and role information.
- *Filter*: Besides the usual administration services the «use filter» service is part of this application. This service performs the actual filtering of traffic and data. It does this by comparing the input against a set of black- and whitelists. Normally, this service consists of different gateway systems such as web application firewalls, proxies, and so on.
- *Administrate Access*: This application consists of the use of the different services of the other applications in order to manage the whole LetMeAccess (I2) pattern. It provides an interface to the administrator, normally a graphical user interface (GUI) in order to manage the system. It is noteworthy that in reality every gateway system has its own interface. This has the negative impact that no coherent view over all access systems is possible.

The application view shows the complexity of this pattern. The access to a resource is a process that is composed of different steps that must remain as unobtrusive as possible for the user in order to maintain a high degree of usability.

Technology View

To gain access to resource (an application), a user must pass different systems which each have distinct tasks. Generally, the chain of activity is as follows (Fig. 9.18) (Table 9.6):

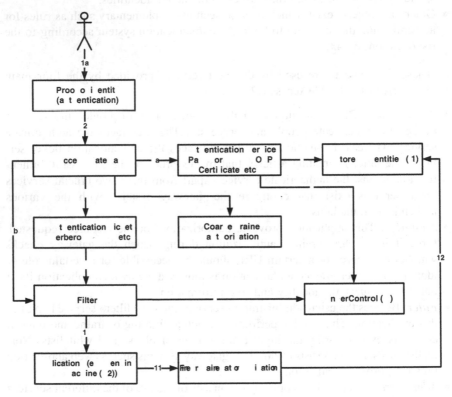

Fig. 9.18 Chain of action in LetMeAccess (I2)

Table 9.6 Step-by-step explanation of the activity chain

Step	Activity
1	A user (or a service or a process) request access to a resource. They are received by the gateway system
2	The access gateway asks them to provide proof of their identity. This may be a password, a OTP, a certificate, a biometrical attribute, or any other proof deemed reliable enough
3a	The access gateway passes the provided authentication token to the authentication systems, which validates it
3b	For anonymous access as well as for an access when the application requested handles all authentication tasks, steps 3a–7 are skipped
4	In order to perform this task, the authentication system must ask identity information from the StoreMyIdentities (I1) pattern

(continued)

Table 9.6 (continued)

Step	Activity
5	Any action is logged to the UnderControl (I3) pattern. This logging is exemplary, as all the other systems must also create an audit trail
6	The access gateway is able to perform a coarse-grained authorization, e.g., it can decide whether access to a certain resource URL is allowed for a certain user or role
7	If the authentication and the coarse-grained authorization had been successful a ticket proving this is granted. This can be Kerberos or SAML or any other technology deemed secure enough
8	After being successfully authenticated, traffic is passing a filtering device, validating the traffic. In the case of anonymous access (see 3a) the filtering helps to raise security to an acceptable level and is mandatory. Filtering can consist of various types such as DNS blacklists, protocol filters such as HTTP, malware filters, and others
9	Filtering must always be logged
10	After having successfully passed all filtering mechanism access to the resource is granted. If the application supports the authentication ticket created at step 7, no further action by the user is needed and access is granted. This is also called Single-Sign-On (SSO)
11	The fine-grained authorization is done by the application
12	In order to get the necessary information such as roles and rights, the application queries the StoreMyIdentities (I1) pattern

The actual technical implementation may differ between organizations and the products used by them, but there are common concepts and protocols. Figure 9.19 shows a possible implementation of a CAZ, with several different gateway systems.

The following access patterns are determined by the parameters «who requests the access» and «from where» «using which protocol» and «requesting which resource»:

- *Traveling Users* need to contact their home base. For achieving this, they use some kind of Remote Access Protocol. In most cases, the protocol used is IPsec or some kind of SSL VPN. The gateway provides them with a full network access that allows them to work as if they were in their office.
- Communication between external users, partner, customers, or suppliers is much more restricted. Mostly they need to use only a handful of applications, which they access via HTTPS. The gateway authenticates them, filters the traffic, and selectively grants access to the resources requested.
- For protocols other than HTTPS the same pattern should be considered. In terms of security, using a proxy as a choke and monitoring proves to be beneficial. If an encrypted communication is broken up to perform a filtering, it must be decided on a per-case basis.

- Communication to and from external systems or applications is often done using web services such as SOAP over HTTPS.
- Internal users may also be routed via the CAZ, especially when accessing web applications. However, it is also possible that they authenticate directly at the AD. If they want to access a resource not in the internal network, traversing the CAZ is mandatory.

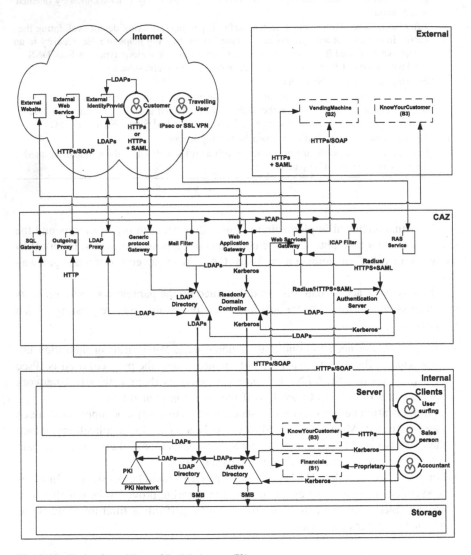

Fig. 9.19 Technology View of LetMeAccess (I2)

- Outgoing connections from the internal network must always pass a forwarding proxy acting as a choke and monitoring point.

The CAZ consists of many different gateways. The exact number and types of gateways, depend on the actual implementation and the requirements of the environment the implementation takes place. The following sample of gateway systems, however, is often seen:

- Outgoing proxy: Filtering all outgoing traffic against malware and protecting the accessing devices from threats of the Internet.
- LDAP proxy: If identity information is exchanged between different organizations and/or networking zones this must either be done by a web service or by traversing an LDAP proxy.
- Generic protocol gateway: As not all protocols can be sent through a proxy, a generic gateway should be put in place that can at least authenticate and route traffic from and to the different networking zones. A common way is to open a certain port after a successful authentication has taken place.
- Mail filter: Outgoing and incoming e-mail should be routed through one central system in order to control and filter the mail flow.
- Web application gateway: This gateway authenticates and protects the various web applications of the enterprise. Sometimes, additional functionality such as rewriting of URLs or coarse-grained authorization are implemented as well. In the case of transport of binary data, the gateway can request a scanning via ICAP protocol from a central scanning service.
- Web services gateway: In order to authenticate, filter, transform, and route these messages a web services gateway is used. Different vendors implement different approaches of such gateways with regard to the functionality provided. Some gateways are more than just a network guardian, providing powerful transformation and routing mechanisms and being in fact enterprise service buses that provide gateway functionality as well.
- ICAP Filter: Internet content adaption protocol (ICAP) is used whenever a gateway needs to scan incoming or outgoing data against malware, URL, or common content patterns that are not allowed to pass.
- RAS Gateway: The RAS gateway serves as the authentication point of collaborators that are in an untrusted network and need to be connected in a way that they become part of the trusted network. Using a VPN technology such as IPSec or SSL VPN is the most common approach.

Behind the gateways the authentication services are positioned:

- One of the most common authentication systems is a domain controller from the AD. In order to increase security it is possible to use a read-only domain controller in the CAZ, thus reducing exposure of the authentication information.

- The Authentication Server solves the problem that every gateway needs to implement all the authentication methods (certificate based, OTP, username and password, etc.). Furthermore, when using a standardized authentication ticket (i.e., using a SAML authority) you will want to have only one issuing authority. Therefore, it is often reasonable to decouple the authentication from the actual gateways and use a dedicated system that is only responsible for providing the different authentication mechanisms. The communication between the Gateway and the Authentication Server is often Radius, protected by the use of SSL or a Web service using HTTPS.
- Sometimes, even further functionality is added such as Authorization and Accounting. This is when a so-called triple-A server (Authentication, Authorization, and Accounting) is used instead of the Authentication Server. The triple-A server decouples the authentication and authorization from the gateway and provides the capability to centralize these functions for different gateways. The triple-A server provides the different authentication methods and the management thereof in a central spot. Whether or not to use a triple-A server depends on the actual environment. It is possible as well to omit this system and to have the gateway deal with different authentications.
- Another possibility is that identity and authentication information is stored in the same system, mostly an LDAP server.

After a successful authentication, the gateway or the authentication service provides an authentication ticket that is presented to the resource requested. If this resource trusts the authentication service it accepts this ticket and lets the user access without any additional authentication procedures taking place. If this mechanism is enabled throughout the enterprise, a SSO system is achieved.

- The most often-used authentication ticket, especially for internal systems, is Kerberos.
- For web applications, SAML is a good choice for an authentication ticket as it is widely used and well supported.
- There exist other authentication tickets, the simplest being a cookie.
- For the implementation of the LetMeAccess (I2) pattern it does not matter which type of authentication ticket is chosen; however, we suggest using a secure and robust protocol that is not susceptible to replay attacks.

The LetMeAccess (I2) pattern is challenging in terms of the technical infrastructure. It can be implemented step-by-step thus dispersing costs over a longer time frame. The reward of a successful implementation is great, not only in terms of cost reduction and increased security but also in terms of a much better user experience.

9.2.6 Resulting Context

Interaction

Figure 9.20 shows the interaction of the pattern with the surrounding EAPs.

Being a typical Infrastructure Pattern, LetMeAccess (I2) offers an interface to all other patterns that require authentication, filtering, and coarse-grained authorization. It requires an interface to the StoreMyIdentities (I1) pattern to access identity information of the person or process that is to be authenticated or authorized. As LetMeAccess (I2) is a crucial pattern not only from the business perspective but also from a security point of view, it is strongly recommended to use the security pattern UnderControl (I3).

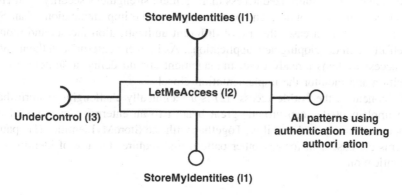

Fig. 9.20 Resulting context for the LetMeAccess (I2) pattern

Consequences

Having a centralized access management concentrated in one special networking zone allows to monitor closely who accesses which resource and from where. This simplifies intrusion detection as well as uncovering abuse from internal employees as it strengthens accountability.

For developing new applications or for enhancing access to internal applications from the outside, the time to production is reduced as the difficult task of authentication is standardized by the use of the authentication token. By decoupling the authentication method from the actual application that demands an authentication the enterprise gains much freedom in choosing the authentication method most suited for the degree of protection needed and the environment used for access. It also lowers the dependence on a sole vendor of an authentication technology as most gateway products support a standard set of authentication methods such as X.509 certificates, OTP tokens, and passwords.

A successful implementation of LetMeAccess (I2) strongly relies upon a well-designed identity management. Although it is possible to build a centralized access management system without solving the question about the provisioning of identities first, it makes hardly any sense as many advantages, especially in the security domain, are lost or cannot be fully realized. Whereas the StoreMyIdentities (I1) pattern has the greatest challenges at the process level, the LetMeAccess (I2) pattern is technologically challenging. Often the important redesign of networking zones can be done step-by-step. However, it is important to note that security benefit may only be reaped when this step is finished and resources are exclusively reachable after having passed the CAZ. One important point to consider is the propagation of authentication tokens in a secure way and only after having done a reliable verification of the person's claimed identity.

Implementing a centralized access management strengthens security, as there is one choke point to monitor. The pattern supports the implementation of an SSO system as well, as it eases the use of different authentication factors and reduces the effort when developing new applications. As in every enterprise authentication and access systems already exist, management should define a strategy for the transition and monitor the implementation closely.

To conclude, the LetMeAccess (I2) is a technically challenging pattern that – once implemented – can provide great benefit to an enterprise in terms of cost reduction, security, and usability. Together with the StoreMyIdentities (I1) pattern it forms the basement for any other pattern that requires the use of identities and authentication.

9.3 UnderControl (I3)

«Can you look me in the eye and tell me you've got this UnderControl and it's not gonna end up in a disaster?»

Tim Lockwood in the film «Cloudy with a chance of meatballs»

9.3.1 Introduction

Name and Overview

Name	UnderControl
Number	I3
Type of pattern	Infrastructure
Abstract	This pattern describes all the measures taken to keep the ICT infrastructure UnderControl in terms of availability, confidentiality, integrity, and auditability
Capabilities	Logging events, storing and analyzing logs centrally, ensuring the integrity of systems, detecting and alerting security incidents, Vulnerability management, and preserving the defined segmentation of the network
Referenced patterns	All patterns
Bricks	Log management, Intrusion detection, Vulnerability management, Log service, Firewall rule management, Security management system, host-based IDS, network-based IDS, Vulnerability management system, Log correlation engine, Management system for firewall, Integrity checker, IDS probe, Vulnerability scanning probe, Log system, Firewall, and Database/storage
Impeding forces	Initial and recurring costs, privacy concerns
Supporting forces	Security, regulatory needs, prevention, and mitigation of security incidents
Invariance	Medium: The pattern can be applied as described but there exist a variety of different approaches for this problem
Complexity	High: The pattern has many different bricks and many of them are interconnected
Connectivity	High: The pattern is connected to all other patterns
Keywords	Security, logging, availability monitoring, vulnerability management, and network segmentation

Definition

The UnderControl (I3) pattern treats the problem of how a complex and quickly changing ICT infrastructure can be kept under control. This requires the definition and implementation of different controls in the field of information security and performance monitoring ensuring the detection of deviations in confidentiality, integrity, availability, and auditability.

ISACA (Information Systems Audit and Control Association) defines confidentiality, integrity, availability, and auditability as follows:

«The protection of sensitive or private information from unauthorized disclosure»
«The accuracy, completeness and validity of information»
«Information that is accessible when required by the business process now and in the future»
«The level to which transactions can be traced and audited through a system»

(ISACA 2012)

Control is defined by ISO 27002 as

«means of managing risk, including policies, procedures, guidelines, practices or organizational structures, which can be of administrative, technical, management, or legal nature. NOTE Control is also used as a synonym for safeguard or countermeasure.»

(ISO/IEC 2007)

Derived from these statements, we define the UnderControl (I3) pattern as follows:

«UnderControl (I3) is to ensure that loss in confidentiality, integrity, availability and auditability are prevented, detected, contained and resolved during all phases of the information life cycle and of the ICT systems that are used in order to create, modify, process, store, archive and delete this information by defining and implementing the necessary controls.»

It has the following capabilities:

- Logging events on network, operating system, database, and application level.
- Storing and analyzing these logs centrally.
- Ensuring the integrity of systems.
- Detecting and alerting security incidents.
- Vulnerability management.
- Preserving the defined segmentation of the network.

We intentionally focus the capabilities of this pattern on three core services:

- Detection of intrusions by means of Log File Analysis, Host, and network-based intrusion detection (NIDS).
- Reducing the attack surface by an active Vulnerability Management.
- Controling and channeling network flows.

There are different fields that are in the vicinity of UnderControl (I3) but are not treated within this pattern, as the ties to processes outside of this pattern are stronger than those within this pattern. One such process is monitoring and measuring the availability of systems or applications. Although it treats one of the security goals (availability) and could be performed within this pattern, in most organizations the availability management is not done by the security operation/ management but rather by service management. Therefore, we do not cover it within the pattern but advise that it must be done and should always be done in an end-to-end way monitoring the availability as the end-user perceives it.

The condensed information generated in the UnderControl (I3) pattern serves as an important input to Risk Management. We do not consider Risk Management as part of this pattern as it covers many more topics and goes far beyond information technology.

9.3.2 Example

After having visited an ethical hacking course and having seen how easy it can be to gain access to systems, the CEO of TheWineBottle decides to strengthen security. Accepting the fact that attacks cannot be completely rendered unsuccessful and in order to keep the systems user friendly, focus should be laid upon the detection and containment of security incidents.

9.3.3 Context

The underlying concept of UnderControl (I3) can be applied to any organization. The actual implementation and the associated costs may vary depending on the size and business of the enterprise.

The main actor is the person who has been charged with the detection and handling of anomalies. Anomalies can have a natural cause that does not have any relation to an actual attack or technical disruption: That is when we are talking about false positives. Improving the differentiation between false positives and actual attacks is one of the main goals of UnderControl (I3), as well as generally increasing the rate of detection and the reduction of damage. Normally, the main actors are a team of *Security Operators* and one or more *Security Managers* who are responsible for decision making and the *Firewall Administrators*.

9.3.4 Problem

With ICT becoming one of the critical factors for successful business process implementation, the exposition to attacks has increased simultaneously in the past few years. The main threats do not come from individuals any more but from criminal organizations, hacktivists, and from secret services.

The following story is – unfortunately – very realistic as many security projects are only started after some serious security incident has happened.

After a serious data leakage, which exposed several hundred customer files
to the Internet, TheWineBottle's management decides to take action. An
external auditor analyzes the situation and proposes to strengthen the
detection of security incidents as well as the auditability of all actions. In
order to reach these goals, he proposes centralizing the log management and
implementing an integrity checking system for every critical server as well
as investing in security personnel and develop and live the necessary processes for detection and reaction. Concerning the networking structure he
has some proposals to streamline and improve connections between the
different zones as well as restricting access to the critical systems.

Organization's View

Any enterprise doing business on the Internet can fall victim to an attack, be it
specifically targeted against the enterprise in order go gain information or be it just
coincidentally by mass attacks. Advanced persistent threats (APT) have hit large
enterprises, governments, nongovernmental organizations (NGO), as well as small
enterprises. This kind of threat is the most dangerous as the motivation is mostly to
steal information, motivated by classic or by industrial espionage. The attacker has
all the resources he needs for a successful attack (that is why it is called advanced)
and he wants to remain undetected in the internal network for as long as possible
(that is why it is called persistent).

In order to avoid attacks, threat mitigation must be done. One important part is
to reduce the attack surface in such a way that an attacker has fewer options of
where and what to attack and to increase chances of detection. One important part
is to manage the vulnerabilities in an ICT infrastructure. As software still is a
quickly changing field of technology, there are always vulnerabilities that need to
be patched. In order to have an overview of all unpatched or misconfigured systems, a central Vulnerability Management System is most helpful.

Even with all precautions taken, successful attacks are going to happen. In order
to detect them and mitigate the effect, it is important that security incidents are
detected, reported, tracked, and actively managed. Registering events that deviate
from a baseline is considered a normal form of the basis of any detection strategy.
Analyzing log files and deploying host-based and NIDS systems as well as software that ensures the integrity of systems are of great help to quickly detect any
security breach. The mitigation of the effect can also be supported in a passive way
by a suitable networking infrastructure with zones that reduce the impact of a
successful attack.

Enterprise Architect's View

Although security often is not the primary concern of the typical Enterprise
Architect he can be one of the most important drivers. As it is most beneficial to an

enterprise to solve security concerns in a holistic and comprehensive way, the Enterprise Architect is most interested in building a reusable infrastructure that solves the problems of managing vulnerabilities, detecting security incidents, and ensuring traceability and auditability. Therefore, he must ensure that protocols to be used for logging, processes, and responsibilities are defined. Designing network zones and placing systems correctly is a task that is well known to Enterprise Architects. In order to implement security from the beginning of a new application and to avoid problems later on, this task should be taken with great care and included in any project work as well as in an ongoing governance task. If the network is clearly structured and policies exist, this is much easier to achieve other than the necessary analysis to be done again and again for every new system or application. When trying to increase security capabilities of the organization, the Enterprise Architect must talk with many stakeholders to gain consensus of the action plan. He must show to the management that the money spent on security is well invested and he must take seriously privacy concerns and try to solve any privacy issues by clearly defined policies and active information of all employees.

End-user's View
End-users do not want to be bothered by security – be it a security measure that reduces the end-user experience – or a security breach endangering the end-user's privacy. The problem that UnderControl (I3) faces is to implement reasonable security without the end-user noticing it.

Although it is impossible to completely avoid attacks and it is never easy to detect them, UnderControl (I3) raises the bar for a successful attack and enables the enterprise to deal with all lower rated attacks on a routine basis without needing to trigger an alarm bell too often. The pattern follows the approach of focusing on the processes and the data to be analyzed and is compatible with any of the – often very different – solutions available on the market.

9.3.5 Solution

Vision

> The ICT infrastructure of TheWineBottle is constantly monitored. Any anomaly is detected, analyzed, and leads to a reaction by the operation team. The analysis of all log files is done at a central facility that allows correlation between individual events. The availability is monitored on an end-to-end basis, exactly as the customer experiences it.

Principles

---

1. *Principle*   *It is all about risks*

Statement   The organization is aware of information security risks and manages these actively

Reasoning   Information risks are ubiquitous and cannot be avoided in their entirety if the business wants to realize new opportunities. The risk appetite may differ between organization and business sectors

Consequences   Information risks must be analyzed, managed, communicated, and continuously monitored. UnderControl (I3) provides comprehensive risk reports to the enterprise-wide risk management

2. *Principle*   *Log files are the gold mines of security*

Statement   Log files must be stored centrally and analyzed on a regular basis

Reasoning   Most if not all attacks leave traces in log files (if the systems are configured to log events). By analyzing events and comparing them to an expected behavior, it is possible to detect an attack thus reducing its impact

Consequences   All systems, databases, and application must provide their log information via a standardized interface to a central facility. The log files must be protected in their confidentiality and integrity. Experienced administrators must check the log files on a regular basis for malfunctioning, anomalies, and other traces of attacks or deviations from normal operation

3. *Principle*   *Detection must be done in a multi-layered way*

Statement   Detection must involve all levels, from the network to the operating systems, to the applications, and also the employees who must be security aware

Reasoning   It cannot be said on which level traces of a particular attack can be seen. By observing all layers, chances for a detection and defence are greatly enhanced

Consequences   All devices and applications must transfer their log files to a central system. It is absolutely crucial that all systems at all layers have exactly the same time to be able to trace an attack. A mandatory training on a regular basis raises the awareness and empowers the employees to detect anomalies in their daily work

4. *Principle*   *Integrity of systems is crucial*

Statement   It must be possible to prove the integrity of a system at any time

Reasoning   After having discovered traces of attacks, the extent of the attack must be quickly and reliably assessed

Consequences   All systems must have an integrity checking mechanism that reports any alteration of system files to a central console where the history of all changes is stored

5. *Principle*   *Clearly defined communication patterns lead to security*

Statement   All network traffic must follow a defined path between different networking zones

Reasoning   Anomalies at the network level can only be detected if the complexity is not too big. A well-structured network leads to a better security and to lower costs caused by outages. In case of a security breach, the impact can be minimized

Consequences   The network must be divided into different zones with assigned communication protocols that interconnect the zones where necessary

---

Holistic View

As Fig. 9.21 shows, UnderControl (I3) is rather complicated but the following main parts can be distinguished:

- Intrusion Detection, Log File Analysis
- Vulnerability Management
- Firewall Management

The first area is a typical domain of a Computer Emergency Response Team (CERT) that acts in the domain of operational security.

Intrusion detection is defined as

«Intrusion Detection System or IDS is software, hardware, or combination of both used to detect intruder activity» (Rehman 2003).

Vulnerability Management can be seen as a part of security operations as well. Contrary to the Intrusion Detection and Log File Analysis, which are detective controls, Vulnerability Management has a strong preventative component. Vulnerability Management consists of three areas: Vulnerability Discovery, Vulnerability Analysis, and Vulnerability Remediation. (Buecker et al. 2011). The proposed Vulnerability Management covers all these areas, as the discovery is done by scanning, whereas the analysis and remediation rely on correct operation of the appropriate business processes that are backed by the Vulnerability Management application.

Although firewalling is often seen as a dedicated field done within networking divisions, we count it to this pattern as it provides help in keeping the network traffic «under control» which is an absolute necessity to be able to detect attacks at the network level. A firewall in the context of this book should be considered as a concept and not just as a filtering device on OSI layer 3. Depending on the protocol to be filtered, securing of the communication should go up to layer 7 (e.g., Web Application Firewalls, Proxy Servers). Basically, a Firewall is a Policy Enforcement Point:

«a firewall is a device that enforces an access control policy between two or more security domains» (Hucaby et al. 2012).

The main actor of *Intrusion Detection* and *Log File Analysis* is the security operator responsible for detecting security breaches and the security manager whose responsibility is to manage security incidents and to keep an eye on the attack surface of an enterprise measured by vulnerabilities. Another actor is the sender of log files. Normally this is a service of a device, an operating system, or an application that delivers the log information to a central instance. However, the normal user may play an important part as well, as sometimes it is he who witnesses an anomaly and alerts the security team. In order to make any reporting as easy as possible, it is recommended to provide a reporting form on an internal webpage and to train users on how to detect anomalies and how to report these. On the application level of the *Intrusion Detection* and *Log File Analysis* four applications exist, namely:

- the *Log Management*,
- the *Intrusion Detection*,
- the *Log Service*, and
- the *Vulnerability Management System* that serves to reduce the attack surface and often is an important part of compliance measurement. Its main actor is the security manager who observes the security lifecycle of the systems and insists in reducing vulnerabilities by patching systems, databases, and applications.

Another important actor, especially for the *Log Management*, is the administrator of a system who can use the *Log Management* for error analysis and performance improvement.

Manage Firewall is the visible process and application originating from the network zonation. Firewall rules need to be created, managed, and audited. In the case of a security breach, additional rules may help to contain the damage within one zone.

On the application layer the main components are clearly visible, namely the *Log Management*, the *Intrusion Detection*, the *Vulnerability Management*, the *Reporting Interface* for security incidents and the firewall rule set being managed. In the middle, an interesting part is the *Log Service* that marks the interface to every other pattern or more precisely to any system, service, database, or application that writes log files, which subsequently are transported to UnderControl (I3).

The technical layer is complicated and features many components. Figure 9.21 shows that the *Log System* lies in the heart of the technical layer and offers interfaces to most of the other components. The *Log System* is where the log files are transported, stored, normalized, and indexed for analysis. The *Log System* is really the heart of this pattern as it solves the problem of collecting all information from all other patterns and enabling the organization to extract the information needed. The different components for the security operations such as the *host-based intrusion detection* (*HIDS*), the NIDS, the *Log Correlation Engine,* and the *Vulnerability Management System* are integrated in a portal-like application called *Security Management System*. The Security Management System should feature a role-based access model to provide only the information to the different actors that they really need. The HIDS can differ strongly depending on the vendor but it should be ensured that a reliable *Integrity Checker* is in place as this enables to prove that a system has not been affected by an attack. The *Log Correlation Engine* is an important element, as by correlating different events from different systems, attacks can be detected that would have otherwise not been seen. The *Vulnerability Management System* and its associated *Scanning Probes* form the

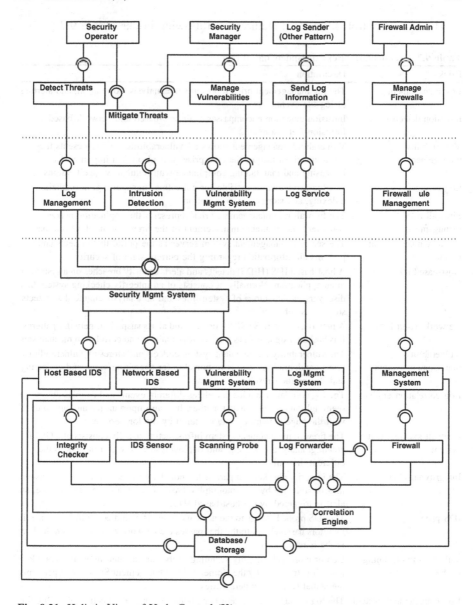

Fig. 9.21 Holistic View of UnderControl (I3)

technical environment needed for actively scanning for vulnerable systems and tracking these vulnerabilities. Firewall administration can be quite complex on a technical level and strongly depends on the size and technology used. One basic similarity between all solutions is that up from a certain number of firewall rules are kept separately in a *Management System* and deployed to the firewalls.

The UnderControl (I3) pattern features the following bricks (Table 9.7):

Table 9.7 Architecture bricks of UnderControl (I3)

Brick	Description
Log management	The log management brick represents the analysis, correlation, and alerting of log file events
Intrusion detection	Intrusion detection encompasses both host-based and network-based Intrusion Detection
Vulnerability management	Vulnerability management shows all vulnerabilities and represents the actual attack surface of the enterprise. It is also often important for increasing and maintaining compliance with regulatory specifications
Log service	The log service is responsible for collecting, transporting, normalizing, indexing, and storing log information
Firewall rule management	The firewall rule management brick represents the application needed for a consistent and auditable management of the firewalls and their rule base
Security management portal	The security management system serves as the portal that collects and presents all information regarding the current state of security
Host-based IDS	A host-based IDS (HIDS) detects and alerts security breaches on a system or in an application. Normally, it consists of an integrity checking system that discovers modifications of system files and an analysis engine that detects suspicious behavior
Network-based IDS	A network-based IDS (NIDS) detects and alerts suspicious network patterns. It is based on signatures as well as flow analysis and correlation mechanisms
Vulnerability management system	The vulnerability management system collects and stores all vulnerabilities, scans configurations, and is responsible for triggering scans and collecting and storing their results
Log correlation engine	The log correlation engine correlates different events and couples otherwise seemingly unrelated events together. It is an important technology to deal with the huge amount of data gathered by the log service
Firewall management system	The firewall management system infrastructure usually consists of a GUI for creating, analyzing, storing, and deploying the firewall rule sets to the different firewalls
Integrity checker	The integrity checker is a part of the host-based IDS and secures all system files on a device by a cryptographic hash. If an attacker modifies a file, an alert is triggered by the host-based IDS
IDS probe	The IDS probe belongs to the network-based IDS and is a sniffing device. It monitors passively all traffic that passes the network zone for which the IDS Probe is responsible
Vulnerability scanning Probe	One or more vulnerability scanning probes are located in every network zone. It is triggered by the Vulnerability Management System and performs the actual scan for vulnerabilities
Log management system	The log management system is responsible for the collection of all log file information from the various systems, services, and applications. It offers different interfaces for standardized protocols such as syslog. It not only collects log data but also normalizes and indexes it
Log forwarder	The log forwarders collect log information in different network zones and forward it to the log management server
Firewall	The firewall is the device that divides the different network zones with different security requirements and guards these junction points
Database/storage	There is a lot of information that needs to be stored. This is done in one single database or in flat files on a data store depending on the technology chosen

Business View

The business view shows that there exist many different business processes. This clearly reflects the fact that security cannot be achieved on a purely technical level and that every solution that neglects the process level is destined to fail. However, if the necessary business processes are clearly defined and continuously improved, an organization has a good chance to ward off many attacks that would have otherwise been successful. Even if an attack has been successful, the implementation of efficient detection and reaction mechanisms at the business level helps to reduce the potential damage in terms of cost and reputation loss. Reputation loss is also a big concern in the case of availability issues, but many cases can be eased if a customer or user has a simple possibility to report a problem with an application and if he quickly gets a reaction (and of course the problem is solved fast).

Figure 9.22 shows the most important business process of UnderControl (I3) with its main actor, the *Security Operator*. The goal of the process is to detect attacks and to mitigate the occurring threats. It follows the often-cited reaction process, which is a core competency of any Computer Emergency Response Team. The first field of action is to detect the attack as early as possible and to do a triage to allocate resources to the most critical findings. The second process group deals with the reaction to the attack. The reaction consists of enforcing countermeasures and – if deemed necessary – do a forensic analysis. The reaction process must continue until the success of the countermeasures can be confirmed. One important point is to do a *Lessons Learned* follow-up as this leads to a continuous improvement of the process and the technical environment and helps avoiding attacks in the future or reducing their impact. All findings by Security Incident Response should be considered as input *to Risk Management* as it may have an impact on the risk landscape of an organization and helps in calibrating the risk analysis and management process.

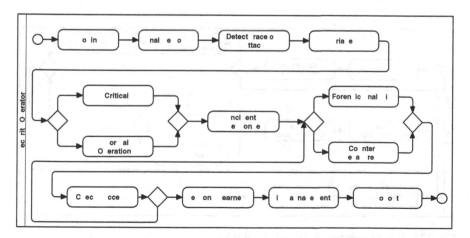

Fig. 9.22 Security operator detecting attacks

The second business process shows how the *Security Manager* reduces the attack surface by managing vulnerabilities (Fig. 9.23).

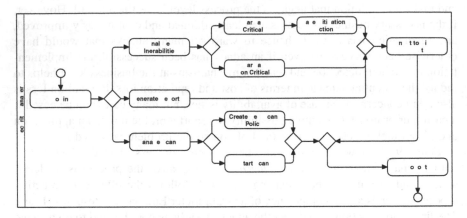

Fig. 9.23 Security manager doing vulnerability management

There are two paths the *Security Manager* can follow. After the mandatory *Login*, he chooses to analyze current vulnerabilities. The results of analyzing vulnerabilities, especially if these happen to be of critical nature, are an important input to the Risk Management of an organization. The second path shows how vulnerabilities are found. The vulnerability-scanning infrastructure needs to be configured and the appropriate scan must be defined and started. The scan produces results in the form of vulnerabilities, which are analyzed within the first path.

The third process shown in Fig. 9.24 is also within the responsibility of the *Security Manager* and shows how firewall rules are checked for compliance and risk.

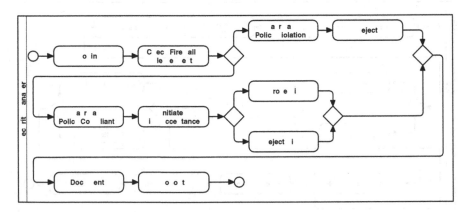

Fig. 9.24 Security manager checking firewall rules

If a rule is noncompliant or if the risk is unacceptable, the rule change is rejected. Checking rules for compliance is important to keep the networking zones stable and to avoid any mixing of systems that do not belong in the same zone due to their role or due to security requirements. It must be ensured that rules are re-controlled regularly to find obsolete rules. Any change to the firewall rule set and the approval or rejection of it must be documented in a way that is auditable. It is important to note that the firewall rules are not yet implemented at this moment but are merely requests.

Figure 9.25 shows that after a firewall rule has been approved it needs to be implemented. This can be done by creating a new firewall rule or by modifying an existing rule. In order to have a segregation of duties, another person preferably in another organizational unit should do this. Normally, this actor is the *Firewall Administrator*. The process is quite straightforward but just as with the approval process, documentation is a key issue here. Firewall rules should be tested exhaustively before documenting them and finishing the process by logging out of the firewall management system.

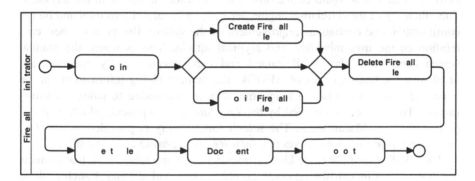

Fig. 9.25 Administration of firewalls

No human actors drive the business process in Fig. 9.26, but systems such as applications, services, and databases that deliver log information to the Under-Control (I3) pattern. In fact, every pattern that implements UnderControl (I3) has

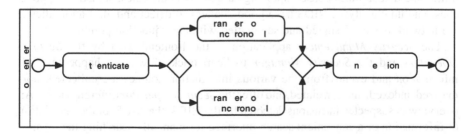

Fig. 9.26 Log transfer

different actors that send log information. In order to keep confidentiality, integrity, and authenticity of log file information confidential, an authentication process of the sending entity is necessary. There are two main methods of how log information is transferred; logs can be transferred synchronously or asynchronously.

In conclusion it can be said that there exist many important business processes that are crucial for maintaining an adequate level of security in terms of confidentiality, integrity and availability.

Data and Application View

Figure 9.27 represents the Data and Application View of the detection part of UnderControl (I3). The detection of attacks and anomalies rests on three pillars, the *host-based IDS*, the *Log Management*, and the *network-based IDS*.

Detection would not be effective if these three applications were separated, as they are only to reveal one isolated view on what is happening. But if they are interconnected and the results are correlated, chances are that an attacker can be detected before damage has been done. A correlation engine offers the service to do the correlation and to help the Security Operator to find the relevant log file entries. Otherwise it would be the oft-cited search for the needle in the haystack. The efficiency of the correlation engine depends on the algorithms used and on the configuration and continuous improvement of the system. But even the best correlation engine may miss new and atypical attacks. This is where the manual search comes into play. Well trained and experienced security operators are invaluable for finding traces of APT. As the amount of log information can be huge and searches can take a long time, it is recommended to index the information. This service is provided by the *Log Indexer* component, which is also a part of the Log Management. The search functionality is provided by the *Log Management* and is accessed via the *Security Management* component.

The HIDS should use some kind of integrity checking mechanism that protects the system files by calculating cryptographic hashes and alerting if such a file is modified or if a new file is added. The service *Monitor Integrity* enables the monitoring of the system files, whereas the service *Detect Intrusion* alerts if unauthorized modifications have been detected. Using such a system is the best way to have an auditable proof that no system has been compromised. Even in the case of a security breach the integrity checker allows a quick diagnosis of what has happened.

The NIDS must be distributed over the whole network with sensors that sniff the traffic and detect attacks based upon signatures, dynamic rules, statistical approaches, and flow analysis. NIDS have good chances to detect and alert anomalies if the network is well designed and segmented with clear junction points.

The *Security Management* application is the frontend used by the *Security Operators* and the *Security Manager* to keep track of what is happening. All information and events from the various information sources are collected, normalized, indexed, and correlated, and offer the *Security Operator* different views: An overview of suspected intrusions detected by the HIDS, the NIDS, or the correlation of information or a convenient search interface for manually searching the logs.

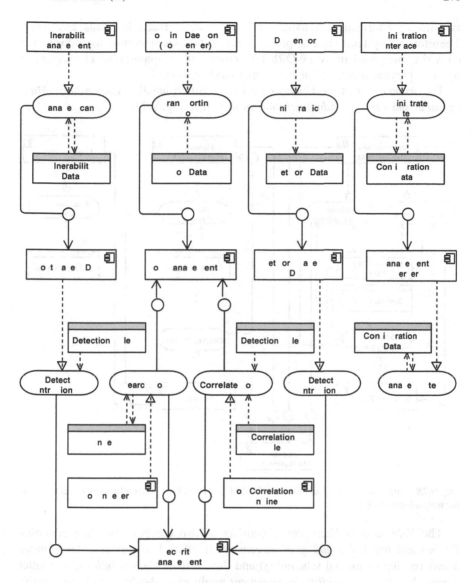

Fig. 9.27 Data and application view of UnderControl (I3) - detection

The data objects used are basically the log information that is collected, transported, and stored. This information makes the biggest part of all data and its enormous amount, and makes the storage and processing a challenging task. The other data objects are the index of the log data, detection rules both of the HIDS and NIDS, *Correlation Rules*, and *Configuration Data* of the systems involved. The protection of the confidentiality, integrity, and authenticity as well as the availability of the data and the systems is crucial. If an attacker can modify systems or information, UnderControl (I3) cannot reach its goals any more. Therefore, all systems must be protected and it is advised to store log information on write once read many (WORM) together with cryptographic checksums in order to prevent accidental or intentional modification.

The second part of the UnderControl (I3) pattern handles *Vulnerability Management* and *Firewall Administration* as shown in Fig. 9.28.

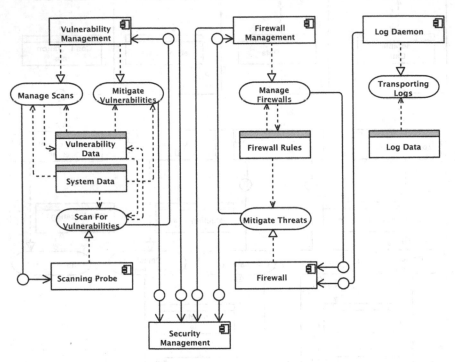

Fig. 9.28 Data and application view of UnderControl (I3)—vulnerability management and firewall administration

The *Vulnerability Management* consists of two components – the *Scanning Probes* and the *Vulnerability Management*. It offers two services, the *Manage Scans* (configuration and scheduling) and the *Mitigate Vulnerabilities*. The latter means that the *Vulnerability Management* application should be able to identify vulnerable systems and to send a ticket to the responsible administrators with all relevant information about the mitigation procedure (patching or configuration change). Ideally, this is integrated into an existing ticketing application.

The *Firewall Management* consists of three components with their associated services. The goal of the whole application is to protect the network internally and externally and to provide a channeling of the different communication streams. A centralized firewall management is strongly recommended to keep the different rules of the different firewalls consistent. The functionality of a *Firewall Management* application is not limited to the administration and the deployment of the rule sets but can be enriched by functions that provide a validation of new rules in terms of security and performance. An interesting feature would be a firewall simulator capable of answering questions such as «which system is accessible on which port if the attacker gained a foothold in another networking zone». The firewall itself mitigates threats by blocking access attempts that violate the policy as well as reporting these attempts to the log daemon that transports the information to the *Log Management* described in Fig. 9.27.

Basically, there exist three data objects that are important to this part of the Data and Application view. *Vulnerability Data* consist of a description of vulnerabilities, which are mapped to the System Data that basically is an inventory of all systems to be scanned for vulnerabilities. Ideally, the configuration management database (CMDB) in which all Configuration Items are stored feeds this Data Object with the necessary attributes such as system name, IP address, system owner, and so on.

The Data and Application view of UnderControl (I3) reflects the detective and the preventive parts of information security. It provides three core services, the *Intrusion Detection*, the *Vulnerability Management*, and the *Firewall Management*. There are just a few types of data objects but the amount of data to be processed is huge and requires processing power as well as storage capability.

Technology View

The Technology View introduces a new networking zone within the internal zone. It is called *Secure Management* (*Secure Mgmt.*) as it harbors all systems that store and analyze data produced by UnderControl (I3), and thus are needed for the management of these security devices. Each production networking zone known from the other patterns has at least the following components that serve as information source or relaying system:

- Log Forwarder.
- NIDS.
- Server systems equipped with HIDS.
- Vulnerability Scanning Probes.
- Firewalls that do the segmentation between the different networking zones.

Just as in the Data and Application view, we divided the infrastructure into two pictures: Fig. 9.29 shows the infrastructure needed for the *Log Management* and *Intrusion Detection*, Fig. 9.30 displays the *Vulnerability* and *Firewall Management*. Both share the same concept that the relevant systems are placed within a specially secured networking zone, whereas the information gathering systems reside as close as possible to the information sources.

The *Security Management Portal* acts as the entry point for the *Security Operator* and the *Security Manager*. They access the portal by the use of HTTPS, preferably authenticated by two factors. They can use typical functions such as dashboards or graphs that give an oversight of the state of security as well as the specialized functions such as searching the logs, analyzing alerts, deciding upon actions, and reconfiguring detection rules. The Security Management Portal

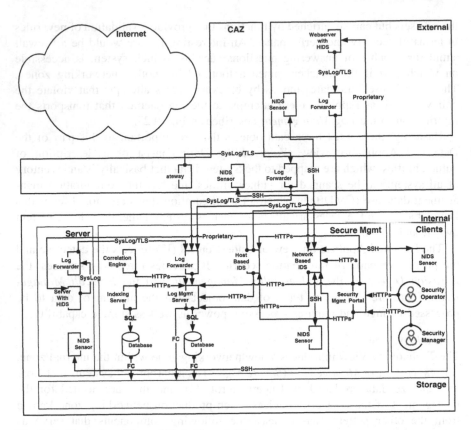

Fig. 9.29 Technology View of UnderControl (I3)–log management

interconnects by the use of HTTPS with the three main elements of *Intrusion Detection*, the HIDS, the NIDS, and the *Log File Management System*. Sometimes this system is also called security incident and event management system (SIEM).

The *Log Management System* stores all log information. Depending on the technology chosen this is done by the use of a database or in a file system. It provides web service interfaces to the *Correlation Engine* and to the *Indexing Service*. These two are sometimes integrated into the *Log Management System*. The *Log Management System* gets all information by the syslog protocol, secured with transport layer security (TLS). Each networking zone has a *Log Forwarder* that acts as a local collection and relaying system. The *Log Forwarder* can have storage capabilities itself, so it can act as a store and forward system, caching information when the central log management system becomes unavailable. It is important to note that all transfers of log information should take place on its own networking segment as otherwise the production network would have much additional load. In the case of a distributed denial of service (DDOS) attack, the logging could even lead to a total outage as systems sending much more information than normal on an already saturated network. This is why this information should always be sent over a dedicated network segment.

The NIDS is distributed over the whole network with sensors residing in every network segment. The sensors sniff all traffic passing by and alert if a packet matches to an attack pattern or if certain thresholds are exceeded. The sensors communicate with the central IDS console using SSH as the protocol. The NIDS server in the Secure Zone contains the detection rules and performs anomaly calculations using statistical and flow-measuring techniques. New rules are pushed to the different sensors using SSH.

The HIDS System is installed on every server (and if feasible on the clients as well). Limitations in the deployment may occur when appliances are used that do not allow the installation of custom software. Apart from that it is strongly advised to protect all systems by an intrusion detection system. The basic function is to provide cryptographic hash values calculated over all system files. These hash values are stored within the central HIDS management system in the *Secure Management* zone. Any modification of a system file leads to another hash value that triggers an alert. Some HIDS offer the analysis of log files as well or the monitoring for suspicious processes or networking sockets.

Figure 9.30 shows the second part of UnderControl (I3) with the *Firewall Management* and the *Vulnerability Management*. Both are distributed over different network zones and resemble in their architecture the detection system.

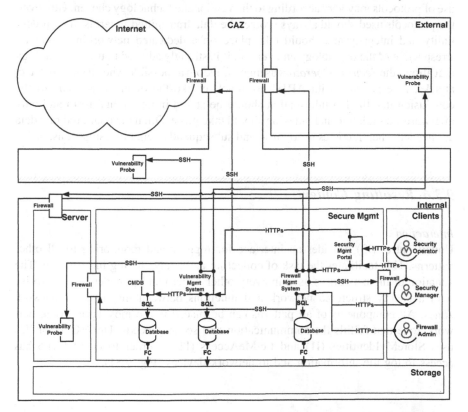

Fig. 9.30 Technology View of UnderControl (I3)—vulnerability and firewall management

The Vulnerability Management stores all known vulnerabilities, together with detection routines and remediation advice. Using an interface to the CMDB allows the mapping of vulnerabilities to systems with their respective owners. If a vulnerability with a serious impact is found, the owner of a system is alerted using a ticket that contains the description for remediation or mitigation of the vulnerability. The *Security Management Portal using HTTPS* accesses the *Vulnerability Management System*. The main actors, the *Security Operator* and the *Security Manager*, use the *Security Management Portal* in order to obtain information about vulnerable systems or to plan and perform scanning tasks. The *Vulnerability Management System* automatically chooses the best suited *Probe* for a scanning task based on the networking topology. It communicates with the *Vulnerability Scanning Probes* using SSH, thus deploying new scanning tasks and retrieving the results.

The firewall environment in an enterprise consists of the *Firewall Management System* and the different firewalls that control and channel the traffic in and out of the different networking zones. Firewall rules are designed, created, modified, deleted, and approved using the *Firewall Management System* from where they are deployed to the appropriate Firewall using SSH.

The UnderControl (I3) features a variety of systems that form an effective base for detecting attacks and mitigating threats. Its actual implementation and especially the use of protocols may vary according to the vendor and technology chosen. However, the protocols used should always protect the data transmitted in terms of confidentiality and integrity and should take place on a dedicated networking segment. Irrespective of the technology and vendor, it is strongly advised to use a technology that allows the *Security Operators* as much freedom as possible when trying to detect attacks, as especially with APTs, no attack is like the other. This leads to the conclusion that the log information should be stored in its original form and only afterwards, correlation and indexing should take place. Often the unaltered raw data are needed when it comes to forensic and subsequently penal investigations.

9.3.6 Resulting Context

Interaction
UnderControl (I3) provides an interface for logging and monitoring to all other patterns. This facilitates the task of collecting and analyzing log information. The zonation of the network is used in every other pattern and provides the enterprise with a clearly structured network and junctions between the different network zones. All components of all patterns can be placed in the most appropriate network zone that fulfills the communication and security needs. UnderControl (I3) uses StoreMyIdentities (I1) and LetMeAccess (I2) in order to decide who has access to log file information and to network devices (Fig. 9.31).

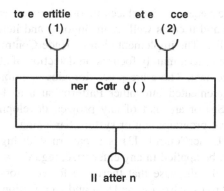

Fig. 9.31 Interaction of UnderControl (I3) with other patterns

The UnderControl (I3) pattern uses the following EAPs:

- StoreMyIdentities (I1) and LetMeAccess (I2): These EAPs are referenced practically in all patterns as the implementation of these central services is of great benefit for the Enterprise Architecture as a whole.

As an Infrastructure Pattern, UnderControl (I3) provides important functionality to other patterns.

- Transporting, storing, and analyzing log information.
- Ensuring auditability.
- Detecting security breaches.
- Structuring the network.

Consequences
Implementing UnderControl (I3) forms the base for the detection and analysis of security breaches as well as for monitoring vulnerabilities. In regard to networking it ensures a clear, coherent, and secure zonation of the network. It helps to accomplish any auditability requirements imposed by regulation and reduce overall risks and costs by security breaches.

It is crucial to understand that an organization only has the chance to reap the benefits of implementing this pattern, when the appropriate business processes are created and continuously improved in their maturity. It is necessary to hire skilled people capable of running the processes, understanding the technology, as well as the psychology of attackers. This leads to the conclusion that the implementation of this pattern needs strong and ongoing management support and careful planning. It should be accompanied by the implementation of an Information Security Management Systems (ISMS) such as ISO 27001 and other frameworks defined.

This ensures that the necessary interfaces to other processes such as Risk Management are defined and used as well as an ongoing and iterative process for the improvement of quality. The implementation of UnderControl (I3) alone does not provide enough security as it mainly focuses on detection of attacks, Vulnerability, and Firewall Management. There are other domains of information security that are either partly implemented into other Patterns such as LetMeAccess (I2) or ForYourEyesOnly (S5) or are part of any project, development, or engineering task such as defensive programming or system hardening.

We believe that UnderControl (I3) is a pattern with high invariance on the business level. It can be applied in any enterprise, regardless of its size or field of business, but it may be the case that there are fewer actors as one actor might incorporate different roles. Also, on the Data and Application View we consider it to have a medium to high invariance, even though the applications may slightly differ depending on the size of the business and on its sourcing strategy. On the technical level, we expect a bigger invariance for the reason of vendor-specific implementations. The philosophy of having distributed sensors but a centralized analysis environment in a separate and secured networking zone, however, remains the same and should always be adhered to.

The complexity of UnderControl (I3) is high and parts of it are rather difficult to implement. The firewall management part is already in place in many organizations as well as some kind of vulnerability management. The challenging task is the implementation of the log management part as it covers many different aspects ranging from the network level up to the application level and from business processes that need to be implemented and trained down to difficult technical configuration and adaption issues. However, if UnderControl (I3) is successfully implemented the reward is in terms of increased security and resilience against attacks and improved compliance with regulatory requirements and reduced damage caused by security breaches. In the time of ever-increasing risks caused by attackers with vast resources and at the same time the high demand for mobility and access to sensitive information from everywhere at any time, the capabilities provided by this pattern may be considered as critical for any organization.

In conclusion, we would like to emphasize how important it is to be aware of the fact that security cannot be achieved without factoring in the employees. If well trained and with a culture of security and risk awareness in their minds they can influence security much stronger than any Firewall or Intrusion Detection System ever could.

9.4 YouHaveMail (I4)

«Strange as it may seem, I still hope for the best, even though the best, like an interesting piece of mail, so rarely arrives, and even when it does it can be lost so easily.»

Lemony Snicket

9.4.1 Introduction

Name and Overview

Name	YouHaveMail
Number	I4
Type of pattern	Infrastructure
Abstract	This pattern describes how E-mail is used for communication within the enterprise and with external parties such as customers and suppliers
Capabilities	Reading E-mails with different clients such as a full-featured E-mail client on a PC, mobile access and synchronization and webmail access
	Managing E-mails, which consists of sorting, searching, archiving, and other tasks
	Sending E-mails internally and externally
Referenced patterns	All patterns
Bricks	Messaging frontend, Messaging backend, Administration interface, Mobile messaging, E-mail client, Webmail, Mail Gateway, Mailbox server, Web frontend server, and Mobile access
Impeding forces	Legacy applications, long grown habits
Supporting forces	Access to E-mails from everywhere, also with mobile devices
	Increased security and resilience against malware and spam
Invariance	High: The pattern can be applied as described
Complexity	Low: The pattern consists of only a few bricks and is not very difficult to implement
Connectivity	High: The pattern is connected to many other patterns
Keywords	E-mail, messaging, and asynchronous communication

Definition

The YouHaveMail (I4) pattern solves the problem of written, asynchronous, and electronic communication. The following definitions describe E-mail and messaging in an enterprise environment:

«The Internet mail system can be easily conceptualized by introducing the key elements. A message is a piece of information that one Internet user wishes to send to another. It may include multiple parts, including binary files, that may be attached to the message»
(Wood 1999).

Another important property of E-mail is the fact that it is asynchronous communication method:

«Electronic mail is an asynchronous messaging technology. The person that you are trying to reach does not have to be available that instant. She will receive your message the next time she checks her mail. This simple fact allows nearly every netizen to send a message to any other at any time»   (Wood 1999).

Technically spoken, E-mail consists of different elements that are grouped together:

«The Internet Mail Model, like the Internet itself, is a collection of standardized components all acting with a common goal. In the case of E-mail, the goal is to provide the framework for carrying electronic messages between one user and another. Each of the end-users may be on very different platforms. Their respective sites may have vast geographic, technological, and social differences. Those differences demand that the framework be at once both robust and flexible. The Internet's E-mail framework consists of agents, E-mail stores, and standards»   (Mullet and Mullet 2000).

As many messaging systems tend to broaden their focus in the direction of unified messaging, we consider this a new Business Pattern (WorkTogether (B1)) and do not include it in the Infrastructure Pattern YouHaveMail (I4). The reason is that business processes should drive WorkTogether (I4) while YouHaveMail (I4) is clearly an Infrastructure Pattern whose objective is to provide a service to other patterns. Derived from these statements, we define the YouHaveMail (I4) as follows:

YouHaveMail (I4) is an Infrastructure Pattern with the aim to enable asynchronous messaging services for all purposes in an enterprise. We do this by following the paradigm of Internet E-mail as it is intended by the according requests for comment (RFCs).

It has the following capabilities:

- Sending E-mails using a central Messaging Backend system.
- Receiving E-mails from internal as well as external users.
- Managing E-mails using folders, filters, searches, and indexing.
- Filtering E-mails based on interfaces provided by LetMeAccess (I2) and UnderControl (I3).
- Accessing E-mails from different devices such as E-mail clients, webmail clients, and mobile devices.

9.4.2 Example

The company, TheWineBottle, wants to update its messaging system in a way that new requirements for access such as from mobile devices can be implemented without a major redesign of the whole infrastructure. The messaging system should be accessible from other applications as well as for users with different E-mail clients.

9.4.3 Context

This pattern can be used universally; it is well suited for any kind of business and size of enterprise.

Basically there are two actors, internal users for whom E-mails are stored and external users who send and receive E-mails from internal users. These parties want to communicate in an asynchronous way without being hassled by spam or malware. E-mail still is one of the most important electronic communication technologies and many business workflows rely heavily on the use of E-mail.

9.4.4 Problem

E-mail is historically grown and has many interdependencies that often are not documented. As a protocol defined in the very first hours of the Internet it lacks many security features that are crucial today. But as an important communication channel, high reliability and well-designed interfaces are fundamental for any enterprise. As many vendors enrich their E-mail solutions in the direction of groupware and/or unified communication solutions, we nevertheless try to lay a focus on the initial idea of how messaging systems have been designed as this makes it possible to draw a vendor-independent pattern with clear and well-designed interfaces.

The following story has been often heard and witnessed in many variations. But all share the same deeper reason – a proven technology has aged and does not live up to the expectations of its users anymore.

> The CEO of TheWineBottle is very fond of his new smartphone. He enjoys the immediate arrival of new E-mails from his private G-Mail Account. Unfortunately he cannot access his business mailbox in that way. He must use a rather uncomfortable web interface, as this is the only way to access his mailbox from the Internet. Using a smartphone makes this really uncomfortable. After having talked to several of his best sales persons who have the same bad feelings toward the aged E-mail system he is convinced that E-mail at TheWineBottle needs renovation.

Organization's View
Despite all the Social Networks E-mail is still one of the most important asynchronous communication channels in any organization. It is not only used for communication between employees and customers but also as an important carrier of notifications and system information. The way E-mail is integrated and the

feature catalog available is often vendor dependent, which can pose problems when trying to implement new applications that need to use E-mail as a communication channel. With the rise of mobile devices, a new interface for accessing E-mails is needed. Users not only want to access their E-mails by a webmail interface but also wish to have new E-mails pushed to their smartphones or tablets.

Enterprise Architect's View

As in many enterprises messaging just works and is enhanced gradually by upgrading versions; this topic does not make it regularly to the Enterprise Architects desk. However, considering the importance of E-mail as an asynchronous communication channel, Enterprise Architects should have the opportunity to reconsider the E-mail infrastructure and to define and enforce well-standardized interfaces and protocols. The main focus of the Enterprise Architect should be therefore laid on how other applications work with YouHaveMail (I4) and how information is stored, searched, and retrieved from messaging systems. This should be done in a modular way, so that later on parts of the system can be changed without affecting the others. Another important point is to improve access to mailboxes so that it does not matter from where and using which device a user connects. Especially interesting is a push function that automatically informs users who are on the road if new mails have arrived. Apart from the definition of interfaces, protocols, and the realization of ubiquitous access, the Enterprise Architect should also keep an eye on long established and often informal workflows, which depend at least partly on E-mail as the main transport channel. It can be challenging to identify and integrate such workflows into the new system. However, it is a great opportunity to make such processes visible and more reliable. Old E-mail systems tend to have poor security, especially in terms of confidentiality and authenticity. As more and more crucial information is passed through this channel, the Enterprise Architect should seize the chance to implement security controls both on the message layer and on the transport layer.

End-user's View

End-users have high expectations to E-mail: it should just work and should be available anytime and everywhere. They wish to use whatever device they have at hand in order to access their E-mails. If an E-mail is sent, the end-user expects it to be delivered immediately. Another important consideration to be made is that E-mail should be as spam-free and malware-free as possible as no one likes to be bothered by these annoyances when communicating with co-workers or customers. If additional security is implemented, end-users are willing to accept it as long as it does not interfere with the workflows they are used to.

9.4.5 Solution

Vision

The messaging solution of TheWineBottle has well-designed interfaces to all applications requesting, sending, and/or receiving E-mails. Any user can access his/her E-mails from anywhere using any device in a secure and user-friendly way.

Principles

1. *Principle*	*Access from anywhere with any kind of device*
Statement	The YouHaveMail (I4) pattern must be accessible from everywhere with any kind of device. Strong emphasis must be laid on mobile use
Reasoning	As E-mail is one of the most important communication channels, users wish to access their E-mails from everywhere using any kind of device that comes in hand
Consequences	The messaging system must provide interfaces that are accessible from everywhere with any kind of device. In order to reach this goal, it is inevitable that multiple interfaces are created and different protocols are supported
2. *Principle*	*Security*
Statement	The YouHaveMail (I4) pattern must be protected against spam, malware, and must ensure integrity and confidentiality
Reasoning	E-mail systems are often attacked in order to gain information. While the spam problem nowadays is mostly contained, the problem of targeted attacks using malware is still prevalent
Consequences	Security is a mandatory requirement. It is advisable to integrate other patterns such as LetMeAccess (I2) and UnderControl (I3) into the YouHaveMail (I4) pattern in order to have a coherent security
3. *Principle*	*Implementation of standards and well-defined interfaces*
Statement	The YouHaveMail (I4) pattern must implement standards such as simple mail transfer protocol (SMTP), Internet message access protocol over SSL/TLS (IMAPS), HTTPS, and TLS correctly. It must provide well-defined interfaces for use by other patterns and applications
Reasoning	The use of well-known, widely used standards will support a better interoperability with the existing systems and forms the base for other patterns to use the YouHaveMail (I4) pattern
Consequences	A strong focus on the use of standardized protocols and well-defined interfaces must be made
4. *Principle*	*Modularity*
Statement	The YouHaveMail (I4) should be built in a modular way in order to be able to exchange modules when new requirements or features appear
Reasoning	In a modular design, new requirements can be easily adopted without changing the whole system and while preserving the existing interfaces
Consequences	The paradigm of Internet E-mail that postulates different protocols and tools for different use cases (such as sending and receiving E-mail) should be adhered to

Holistic View

E-mail uses protocols described in the old days of the Internet and now have become a critical infrastructure. E-mail per se does not guarantee any security or privacy; there is no guarantee of a successful delivery and that a failed delivery gets noticed. This fact must be kept in mind when using E-mail as a communication channel and additional measures should be planned and integrated.

Figure 9.32 shows how the YouHaveMail (I4) pattern is organized. The business layer shows the main actors of the pattern, namely the internal users who can send, receive, and manage E-mails and the external users who just can send E-mails to internal users. In order to emphasize the importance of application interfaces, these are drawn as a separate actor.

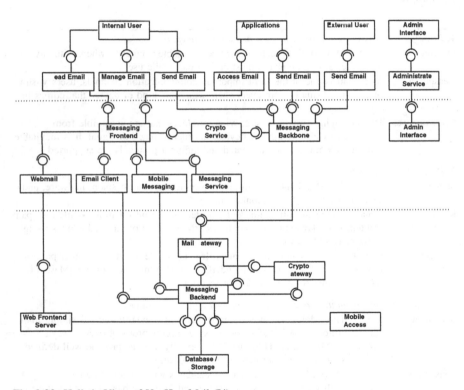

Fig. 9.32 Holistic View of YouHaveMail (I4)

On the application layer there are two main components of the YouHaveMail (I4) pattern, namely the messaging frontend and the messaging backend. The frontend consists of different interfaces for the various access methods such as a normal E-mail client, a web interface, and mobile access as well as an application interface.

At the technical layer, the Holistic View shows only the elements that are absolutely necessary to implement the pattern. First of all, mail traffic should be accepted by a different system than that which stores the E-mail (the Mailbox Server). In order to provide access with different access methods, a web server for the web frontend and a server for mobile access are shown.

To administrate the service, every layer has the necessary elements, such as an interface for administration and the actual administration server. The main actor here is the system administrator.

The YouHaveMail (I4) pattern features the following bricks (Table 9.8):

Table 9.8 Architecture bricks of YouHaveMail (I4)

Brick	Description
Messaging frontend	Is used by the internal users to access their E-mails and combines the following three bricks to the logical frontend
Webmail	Offers a webmail interface in order to access E-mail without a client needed (apart from a browser)
E-mail Client	The E-mail client is the classical method of accessing one's inbox. Usually it is also the method that offers the largest functionality
Mobile messaging	Mobile use of E-mail has different requirements than using an E-mail client or a webmail client. Most notably there is a demand for a push functionality that immediately alerts the user of a new message in his inbox
Messaging service	As E-mail has become a crucial communication channel for many business processes a tight integration in many other patterns and applications is important. Provisioning a service that grants access to applications with a well-defined interface and standardized protocols can do this
Messaging backbone	The messaging backend mainly serves as the transport backbone between the sender and the mailbox server. It may receive E-mails from the outside or deliver E-mails with external destinations to other mail servers on the Internet. As it serves as a gateway between internal and external users it has a security component as well and must be tightly connected to the UnderControl (I3) and LetMeAccess (I2) patterns
Admin interface	The admin interface is the application used to administrate and manage the whole messaging infrastructure
Mail gateway	The mail gateway is responsible for connecting the internal to the external mail systems
Messaging backend	The messaging backend is the mailbox server that stores the users' mailboxes
Web frontend server	The web frontend server presents a web frontend that allows the user to access his E-mails via a web browser
Mobile access	Mobile access is often integrated in the mailbox server. It features the push and synchronization technologies requested by mobile users
Database/storage	How E-mails are stored depends upon the solution chosen. Some vendors use databases, others prefer storing them directly on a file system

Business View

The Business View shows that the main business processes are rather simple, especially writing and sending E-mails by an external user (Fig. 9.33).

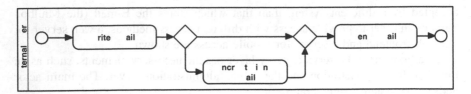

Fig. 9.33 External user sending an E-mail

The second business process describes the actions an internal user may undertake. These are not limited to send E-mails, he can manage and read his E-mails as well as receive E-mail from internal and external users. Managing E-mail may include different tasks such as searching, editing, filing, and archiving. Some of these tasks may be executed in other patterns such as WorkTogether (B1) or InformationChest (S2). It is important to note that all actions need an authentication, meaning a login/logout procedure (Fig. 9.34).

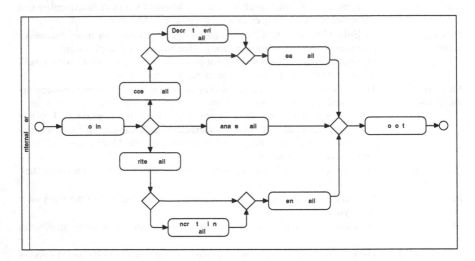

Fig. 9.34 Internal user managing E-mails

As E-mail is an important communication and transport channel in an enterprise; it is also common that applications require access to a mailbox or need to send E-mails (or both). Both cases need an authentication and a session termination. Access to mailboxes must follow a standardized protocol and needs to ensure that no interference with another business process, such as a user managing a mailbox, occurs. E-mail should be signed and encrypted if the information transported needs protection of its integrity, authenticity, and confidentiality. Especially, signing should be done by default to raise the level of protection against different attacks such as malware and phishing attacks (Fig. 9.35).

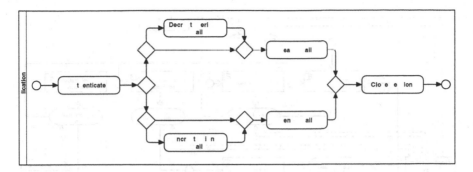

Fig. 9.35 Application using YouHaveMail (I4)

There is a lot of administration work that needs to be done. After a successful authentication, the administrator can choose which component he must manage. Whether an administrator has access to all tasks or just to one depends on the size of the enterprise. When performing very sensitive tasks such as accessing a mailbox of a user adhering to a four-eyes principle avoids privacy issues (Fig. 9.36).

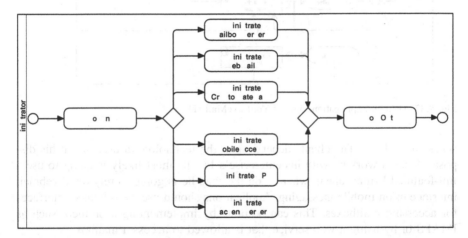

Fig. 9.36 Administration of YouHaveMail (I4)

In conclusion, the business processes are rather simple, but nevertheless E-mail is a crucial communication channel for nearly every enterprise.

Data and Application View
Figure 9.37 shows the Data and Application View of YouHaveMail (I4). Most notably, the *Messaging Frontend*, the *Messaging Backend*, and the *Messaging Backbone* are clearly visible.

Especially the *Messaging Frontend* uses many services, as it is a virtual construct that consists of different elements that allow a user or an application to

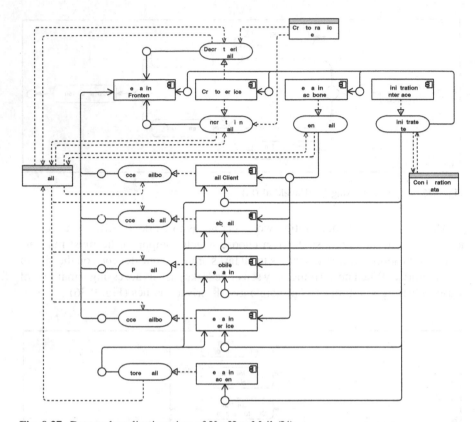

Fig. 9.37 Data and application view of YouHaveMail (I4)

access a mailbox. The clients depend upon the technology a user has at his disposal. If he is working with his enterprise's PC, he most likely is going to use a full-featured E-mail client, whereas on the road he is going to rely on a webmail interface or on mobile messaging. Applications should use well-defined interfaces for accessing mailboxes. This can be done by implementing a protocol such as IMAPS or by using a web service that is allowed to access a mailbox.

The mailboxes are stored within the *Messaging Backend* whose storage service is used by all frontend components. It is important that – to avoid data redundancies – all E-mails are stored within the same system. Speaking of data, the main data object is unsurprisingly the E-mail itself; other data objects include configuration data and cryptographic keys.

Sending E-mails, regardless of whether internally or from/to external parties, should be done using the *Messaging Backbone*. This ensures that all E-mails are scanned against malware and spam and are routed correctly.

E-mails that need to be protected in their integrity, confidentiality and authenticity must pass a cryptographic system. This can either be integrated in the frontend component or a gateway that encrypts and signs E-mails on behalf of the

user and vice versa. The actual implementation depends upon the needs of the
enterprise and the technical conditions.

All these components, services and systems need to be managed. Preferably this
is done from a central administration interface that has access to all systems. This
interface can be a virtual one in the form of a portal or a jump host or an
application of its own.

The application view of YouHaveMail (I4) shows an often-encountered messaging architecture with *Messaging Frontend, Backend* systems, and a *Messaging
Backbone*. The precise form depends on the vendor chosen as well as on the size of
the enterprise.

Technology View
The Technology View in Fig. 9.38 shows that the main infrastructure of
YouHaveMail (I4) is within the internal network. It is advisable to position the
externally reachable mail server in the external networking zone to prevent direct
attacks against the internal zone. Every access must pass the CAZ in order to use

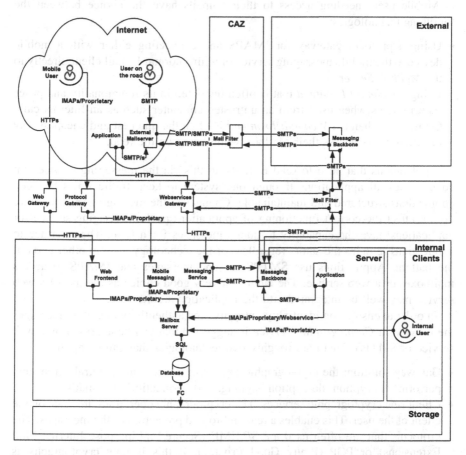

Fig. 9.38 Technology View of YouHaveMail (I4)

any resource of the YouHaveMail (I4) pattern. The *Messaging Backbone* delivers E-mails: This communication passes different stages in the *Messaging Backbone*. The most important stage is the Mail Filter that is part of the LetMeAccess (I2) pattern. The Mail Filter provides malware and spam filtering capabilities.

The *Messaging Backbone* itself is responsible for the mail transport. As internal communication protocol, SMTPS is used, the TLS secured variant of SMTP. When communicating with external parties TLS should be offered as an option, but it is not feasible to enforce it, as too many mail servers would not be able to cope with TLS-based encryption.

The *Mailbox Server* offers IMAPS as the standard protocol to access a user's mailbox. However, depending on the vendor chosen, this may be another protocol such as MAPI (Messaging Application Programming Interface). With the point of view of avoiding data redundancy and to ensure availability of mails throughout the data lifecycle, using a protocol where E-mails remain stored on a server is strongly advised.

Mobile users needing access to their E-mails have the choice between the following technologies:

- Using a protocol gateway for IMAPS and connecting either with a mobile device to the mobile messaging service or with a normal E-mail client directly to the *Mailbox Server*.
- Using a *Webmail Frontend* that is often restricted in its functionality and poses security risks when used from an untrusted computer such as an Internet café. On the other hand, a *Webmail Frontend* is often the quickest and cheapest way of letting users access their Mailbox while being on the road.

Applications that need to send E-mails do this via the messaging service that concentrates all applications through one system to keep traffic flows between applications structured and maintainable. Changes to the messaging infrastructure do not affect the correct functioning of applications as the messaging service for applications have the capability to queue messages for a time. The interface to applications remains the same, regardless of the technology used in other parts of the pattern. Applications use SMTPS to send messages and IMAPS to access mailboxes or a web service. The latter is a very good choice as the use of a web service may well be integrated into the application architecture.

In order to ensure confidentiality, integrity, and authenticity of certain messages the usage of a *Cryptographic Service* is suggested that can be accessed by a web service or SMTPS. There are roughly two technologies that can be applied:

- Gateway solution: the cryptographic treatment is done on a central server that performs encryption, decryption, signing, and verification of E-mails.
- Client side cryptographic services: The cryptographic operations are done on the client of the user. This enables a real end-to-end protection of the messages. The protocols that are often used are S/MIME (Secure/Multipurpose Internet Mail Extensions) or PGP (Pretty Good Privacy). If this is how cryptography is

implemented into the YouHaveMail (I4) pattern, the use of a central crypto-graphic service is not necessary.

When dealing with cryptography, the implementation of a PKI is strongly advised to enable that a secure and traceable issuing of certificates is possible. Whether the enterprise chooses to implement its own PKI or to purchase the service externally depends on the technological and organizational context of the enterprise.

In conclusion, it can be said that the technical solution of this pattern is a rather simple one to implement. The actual implementation in an enterprise might differ based on the vendor chosen or on the size of the enterprise.

9.4.6 Resulting Context

Interaction
As an Infrastructure Pattern, YouHaveMail provides an interface to all other patterns. As shown in Fig. 9.39, the pattern depends on the use of three other Infrastructure Patterns, StoreMyIdentities (I1), LetMeAccess (I2), and Under-Control (I3). The use of the first two Infrastructure Patterns results from the fact that YouHaveMail (I4) must protect access to its data and using StoreMyIdentities (I1) and LetMeAccess (I2) are best suited to fulfill this. LetMeAccess (I2) has also the task of controling inbound messages and initiating Malware and Spam filter-ing. UnderControl (I3) is important for the detection of things that went wrong.

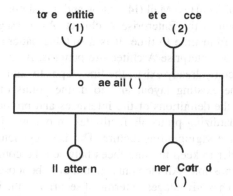

Fig. 9.39 Interaction of YouHaveMail (I4) with other patterns

The YouHaveMail (I4) pattern uses the following EAPs:

- StoreMyIdentities (I1), LetMeAccess (I2) and UnderControl (I3): These EAPs are referenced practically in all patterns as the implementation of these central services is of great benefit for the Enterprise Architecture as a whole.

As an Infrastructure Pattern, YouHaveMail (I4) provides important functionality to other patterns.

- YouHaveMail (I4) provides an interface to send and access E-mails to all other patterns.

Consequences

Implementing YouHaveMail (I4) provides a secure and reliable messaging infrastructure that forms the core of asynchronous communication in most enterprises. The business processes of this pattern are generic and well known in every enterprise. It is very unlikely that the implementation of this pattern generates new business processes, but it can well be that existing business processes and their applications need to be slightly adapted to fit in this pattern. Older applications might use protocols or protocol versions that neither guarantee confidentiality and integrity, nor authenticity on the transport layer. Therefore, it might become necessary to grant an extended time period during which these protocols are still supported.

Another area of concern might be applications that use SMTPS as a data exchange service and access and modify E-mails directly on the file system. Such applications should be carefully analyzed. It might be that using another pattern such as ForYourEyesOnly (S5) might give the greater benefit than an adaption of the application to YouHaveMail (I4).

We believe that YouHaveMail (I4) is a pattern with a high invariance on the business and application levels. It can be applied in any enterprise, regardless of its size or field of business. On the technical level, however, vendor-specific implementations can lead to invariance. These deviations neither change the core of the pattern nor the philosophy behind its shape.

The complexity of YouHaveMail (I4) is low and it is simple to implement, so it can offer a quick win to the Enterprise Architect. As messaging infrastructures must be redesigned from time to time, it is a suitable pattern to gain first experience with the use of Enterprise Architecture patterns. As in most enterprises, a messaging infrastructure already exists; the first step is to compare the blueprint of this pattern with the existing layout and to define points of action. The most important parts are the definitions of the interfaces and protocols used. Defining interfaces and standardizing protocols facilitates an ongoing interaction between the elements of the messaging infrastructure. This is a key element in the structure of the pattern in order to keep the interfaces between the components and to the outside as stable as possible. All elements should only be loosely coupled or even decoupled. This also has advantages in terms of security as the isolation of a single element increases, and thus decreases the impact a security breach on one element might have. Depending on the size of the enterprise and the vendor chosen, it is possible that some elements are concentrated in one system or service, which is not an obstacle to a successful implementation of the pattern.

9.5 TalkToMe (I5)

«Next time I see you, remind me not to talk to you.»

Groucho Marx

9.5.1 Introduction

Name and Overview

Name	TalkToMe
Number	I5
Type of pattern	Infrastructure
Abstract	This pattern describes how synchronous communication is done using Voice over IP (VoIP) or Video Telephony
Capabilities	Communication with internal or external users by voice or video Getting status information of co-workers Looking up phone numbers
Referenced patterns	StoreMyIdentities (I1), LetMeAccess (I2), UnderControl (I3), WorkTogether (B1), and KnowYourCustomer (B3)
Bricks	Brick, VoIP Frontend, VoIP Backend, Plain Old Telephone, Feature Server, Registrar Server, Self-Service Portal, Proxy Server, session border controller (SBC), Gateway, Admin Interface, and Database
Impeding forces	Reliability and availability concerns, need for bandwidth
Supporting forces	Cost reduction, integration of different communication channels
Invariance	Medium: The pattern can be applied as described but it may differ depending on the vendor chosen
Complexity	Low: The pattern consists of only a few bricks and is not very difficult to implement
Connectivity	High: The pattern is connected to many other patterns
Keywords	VoIP, Video Telephony, and synchronous communication

Definition

The TalkToMe (I5) pattern solves the problem of spoken, synchronous communication over the data network of an enterprise. When we speak of synchronous communication we mean conversation that can be defined as follows:

> «Conversations are the basis of human communication. Conversations can be spoken, written, or gestured. Conversations can even be one directional, such as a coach bawling out his star quarterback after an uncharacteristic interception. Conversations may be «one-to-many» (such as a political candidate giving a stump speech) or «many-to-one» (such as a constituency lobbying that candidate after she's in office). Conversations are more than just an analogy for networks – they literally are modern networking.»

(Wallingford 2005)

The following definition describes the terms VoIP (Voice of IP), IP Telephony, and Converged Networks:

«Although VoIP, IP Telephony, and Converged Networks all have slightly different definitions, they often are used interchangeably. In this book, we will do the same. When using any of these terms, we are talking about the structures and processes that result from design and implementation of a common networking infrastructure that accommodates data, voice, and multimedia communications.»

(Chaffin et al. 2006)

When it comes to visual communication, telepresence enters the scene, which denotes the latest development in the field of visual communication. Roebuck defines it as follows:

«A videophone is a telephone with a video screen, and is capable of full duplex (bi-directional) video and audio transmissions for communication between people in real-time. It was the first form of video telephony, later to be followed by videoconferencing, webcams, and finally telepresence.»

(Roebuck 2011)

As many messaging systems tend to broaden their focus in the direction of unified messaging, we consider this a new Business Pattern. Like YouHaveMail (I4) we consider TalkToMe (I5) an Infrastructure Pattern that provides services to other patterns. In case of unified communication, the business process is driven by the need to collaborate, which is described in the WorkTogether (B1) pattern. Following these considerations, we define TalkToMe (I5) as the synchronous way of audible and visual communication between two and more persons. It has the following capabilities:

- Talking to other persons such as co-workers, customers, and suppliers.
- Talking face-to-face using video telephony.
- Organizing and joining voice or video conferences.
- Publishing and reading status information (whether a certain person is online and available).
- Looking up phone numbers in a directory.
- Leaving a message on a voice mailbox if the communication partner is not in his office.

9.5.2 Example

The telephony system of TheWineBottle has grown old and does not provide any possibility of integration into any other application. Many people have begun to use Skype to have telephony and video capabilities built into their laptops and desktops. Based on this experience, the management decides to exchange their plain old telephone service (POTS) for an integrated VoIP and telepresence solution.

9.5.3 Context

An enterprise of any business in any size is able to use this pattern. Differentiations may arise in functionality provided, especially if an enterprise does not need any visual capabilities.

As in any communication-based pattern, at least two actors exist, namely the ones that are involved in the communication. Speaking of conferencing there can be any number of communication partners within one conference as long as system and network resources suffice. The communication partners mainly interact in a synchronous way; only leaving a message on a voice mailbox is asynchronous by nature.

9.5.4 Problem

Telephony has been traditionally a separate domain and uses a different network than any ICT technology. Convergence of networks and services is nothing new and began in the early days of the Internet when data communication used the telephony network as a carrier for transporting data. However, the networks rather complemented each other than really growing together, not only in technical, but as much in a cultural way. It has not been until these days when things really began to converge and more and more enterprises decided to use their data network to transport voice data as well.

It is not in the scope of the pattern to provide a complete solution schema but rather points out areas of interest for the Enterprise Architecture. VoIP implementations most often have very vendor-specific feature sets, but their core components and capabilities are most often very similar.

The following little story about Jane illustrates the problem that can be solved by implementing the TalkToMe(I5) pattern:

> Jane is working as a procurement manager at TheWineBottle. The phone is one of her most often used work items. Sometimes she is a bit annoyed by the POTS. Well, it just works, but that is it. Sometimes it would be more than convenient just to copy/paste a phone number from the list of suppliers instead of dialling it by hand, especially if it is a foreign phone number.

Organization's View

While one reason for the convergence of telephony and information technology certainly is cost savings another reason is the seamless integration into business processes that are more and more ICT dependent. An interrupt in technology may result in business processes not running that smoothly and not meeting expectations. An automatic tracking of telephone calls to a customer in the customer relationship management is only possible if telephony and CRM are connected.

Therefore, it is crucial to consider TalkToMe (I5) not as something isolated but as a basic infrastructure that has the goal to provide valuable services to other patterns and to be tightly integrated into the business processes of an enterprise.

One of the most important concerns about VoIP technology is availability and quality. The POTS uses a circuit-switched network that has a very high quality as two endpoints are directly connected and do not need to share bandwidth with other services. But as VoIP is maturing and providing services that cannot be offered by the old telephone networks, the concerns are decreasing. However, care must be taken in regard to security and quality of service (QoS) when implementing VoIP in an enterprise environment.

Enterprise Architect's View

In these days, any Enterprise Architect may be confronted with questions of VOIP as many enterprises are in the process of implementing VOIP infrastructures. The Enterprise Architect must ensure that the new VOIP infrastructure fits into the big picture providing all the necessary interfaces for other applications such as CRM systems. Although we speak generally of VoIP and video telephony it can be hard for an architect to choose the right subset of protocols for his enterprise. That is why telecommunication engineers must be present and need to address QoS considerations at the earliest time possible. They must ensure as well that the introduction of VOIP does not lower the performance of other applications due to its bandwidth consumption. Availability and preventive controls in case of any service interruption is an often-neglected task when it comes to VOIP implementations. The Enterprise Architect should take care that the implementation is done in a thoughtful and sustainable way by gathering the different stakeholders and accompanying any implementation project closely.

End-user's View

The end-user expects to work VOIP as reliable and qualitatively superior as the classic telephone system did. He is more than willing to use additional functions and services such as voice mailbox or the integration into other applications as long as the reliability of the system and the quality of the calls remain high. One of the key requirements is that he can use the system from various devices such as Smartphones, Tablets, as well as PCs.

9.5.5 Solution

Vision

The new synchronous messaging system of TheWineBottle provides a seamless integration of voice and video communication into any business process that requests it. It is based on defined and widely used standards that provide a high level of assurance in terms of availability and QoS.

Principles

1. *Principle*	*Protection of the reliability and availability of the service*
Statement	The service must be reliable and available to an extent that matches the one from the POTS
Reasoning	Users have high expectation from VoIP in regard to reliability and availability as the POTS did provide these to an extent that is very difficult to achieve in a packet-oriented network without additional measures
Consequences	Ensure these goals by either a segmentation of the network or redundant deployment of core systems
2. *Principle*	*Performance and quality must match the users' expectations*
Statement	TalkToMe (I5) must have a voice quality and general performance that is equal to that of a POTS
Reasoning	Users generally react sensitively to a new technology with an inferior performance and quality. Especially when it comes to the traditional telephone system, call quality has been seldom an issue
Consequences	Quality of Service (QoS) is mandatory to reach quality and performance goals. Additionally, incident and problem management must be in place, especially during the initial phase of the rollout
3. *Principle*	*Value added services*
Statement	Accompanying services such as fax, video telephony, online status of users, voice mail, call redirection and others, should enrich the classic telephony services
Reasoning	Integrating additional services increases the end-user experience as well as the overall productivity
Consequences	The requirements of additional services must be defined at an early project stage in order to choose the best suiting vendor
4. *Principle*	*Integration into business processes*
Statement	TalkToMe (I5) should be integrated into business processes in a way that no interrupts occur
Reasoning	If TalkToMe (I5) is able to integrate such tasks as making a call or arranging a conference into other patterns such as WorkTogether (B1) or KnowYourCustomer (B3), precious information is created and productivity increases
Consequences	TalkToMe (I5) must provide well-defined interfaces to other patterns

Holistic View

TalkToMe (I5) and its core technology VoIP are currently replacing its predecessor, the classic telephone system. Although it retains strong resemblance from the business process view, the underlying technology has completely changed. It uses a data packet-based networking technology as every other application on the Internet instead of a circuit switched. For interaction with the classic telephone system, gateways that interconnect these two worlds are in place. As a quick orientation a short description of the most common protocols is provided.

Session initiation protocol (SIP) has a peer-to-peer architecture as well as a distributed architecture that consist of user agent clients being the endpoints as well as of different server and proxy services. H.323 is a distributed network that consist of terminals, bridging elements, and gateways. Both protocols rely on real-time transport protocol (RTP) for transporting the data. H.248 in contrast is a centralized architecture that concentrates the logic in media gateways that interconnect the end-user devices. Although mobile communication is on the rise we do not cover global system for mobile communications (GSM) or long time evolution (LTE) specifically as they may be considered as another transportation mechanism for voice data and in nearly all cases is brought as a service and seldom impacts Enterprise Architecture by itself. However, it is noteworthy that with VoIP and wireless LAN (WLAN) mobile in-house telephony is easily achievable.

Figure 9.40 shows how the TalkToMe (I5) pattern is organized. The business layer shows the main actors of the pattern: The internal user needs to make phone calls, or establish a video communication channel as well as to organize or join conferences. The external user may or may not be using some kind of VoIP technology. If he does, he has basically the same possibilities as an internal user. This is summarized in Fig. 9.40 as *VoIP Functionality*. However, depending on the technology used, the configuration, and the security policy there may be differences between internal and external users in terms of functionality provided. If he is relying on the classic telephone service, he is limited to make and receive calls.

On the application layer, the most important elements are the VoIP frontend and the VoIP backend. Frontend is to be understood as the device facing the end-user, whereas backend are the systems containing the logic and the data such as systems for managing and switching calls, storing configuration data, and connecting to the outside. The frontend may be any kind of Software or Hardware phone that is capable of understanding any VoIP-based protocol (e.g., SIP or H.323).

At the technical layer, the Holistic View shows elements such as the *VoIP Soft phone* or *Hardware-based phone*; the first being an implementation or a plugin software that runs on any device such as a PC, Tablet, or even a Smartphone, the latter being a more traditional desktop phone. The *Registrar Server* is responsible to discover current hosts and places them in the discovery service that makes the information available to all participants in the VoIP network. The *Feature Server* adds additional functionality to the system such as voicemail, call queuing, call forwarding, conference calls, and so on. In order to connect to the outside and especially to a public switched telephony network (PSTN), Proxies, SBCs, and Gateway Systems are needed.

The main actor for administration is the administrator for the TalkToMe (I5) system. In order to manage the VoIP infrastructure, there exists an administration interface that connects the administrator to the various systems. Very often, the whole infrastructure is provided by one vendor, which results in a rather well-integrated management console for all the components. In Fig. 9.40, the connections on the technical level are not shown in order to keep the figure readable.

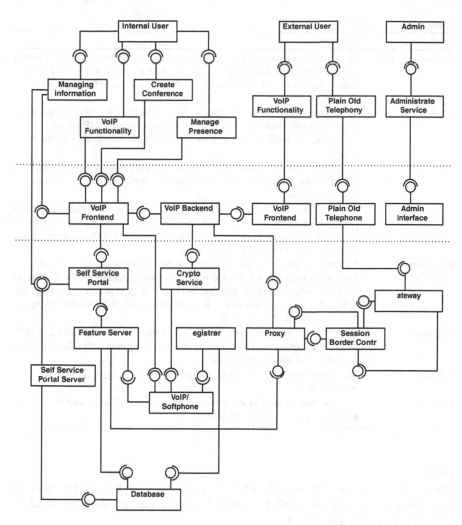

Fig. 9.40 Holistic View of TalkToMe (I5)

The TalkToMe (I5) pattern features the following bricks (Table 9.9):

Table 9.9 Architecture bricks of TalkToMe (I5)

Brick	Description
VoIP frontend	It is used as the interface for the user to the VoIP system and may be a hardware-based VoIP capable phone or a soft phone
VoIP backend	The VoIP backend summarizes the systems that form the foundation of the VoIP infrastructure
Plain old telephone	Many external users, and to a certain extent also internal users, rely on plain old telephones that need to be able to communicate with the VoIP telephones. Connecting the VoIP world to the PSTN world using gateway servers does this

(continued)

Table 9.9 (continued)

Brick	Description
Feature server	The feature server provides the necessary functionality to the VoIP frontend such as call forwarding, call queuing, conference calls, voice mail, and video telephony. Sometimes the feature server is also referenced as a PBX-IP
Registrar server	The registrar server is responsible to store all VoIP endpoints in its database in order to efficiently forward calls to the appropriate VoIP phone. Normally, the VoIP phone initiates this registration right after its boot process
Self-service portal	The self-service portal allows the user to provide additional information not known to the system such as room numbers, preferred contact, or mobile phone numbers
Proxy server	The proxy server acts as an intermediary for incoming and outgoing calls. If one device does not know the address of the device it likes to make a call to the proxy acts as an intermediary. Often the proxy and the session border controller are combined into one device
Session border controller	The session border controller is responsible for the security of the local VoIP infrastructure. It hides the internal network and allows the firewall to have only one inbound destination and one outbound source address for the protocols needed. Additionally, it can interconnect different sites using VoIP and handle QoS aspects
Gateway	The gateway provides connection between the VoIP world and the PSTN world. It is not necessarily placed within the enterprise network; very often it is placed at the VoIP provider
Admin interface	The admin interface is used to administrate and manage the VoIP infrastructure
Database	The database is used to store configuration data, call logs, and other data needed to provide the VoIP services

Business View

The business processes for the TalkToMe (I5) pattern are simple. The first process describes how a user makes a call, by first looking up a number, dialling a number, or joining a conference (Fig. 9.41).

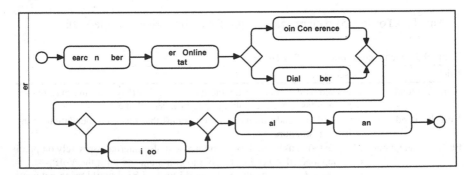

Fig. 9.41 User starting a communication

The second business process describes a user who receives a call. He has the possibility to accept the call immediately to queue it or to refuse it (Fig. 9.42).

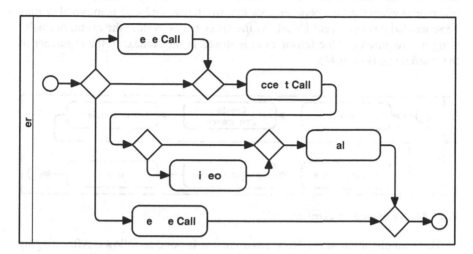

Fig. 9.42 Dealing with incoming calls

Figure 9.43 shows the way a user manages his VoIP environment. Basically, he has the option to manage his voicemail as well as his presence. The latter deals with his online status and with call forwarding. In case he wants to remain unbothered by incoming telephone calls he can forward them directly to his voicemail or if he is out of office he has the option to forward them to his cellular phone or to another co-worker. As these tasks are not done on an interval too frequently and may have an impact on the enterprises security; normally a login process is required beforehand.

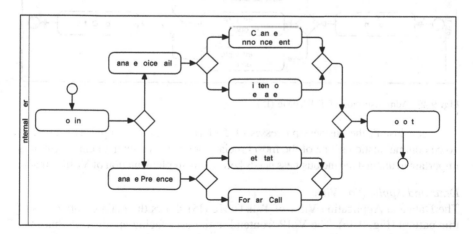

Fig. 9.43 A user managing his VoIP environment

Creating a conference has a few additional steps in comparison to a normal call; the initiator of the conference needs to define the conference schedule, invite the attendees, and finally start the conference. A conference may take place in an ad hoc modus when the time between creation, invitation, and start is minimal or may be scheduled days or weeks ahead. As the latter needs to store the event, normally a login is required and the information is stored in the context of the organizer of the conference (Fig. 9.44).

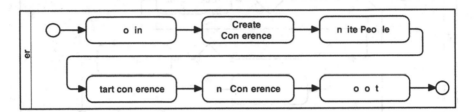

Fig. 9.44 A user creating a conference

The administration of the VoIP environment is done as follows: After logging in, the administrator chooses which device he is going to manage. Figure 9.45 shows the administration of the Proxy Server, the phones, and the server components as different tasks. As the gateway to PSTN networks often is managed by the VoIP provider it is not shown as an administration task. The different server components are aggregated into the task *Administrate Server* and consist of the management of the *Feature Server*, the *Registrar Server*, and optionally other components that form the *VoIP Backend*.

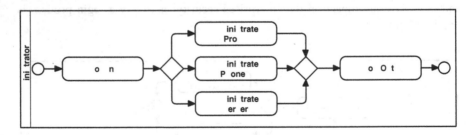

Fig. 9.45 Administration of TalkToMe (I5)

In conclusion, the business processes of TalkToMe (I5) are simple. However, as voice communication is one of the most crucial applications within an enterprise, it is important to understand the business needs before any implementation of VoIP is made.

Data and Application View
The Data and Application View of TalkToMe (I5) shows the main components of this pattern (Fig. 9.46). The VoIP frontend is the user facing application that may be a hardware-based telephone or a software running on a PC, Laptop, Tablet, or

Smartphone. Regardless of its actual technical implementation, it provides core services such as *Video Communication*, *Voice Communication*, and supplemental functions such as *Voicemail*, *Number Lookup*, as well as additional features such as *Presence* and *Conference*.

Most of the data handled by the VoIP frontend is volatile, meaning it is not stored but transferred between the VoIP endpoints (frontends). It may be possible that business requests to record one or more voice or video streams in which case attention to privacy laws is important. Storing calls would be done by the Feature Server or by a third-party server if the vendor does not provide such functionality. If information should be persistent, a transcription service is needed which allows storing, tagging, and searching the information (See also WorkTogether (B1)).

When looking at the VoIP backend system, there are different servers with services provided to the internal functioning of VoIP as well as systems that are responsible for the connection to the outside world. When a new VoIP frontend device boots up, the *Registrar Server* registers it. When the said VoIP device is called by another device, this information is used to find and connect it, which is done by the location service provided by the registrar service or – depending on the implementation – by the *Feature Server*.

The *Feature Server* provides different services such as call relaying, conference relaying, *Voicemail*, and – dependent on the vendor – additional services such as fax. Data that are read and written by the backend systems are *Voicemail Data*, *Conference Data*, phone numbers, *Device IDs*, as well as metadata related to calls such as log files and billing data. As mentioned, normally voice data are not stored, but for the sake of quality control or meeting requirements from law enforcement this may be done by a service provided by the Feature Server.

As discussed in the Holistic View, one problem that may arise by the use of VoIP is that there is no more any automatic matching between user data such as a room number with a telephone directory. In order to keep this functionality and to provide other information, we suggest using a *Self-Service Portal* (see the pattern ResourcesAreScarce (S3)) where the user can provide personal information such as current room number and communication preferences. The portal may also be used as an interface to additional services provided by the *Feature Server*.

The SBC provides protection to the internal VoIP network by hiding its structure and controling traffic flow. It acts as the single entry and exit point for any VoIP connection with the outside world. If there are different locations with their own VoIP network interconnected, *SBCs* are responsible for connecting these different networks together. It can often be seen that the SBC and the *SIP Proxy* are one integrated device. The Proxy Server is responsible to handle connections between the internal VoIP network and the outside world. In order to be able to communicate with the PSTN networks of the POTS, a Gateway Server is needed that provides a service for the call routing between these two network technologies.

To manage the whole VoIP infrastructure an administration interface is provided that reads and writes configuration data. The actual implementation may differ between the various vendors, ranging from simple web interfaces to management and monitoring services with many features. In Fig. 9.46, a *Management*

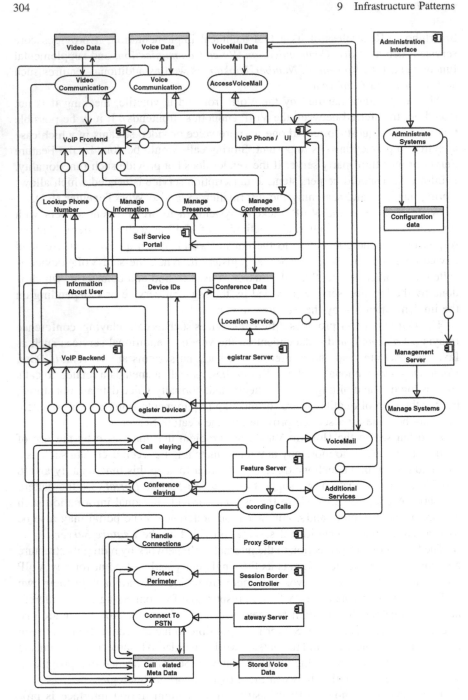

Fig. 9.46 Data and application view of TalkToMe (I5)

Server is shown that combines the different Management Tasks into a single point of entry. The different connections to the components that need to be managed are omitted for better readability.

To summarize, the *Feature Server* is responsible for most of the functionality requested by the users working with the VoIP frontend. In order to be able to communicate with the outside world, a *Proxy Server* and a *Gateway Server* are needed that handle incoming and outgoing connections to other VoIP networks as well as to PSTN networks. It may be said that the application landscape is not too complicated but the migration to such a system can be a challenging task.

Technology View

The Technology View in Fig. 9.47 shows a new network segment that has been introduced by this pattern, the *Telephony Network*. It is strongly recommended to build a network dedicated to the VoIP infrastructure in order to provide the availability and to avoid any disturbance from data streams of other protocols. It does not mean to have a physically separated network; it may well be done using virtual LANs (VLANs) for the VoIP devices.

A large portion of the communication normally takes place between internal users speaking on the *VoIP phone* together. The phone may be a hardware device or a soft phone installed on a PC, laptop, or Smartphone. When such a phone is booted, it registers itself at the *Registrar Server*. This is done using the SIP protocol in its secure version (SIPS) where an additional layer of security is introduced by TLS. When a user calls another user this information is needed to find the other VoIP endpoint (the *VoIP phone* of the requested communication partner). The mapping between device/IP address is stored in the registrar's location service.

The initiation of a session is normally done using SIP; transferring the actual data is done by the RTP. However, alternatives exist and should be considered as well, e.g., H.323 proposed by the ITU (International Telecommunication Union). We strongly recommend protecting voice protocols in their confidentiality, as users tend to trust the telephone infrastructure absolutely and use it to talk about sensitive issues. This is the reason that we always refer to the secured versions of these protocols such as SIPS (SIP over TLS) and SRTP (Secure RTP). Internal communication is done exclusively using VoIP technology using the aforementioned protocols. When it comes to communication with external parties, VoIP is just one possibility, the POTS being the other. For the user this must be completely transparent without any change in the way he uses his phone. In order to communicate with the outside world, data pass the *SIP Proxy* which is able to handle the session initiation and traverse the SBC that is responsible for the protection of the internal VoIP system by defending against DDOS (Distributed Denial-of-Service) attacks and by hiding the internal structure of the VoIP network. It serves as the single point of entry and exit of all VoIP traffic. Normally it is located in the External Zone, however, it could also be located in the CAZ, especially when the *SIP Proxy* functionality and the *SBC* are combined. In order to have phone numbers accessible from the PSTN network, a telephony provider is needed that provides a gateway into the PSTN network. The telephony provider is connected to the own network via the *SBC* by means of SIP trunking.

The *Feature Server* provides all the functionality of a modern telephony service. It is accessed directly by the VoIP frontends for *Voicemail*, presence and other features that are integrated into the VoIP device's GUI. Other services of the *Feature Server* are accessible via a web service using HTTPS or other proprietary protocols such as sending and receiving fax messages. A user can access additional VoIP functionalities using the *Self-Service Portal* in order to manage information such as room numbers, presence options, and preferred communication. Other functionalities are done using the VoIP phone such as accessing the *Voicemail Box* or setting the presence status.

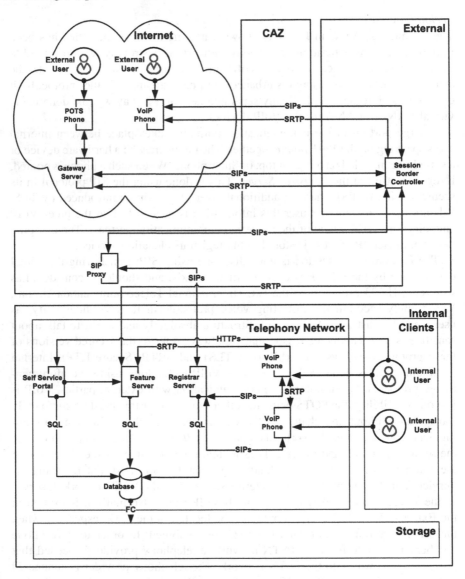

Fig. 9.47 Technology View of TalkToMe (I5)

Although the actual technical implementation may seem simple, it should not be underestimated as a whole new set of requirements in terms of availability, reliability, and QoS for the network infrastructure must be addressed. To fully benefit from the new technology, additional services and systems must be built and integrated into the overall IT landscape. But if all this can be reached, the benefit of a tight integration and the use of additional functions both boost productivity and end-user satisfaction.

9.5.6 Resulting Context

Interaction

TalkToMe (I5) provides interfaces to all other patterns that need one. Basically, the most important requesters of its service are WorkTogether (B1) and Know-YourCustomer (B3). TalkToMe (I5) needs StoreMyIdentities (I1), LetMeAccess (I2), and UnderControl (I3) to function correctly and to avoid redundancies when dealing with IAM (Fig. 9.48).

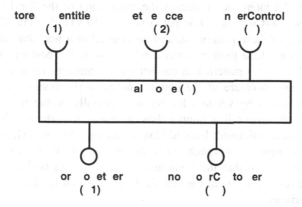

Fig. 9.48 Interaction of TalkToMe (I5) with other patterns

The TalkToMe (I5) pattern uses the EAPs listed below:

• StoreMyIdentities (I1), LetMeAccess (I2), and UnderControl (I3): These EAPs are referenced practically in all patterns as the implementation of these central services is of great benefit for the Enterprise Architecture as a whole.

TalkToMe (I5) provides important functionality to other patterns, which is typical for an Infrastructure Pattern. Not all patterns need a direct interface to synchronous communication but all people work with this pattern. Hence it is useful to have a helpful phone call within the reach of a mouse click or to have a call history available in the actual work environment to have a reminder with whom one has spoken yesterday.

- TalkToMe (I5) provides synchronous communication to all other patterns, especially to WorkTogether (B1) and KnowYourCustomer (B3).

Consequences

TalkToMe (I5) provides a cost-effective and modern synchronous communication environment that allows the user not only to make and receive calls but implements this form of communication into other business processes in a way that would be impossible when relying on the POTS. Additional gain can be taken from the implementation of value added services such as video phone, conference calls, and fax. Unsurprisingly, the business processes are quite simple which is important, as users want to work intuitively with voice communication.

Implementing TalkToMe (I5) may at least partly create new business processes:

- Working with conferences.
- Setting and querying online status.
- Video telephony.

Another impact is the integration into other business processes and into the IT infrastructure. An interesting aspect is the interaction of the WorkTogether (B1) and the KnowYourCustomer (B3) patterns with TalkToMe (I5). If feasible, the implementation of these patterns should be aligned in a way that integration and interaction among these three patterns can be done in the best way possible.

The TalkToMe (I5) pattern is a pattern with a medium invariance. The comparatively simple structure of the pattern increases the invariance, whereas the different approaches by vendors lowers it, especially at the technical layer. It makes a huge difference if a solution has emerged from the existing groupware technology such as Microsoft Unified Communication Solution (Lync) or if it is a more network centric approach such as Avayas Communication solutions. Therefore, we believe that the invariance is high at the business and also the application level but is low at the technical level, which results in the postulated medium invariance.

At the technical level, decision must be taken which protocols to use for communication; the main choice is between the two protocols SIP and H.323. Sometimes these protocols are used as a base but are enhanced with proprietary extensions, which is the case with Microsoft Lync. From a technical point of view, the complexity of the pattern is low but one should not make the mistake to deem its implementation as simple. On the contrary, an implementation of VoIP is a very challenging task that must be carefully approached. The biggest area of concern, however, is the fact that the POTS has proven to be very reliable and of high quality. Living up to this expectation is challenging and needs good planning. Using network segmentation and QoS helps to implement a robust and reliable infrastructure with good performance. Another delicate point to take care of is the situation when a different business unit has been responsible for telephony services and now is migrated to an IT department with an often completely different culture. However, if the goals are met and users are satisfied with the new telephone service, the reward is great, not only in terms of financial and productivity gains but as well as in terms of new possibilities of integrating synchronous voice communication into other ICT backed business processes.

References

Ballad B, Ballad T, Banks E (2010) Access control, authentication, and public key infrastructure. Jones and Bartlett Learning

Buecker A, Browne K, Foss L, Jacobs J, Jeremic V, Lorenz C, Stabler C, Van Herzele J (2011) IBM security solutions architecture for network, server and endpoint. IBM International Technical Support Organization, Poughkeepsie

Chaffin L, Kanclirz J, Porter T et al (2006) Practical VoIP security. Syngress, Rockland

Ciampa M (2009) Security + guide to network security fundamentals. Course Technology/Cengage Learning Boston

Hucaby D, Garneau D, Sequeira A (2012) CCNP security firewall 642–618 official cert guide. Cisco Press, Indianapolis

iDABC (2007) eID interoperability for PEGS. http://ec.europa.eu/idabc/en/document/6484.html. Accessed 24 Aug 2011

ISACA (2012) Glossary of terms. ISACA, Rolling Meadows

ISO (2007) ISO/IEC 27002:2005 information technology – security techniques – code of practice for information security management. International Organization for Standardization, Geneva

Kizza M (2008) A guide to computer network security. Springer, Berlin

Mezler-Andelberg C (2008) Identity management – eine Einführung. Grundlagen, Technik, wirtschaftlicher Nutzen. dPunkt-Verlag

Mullet D, Mullet K (2000) Managing Imap. O'Reilly, Sebastopol

Precht R (2011) Who am I and if so how many. Constable & Robinson Ltd, London

Rehman R (2003) Intrusion detection systems with Snort: advanced IDS techniques using Snort, Apache, MySQL, PHP, and ACID. Prentice Hall, Upper Saddle River

Roebuck K (2011) Unified communications: high-impact technology – what you need to know: definitions, adoptions, impact, benefits, maturity, vendors. Lightning Source Incorporated, La Vergne

Wallingford T (2005) Switching to VoIP. O'Reilly, Beijing

Williamson G, Yip D, Sharoni I, Spaulding K (2009) Identity management: a primer. MC Press, Boise

Windley P (2005) Digital identity. O'Reilly Media Inc, Sebastopol

Wood D (1999) Programming internet email. O'Reilly, Beijing

and always migrated to an IT department with an often completely different culture. However, if the goals are met and users are satisfied with the new telecom services, the reward is great, not only in terms of financial and productivity gains but also in terms of new possibilities of integrating synchronous voice communication into other ICT-based business processes.

References

Bajaj B, [illegible] Banks E (2004) [illegible] quantization and public key [illegible] introduce [illegible]
Bäckström Peyman [illegible] Jardel [illegible] Nubier C Van Bakel I (2011) [illegible] Intern[illegible] and Support [illegible]
Chatt[illegible] Kaeslin [illegible] (2006) [illegible] VoIP security [illegible] Rockland
Chen [illegible] (2007) [illegible] networks security fundamentals. Course Technology Cengage Learning, Boston
Lucasby [illegible] R, Sequeira A [illegible] official cert guide Cisco [illegible] Indianapolis
[illegible] http://[illegible] europa.eu/[illegible]/document/[illegible] 84.html
[illegible]
[illegible] 27001 [illegible] Information technology – Security techniques – code of practice [illegible] International Organization for Standardization, Geneva
[illegible] 2008 [illegible] security [illegible] Springer [illegible]
[illegible] (2008) [illegible] Technical [illegible]
[illegible] (2011) [illegible] O'Reilly [illegible]
[illegible] (2011) [illegible] Prentice Hall, London
[illegible] R (2014) [illegible] using Smart [illegible] Upper Saddle River
Radford [illegible] (2011) [illegible] technology: what you need to know [illegible] Information [illegible]
[illegible]
[illegible] Press
[illegible]
[illegible] O'Reilly [illegible] Sebastopol
[illegible] Berlin

Appendices

«If a man needs his appendix taken out, his gallbladder treated and some brain surgery as well, I don't think too many doctors would do the jobs simultaneously.»

Bob Lavner

Abbreviations

AB	Architecture Brick
ACID	Atomicity, Consistency, Isolation, Durability
ACL	Access Control Lists
AD	Active Directory
AIIM	Association for Information and Image Management
API	Application Programming Interface
APT	Advanced Persistent Threats
B2B	Business-to-Business
B2C	Business-to-Consumer
BaaS	Business-as-a-Service
BPMN	Business Process Model and Notation
BSC	Balanced Scorecards
BYOD	Bring Your Own Device
CAD	Computer Aided Design
CAZ	Central Access Zone
CEO	Chief Executive Officer
CERT	Computer Emergency Response Team
CFO	Chief Financial Officer
CMDB	Configuration Management Database
CMIS	Content Management Interoperability Standard
CMS	Content Management System
CPO	Chief Procurement Officer
CRM	Customer Relationship Management
DASD	Direct Access Storage Device
DDOS	Distributed Denial-of-Service
DMS	Document Management System
DMZ	Demilitarized Zone
DNS	Domain Name System
DoDAF	Departement of Defense Architecture Framework
EAP	Enterprise Architecture Pattern

T. Perroud and R. Inversini, *Enterprise Architecture Patterns*,
DOI: 10.1007/978-3-642-37561-3, © Springer-Verlag Berlin Heidelberg 2013

EIM	Enterprise Information Management
ECM	Enterprise Content Management
EIM	Enterprise Information Management
ERM	Enterprise Records Management
ERP	Enterprise Resource Planning
ESA	European Space Agency
ESB	Enterprise Service Bus
ESS	Employee Self Services
ETL	Extracting, Transforming and Loading Data
FC	Fiber Channel
FEAF	Federal Enterprise Architecture Framework
FTP	File Transfer Protocol
FTPS	File Transfer Protocol over SSL
G2C	Government-to-Citizen
G2G	Government-to-Government
GPS	Global Positioning System
GSM	Global System for Mobile Communications
GUI	Graphical User Interface
HIDS	Host-based Intrusion Detection System
HIPAA	Health Insurance Portability and Accountability Act
HR	Human Resources
HTTP	Hyper Text Transfer Protocol
IA	Information Architecture
IaaS	Infrastructure-as-a-Service
IAM	Identity and Access Management
ICAP	Internet Content Adaption Protocol
ICR	Intelligent Character Recognition
ICT	Information and Communication Technology
IdM	Identity Management
IDS	Intrusion Detection System
IFRS	International Financial Reporting Standards
ILM	Information Lifecyle Management
IP	Internet Protocol
ISACA	Information Systems Audit and Control Association
ISMS	Information Security Management System
ISO	International Organization for Standardization
ITIL	IT Infrastructure Library
ITU	International Telecommunication Union
JBC	Java Beans Component
JDBC	Java Database Connectivity
JMS	Java Message Service
LAN	Local Area Network
LDAP	Lightweight Directory Access Protocol
LTE	Long Term Evolution
MAPI	Messaging Application Programming Interface

MES	Manufacturing Execution Systems
MoReq	Modular Requirements For Records System
NAF	Nato Architecture Framework
NAS	Network Attached Storage
NASA	National Aeronautics and Space Administration
NGO	Non-Governmental Organisation
NIDS	Network-based Intrusion Detection System
NTP	Network Time Protocol
OAIS	Open Archival Information System
OASIS	Organization for the Advancement of Structured Information Standards
OCR	Optical Character Recognition
OES	Operations Execution Systems
OSCI	Online Services Computer Interface
OSI	Open Systems Interconnection
OTP	One Time Password
PaaS	Platform-as-a-Service
PGP	Pretty Good Privacy
PIM	Personal Information Manager
PKI	Public Key Infrastructure
PLM	Product Lifecycle Management
POS	Point-of-Sales
POTS	Plain Old Telephone Service
PSTN	Public Switched Telephony Network
QoS	Quality of Service
RACF	Resource Access Control Facility
RDF	Resource Description Framework
RFC	Remote Function Call
RFID	Radio Frequency Identification
RM	Records Management
ROI	Return On Investment
RTP	Real-time Transport Protocol
S/MIME	Secure / Multipurpose Internet Mail Extensions
SaaS	Software-as-a-Service
SAML	Security Assertion Markup Language
SAN	Storage Area Network
SB	Solution Bricks
SBC	Session Border Controller
SCCSCC	Shared Service Center
SCM	Supply Chain Management
SCOR®SCOR	Supply Chain Operations Reference
SCP	Secure Copy Protocol
SCRM	Social Customer Relationship Management
SFTP	Secure File Transfer Protocol
SIEM	Security Incident and Event Management System

SIP	Session Initiation Protocol
SLA	Service Level Agreement
SMS	Short Message Service
SOA	Service Oriented Architecture
SOAP	Simple Objekt Access Protocol
SOX	Sarbanes-Oxley Act
SRM	Supplier Relationship Management
SSH	Secure Shell
SSL	Secure Socket Layer
SSO	Single-Sign-On
SWIFT	Society for Worldwide Interbank Financial Telecommunication
TLS	Transport Layer Security
TOGAF	The Open Group Architecture Framework
UCC	Unified Communication and Collaboration
UML	Unified Modeling Language
URL	Uniform Resource Locator
US-GAAP	United States Generally Accepted Accounting Principles
VLAN	Virtual Local Area Network
VoIP	Voice over IP
VPN	Virtual Private Network
WebDAV	Web-based Distributed Authoring and Versioning
WLAN	Wireless Local Area Network
WMS	Warehouse Management System
WORM	Write-Once-Read-Many
XBRL	Extensible Business Reporting Language
XML	Extensible Markup Language
XML-DOM	Extensible Markup Language Document Object Model

Index

T. Perroud and R. Inversini, *Enterprise Architecture Patterns*,
DOI: 10.1007/978-3-642-37561-3, © Springer-Verlag Berlin Heidelberg 2013

Printed in the United States
By Bookmasters